Praise for *My Salinger Year*:

'Beautifully captures a moment in history . . . A warm, witty, occasionally sly piece of storytelling' *Harper's Bazaar*

'A year spent in the orbit of a great writer gives rise to an elegant memoir' *Sunday Telegraph*

'Anyone who can remember the fear of feeling hopelessly out of their depth in their first job should get a kick out of *My Salinger Year* . . . Rakoff's prose is precise and often amusing' *Evening Standard*

'This poignant and witty memoir following a year in the life of post-grad Rakoff in her first job at a publishing house in New York – whose client just so happens to be literary legend JD Salinger' *Company*

'An utterly beguiling memoir, not only about Salinger and a bygone era of publishing, but about relationships, finding one's voice, and surviving in the big city' *Bookseller*

'At heart this is a coming-of-age story, evoking the challenge and confusion of surviving your first job and the dawning realisation that your relationship is doomed' *Sunday Express* Summer Reading

'This piquant coming-of-age memoir is Rakoff's tribute to a vanished office world . . . Rakoff writes with wry wit, holding in check a tsunami of feeling' *Intelligent Life*

'This is an impossibly excellent read – a glowingly entertaining, miss-your-subway-stop engrossing, note-perfect piece of storytelling' Charles Bock, author of *Beautiful Children*

A NOTE ABOUT THE AUTHOR

JOANNA RAKOFF is a poet and the author of the novel *A Fortunate Age*, which won the Goldberg Prize for Fiction and the *Elle* Readers' Prize, was a *New York Times* Editors' Pick and a *San Francisco Chronicle* bestseller. As a journalist and critic, she has written for the *New York Times*, the *Los Angeles Times*, *Vogue*, *Time Out* and *O: The Oprah Magazine*. The BBC produced a radio documentary following her as she tracked down the writer of her favourite Salinger fan letter. She has degrees from Columbia University, University College London and Oberlin College. Joanna Rakoff lives in Cambridge, MA.

ALSO BY JOANNA RAKOFF

A Fortunate Age

JOANNA RAKOFF

My Salinger Year

B L O O M S B U R Y

LONDON • NEW DELHI • NEW YORK • SYDNEY

Bloomsbury Paperbacks
An imprint of Bloomsbury Publishing Plc

50 Bedford Square
London
WC1B 3DP
UK

1385 Broadway
New York
NY 10018
USA

www.bloomsbury.com

BLOOMSBURY and the Diana logo are trademarks of Bloomsbury Publishing Plc

First published in Great Britain 2014
This paperback edition first published in 2015

British Library Cataloguing-in-Publication Data
A catalogue record for this book is available from the British Library.

ISBN: HB: 978-1-4088-3017-8
       TPB: 978-1-4088-5550-8
       PB: 978-1-4088-3397-1
       ePub: 978-1-4088-3396-4

2 4 6 8 10 9 7 5 3 1

Printed and bound in Great Britain by CPI Group (UK) Ltd, Croydon CR0 4YY

MIX
Paper from
responsible sources
FSC® C020471
www.fsc.org

To find out more about our authors and books visit www.bloomsbury.com.
Here you will find extracts, author interviews, details of forthcoming
events and the option to sign up for our newsletters.

For Keeril,
with whom this story begins and ends

"It was a day, God knows,
not only of rampant signs and symbols
but of wildly extensive communication via the written word."

—J. D. SALINGER, *Raise High the Roof Beam, Carpenters*

Author's Note

Abigail Thomas describes memoir as "the truth as best she can tell it," and this book is, indeed, the truth, told as best I could. In writing it, I interviewed people I knew during the period chronicled and consulted my own writings from the time and the years shortly thereafter.

To maintain narrative flow, I've fiddled with the chronology of a few events, and I've changed the names—and identifying traits—of most, though not all, of the people.

Those minor adjustments aside, this is the actual story of my Salinger year.

All of Us Girls

There were hundreds of us, thousands of us, carefully dressing in the gray morning light of Brooklyn, Queens, the Lower East Side, leaving our apartments weighed down by tote bags heavy with manuscripts, which we read as we stood in line at the Polish bakery, the Greek deli, the corner diner, waiting to order our coffee, light and sweet, and our Danish, to take on the train, where we would hope for a seat so that we might read more before we arrived at our offices in midtown, Soho, Union Square. We were girls, of course, all of us girls, emerging from the 6 train at Fifty-First Street and walking past the Waldorf-Astoria, the Seagram Building on Park, all of us clad in variations on a theme—the neat skirt and sweater, redolent of Sylvia Plath at Smith—each element purchased by parents in some comfortable suburb, for our salaries were so low we could barely afford our rent, much less lunch in the vicinities of our offices or dinners out, even in the cheap neighborhoods we'd populated, sharing floor-throughs with other girls like us, assistants at other agencies or houses or the occasional literary nonprofit. All day we sat, our legs crossed at the knee, on our swivel chairs, answering the call of our bosses, ushering in writers with the correct mixture of enthusiasm and remove, never belying the fact that we got into this business not because we wanted to fetch glasses of water for visiting writers but because we wanted to be writers ourselves, and this seemed the most socially acceptable way to go about doing so, though it was already becoming clear that this was not at all the way to go about doing so. Years ago, as some of our parents pointed out—as my own parents endlessly pointed out—we would have been called secretaries. And as with the girls in the secretarial pool, back in our parents' day, very few of us would be promoted, very few of us would, as they say, *make it*. We whispered about the lucky ones, the ones with bosses who allowed them to take on books or clients, who mentored them, or the ones who showed massive, rule-breaking initiative, wondering if, somehow, that would be us, if we wanted it badly enough to wait out the years of low pay, the years of answering a boss's beck and call, or if what we wanted, still, was to be on the other side of it all, to be the writer knocking confidently on our boss's door.

Winter

We all have to start somewhere. For me, that somewhere was a dark room, lined from floor to ceiling with books, rows and rows of books sorted by author, books from every conceivable era of the twentieth century, their covers bearing the design hallmarks of the moments in which they'd been released into the world—the whimsical line drawings of the 1920s, the dour mustards and maroons of the late 1950s, the gauzy watercolor portraits of the 1970s—books that defined my days and the days of the others who worked within this dark warren of offices. When my colleagues uttered the names on the spines of those books, their voices turned husky and reverential, for these were names of godlike status to the literarily inclined. F. Scott Fitzgerald, Dylan Thomas, William Faulkner. But this was, and is, a literary agency, which means those names on the spines represented something else, something else that leads people to speak in hushed voices, something that I'd previously thought had absolutely nothing to do with books and literature: money.

Three Days of Snow

On my first day at the Agency, I dressed carefully in clothing that struck me as suitable for work in an office: a short wool skirt, in Black Watch plaid, and a dark green turtleneck sweater with a zipper up the back, from the 1960s, purchased in a London thrift shop. On my legs, thick black tights. On my feet, black suede loafers of Italian provenance, purchased for me by my mother, who believed "good shoes" a necessity, not a luxury. I had never worked in an office before, but I had acted—as a child, in college, after—and I regarded this outfit as a costume. My role being the Bright Young Assistant. The Girl Friday.

I paid, perhaps, too much attention to my dress, because I knew almost nothing about the job that awaited me or the firm that had hired me. In fact, I still couldn't quite believe that I had indeed been hired, it happened so quickly. Three months earlier, I had dropped out of graduate school—or finished my master's, depending on how you looked at it—and flown home from London, arriving at my parents' house in the suburbs with little more than an enormous box of books.

"I want to write my own poetry," I told my college boyfriend, from the ancient pay phone in the hallway of my Hampstead dorm, "not analyze other people's poetry." I did not tell my parents this. I did not tell them anything other than that I felt lonely in London. And they, in keeping with our family's code of silence, asked me nothing about my plans. Instead, my mother took me shopping: at Lord & Taylor, she selected a suit, wool gabardine trimmed in velvet, with a pencil skirt and a fitted vest, like something Katharine Hepburn wore in *Adam's Rib*, and a pair of suede court shoes. The hope, I realized—as the in-house tailor pinned up my sleeves—was that the suit would be a conduit to some sort of acceptable employment.

A week before Christmas, my friend Celeste brought me along to a party, where an old friend of hers spoke laconically of her job at the science-fiction imprint of a large trade publisher. "How did you end up there?" I asked, less because I wanted the mechanicals of the hiring process and more because it struck me as strange that an English major, with an interest in serious fiction, would have taken such a job. By way of an answer, Celeste's friend pressed a business card in my hand. "This is a placement agency," she told me. "All the editors use them to find assistants. Give them a call." The next morning, I hesitantly dialed the number. Publishing had not been part of my plan—though, of course, I didn't have a plan—but the concept of fate appealed to me, a predilection that would get me into trouble soon enough, that it would take me years to shake, and I took it as a sign that I'd happened to get stuck in a corner with Celeste's friend, the two of us quiet and ill at ease within the raucous party. "Can you come in this afternoon?" I was asked by the woman who answered the phone, her accent not exactly English but containing notes of competent Englishness.

And so I found myself, clad in my suit, handing over a

hastily composed résumé to an elegant lady in a skirt and jacket rather similar to my own. "You just finished a master's in English?" she asked, with a frown, her dark hair sliding into her face.

"Yes."

"Well," she said, sighing and putting my résumé down. "That will make you more appealing to some editors, less appealing to others. We'll find you something, though." She sat back in her chair. "I'll give you a call in the New Year. No one's hiring this close to Christmas."

I'd barely made it home from her office when the phone rang. "I have something for you," she said breathlessly. "How would you feel about working at a literary agency rather than a publisher?"

"Great," I said. I had no idea what a literary agency was.

"Fantastic," she said. "This is a wonderful agency. An old, venerable agency. I think it's actually the oldest agency in New York. The job is with an agent who's been in the business a long, long time." She paused. "Some assistants have found her a bit difficult to work for, but others love her. I think you'd be a good match. And she's looking to hire someone right away. She wants to make a decision before Christmas." Later, I would discover that the agent in question had been interviewing potential assistants for months. But for now, on this cold day in December, I tucked the phone into my neck and hung my suit up in the shower to steam out the wrinkles.

The next day, zipped and buttoned back into my suit, I took the train down to Fifty-First and Lex, then walked across Park and over to Madison, to meet with the agent in question.

"So," she said, lighting a long brown cigarette, a gesture that somehow reminded me simultaneously of Don Corleone and Lauren Bacall. Her fingers were long, slender, white, with nonexistent knuckles and perfectly shaped ovoid nails. "You can type?"

"I can," I affirmed, shaking my head stiffly. I had been expecting more difficult questions, abstract inquiries into my work ethic or habits, challenges to the central tenets of my master's thesis.

"On a typewriter?" she asked, pursing her lips and letting out frills of delicate white smoke. Ever so slightly, she smiled. "It's very different from using a"—her face went slack in disgust—"a *computer*."

I nodded nervously. "It is," I agreed.

An hour later, as the sky darkened and the city emptied for the holiday, I lay on the couch rereading *Persuasion*, hoping I'd never have to put that suit back on again, much less the stockings that went with it.

The phone rang once more. I had a job.

And so, on the first Monday after the New Year, I woke at seven, quietly showered, and made my way down the building's crumbling stairs, only to find the world stopped: the street was covered in snow. I'd known, of course, that a blizzard was coming, or I suppose I'd known, for I didn't own a television or a radio, and I didn't traffic in circles where people talked excessively about the weather—we had larger, more important things to discuss; weather was something over which our grandmothers, our dull neighbors in the suburbs, obsessed. If I'd owned a radio, I would have known that the entire city was shut down, that the Department of Education had declared a snow day for the first time in almost twenty years, that up and down the coast people were dying or had died, trapped in cars, unheated houses, skidding on unplowed streets. The Agency utilized a phone tree system for emergency closures, wherein the president of the company—my boss, though I didn't realize that this was her position until a few weeks into the job, for at the Agency all knowledge was assumed rather than imparted—would call the next in command, going down the Agency's hierarchy, until the receptionist, Pam, and the various agents' assistants, and the strange, sad messenger, Izzy, all knew not to come into work. Because it was my first day, I didn't yet figure onto the grid of numbers.

Though the city was indeed in an actual state of emergency, my trains came quickly—the L from Lorimer Street, the 5 express from Union Square—and at 8:30 I found myself in Grand Central, where the various purveyors of coffee and pastries and newspapers were eerily shuttered. Walking north, I arrived in the Great Hall, with its graceful canopy of stars, my heels echoing on the marble floor. I'd made it halfway across the chamber—to the central information booth, where in high school I'd often met friends—before I realized why my shoes were making such a racket: I was alone, or nearly so, in a space always filled with the sound of hundreds, thousands of feet racing across the marble. Now, as I stood stock-still in the middle of it, the hall was silent. I had been the only entity generating noise.

At the station's west side, I pushed open the heavy glass doors and stepped out into the freezing wind. Slowly, I made my way west through the deep snow on Forty-Third Street, until I encountered something even stranger than a silent, unpopulated Grand Central Station: a silent, unpopulated Madison Avenue. The streets had not yet been plowed. The only sound was the wind. An untouched mantle of snow stretched evenly from the shops on its east side to those on its west, marred by not a footprint, a candy wrapper, not even a leaf.

Trudging my way north, I found a trio of bankers running—or trying to run—through the heavy snow and shrieking with delight, their trench coats trailing behind them like capes. "Hey," they called to me. "We're having a snowball fight! Come on!"

"I have to go to work," I told them. *It's my first day,* I

almost told them, then stopped myself. Better to pass as experienced, seasoned. I was one of them now.

"Everything's closed," they called. "Play in the snow!"

"Have a good day," I called back and slowly made my way toward Forty-Ninth Street, where I located the narrow, unremarkable building that housed the Agency. The lobby consisted of a narrow hallway leading to a pair of creaky elevators. This was a building of insurance salesmen and importers of African carvings, of aging family doctors in solo practice and Gestalt therapists. And the Agency, which occupied the whole of a mid-level floor. Stepping off the elevator, I tried the door and found it locked. But it was only 8:45 and the office, I knew, didn't open until 9:00. The Friday before Christmas, I'd been asked to stop by to sign some paperwork and pick up a few things, including a key to the front door. It seemed odd to me that they'd give a key to a complete stranger, but I'd dutifully put it on my key chain, right there in the creaky elevator, and now I pulled it out and let myself into the dark, silent office. I longed to inspect the books that lined the foyer but feared someone might arrive and find me engaged in behavior that would betray me as the grad student I so recently was. Instead I forced myself to walk past the receptionist's desk, down the front hallway, with its rows of Ross Macdonald paperbacks, to turn right at the little kitchen area and walk through the linoleum-floored finance department, arriving at the east wing of the office, which held my new boss's sanctum and the large antechamber where I would sit.

And there I sat, spine erect, feet freezing in my soaked shoes, inspecting the contents of my new drawers—paper clips, stapler, large pink index cards imprinted with mysterious codes and grids—afraid to pull out my book, lest my new boss happen upon me. I was reading Jean Rhys and fancied myself akin to her impoverished heroines, living for weeks on nothing but the morning croissant and café crème provided by their residence hotels, the rents on which were, in turn, provided by their married ex-lovers, as compensation for ending their affairs. I suspected my boss would not approve of Jean Rhys. During our interview, she'd asked me what I was reading, what I preferred to read. "Everything," I told her. "I love Flaubert. I just finished *Sentimental Education* and I was amazed by how contemporary it seemed. But I also love writers like Alison Lurie and Mary Gaitskill. And I grew up reading mysteries. I love Donald Westlake and Dashiell Hammett."

"Well, Flaubert is all well and good, but to work in publishing, you need to be reading writers who are alive." She paused and I suspected that my answer had been wrong. As always, I should have prepared myself more properly. I knew nothing about publishing, nothing about literary agencies, nothing about this specific literary agency.

"I love Donald Westlake, too," she said, lighting a cigarette. "He's so funny." Then, for the first time since I'd stepped into her office, she smiled.

I was tentatively inspecting the books on the shelf above my head—some Agatha Christie paperbacks and what appeared to be a series of romance novels—when the heavy black phone on my desk rang. I picked it up, before realizing that I wasn't sure of the proper greeting. "Hello?" I said tentatively.

"Oh no," a voice shouted at me. "Are you there? I knew you were there. Go home." It was my boss. "The office is closed. We'll see you tomorrow." There was a silence, in which I struggled to figure out what to say. "I'm so sorry you came all the way downtown. Go home and get warm." And then she was gone.

Outside, the bankers were gone, too, presumably toasting their own soaked feet. The wind blew in thick gusts down Madison, twisting my hair into my mouth and eyes, but the street was so silent, so blank and beautiful, that I lingered until my hands and feet and nose grew numb. This was the last Monday on which I'd have no place to be at 9:30 in the morning and there was, I realized, no rush to get home.

There would be other blizzards in New York, but none that generated such silence, none in which I could stand on a street corner and feel myself to be the only person in the universe, none, certainly that stopped the city entire. By the time the next blizzard of such proportions arrived, the world had changed. Silence was no longer possible.

I went home to Brooklyn. Officially, as far as my parents knew, I lived on the Upper East Side with my friend Celeste. After college, when I'd moved to London for grad school, Celeste—whom my parents habitually described as "good" and "nice"—had taken a job teaching preschool and found herself a rent-controlled studio on East Seventy-Third Street, between First and Second. When I stumbled back to New York, she let me sleep on her couch, grateful for the company, then suggested I stay on, splitting her rent. Officially, as far as my parents knew, I had an equally good and nice boyfriend, my college boyfriend, a composer, brilliant and hilarious, in grad school in California. The plan had been for me to come home from London after finishing my master's, visit briefly with my parents, then move out to Berkeley, to the place he'd secured for us in a complex a few blocks off Telegraph, rings of apartments surrounding a bleak courtyard that looked as if it should contain a pool.

But there was no pool. And I had veered from the plan. I had returned to New York and found that I couldn't leave. And then I met Don.

On my second day of work at the Agency, I again arrived uncomfortably early, so fearful was I of arriving late. This time around, I stuck my key in the lock, opened the door a few inches, and seeing that the office was dark, the receptionist's desk unmanned, I quickly closed it and took the elevator back down to the lobby. Madison had been plowed, as had Fifth and the rest of midtown, but the city still felt sleepy, the curbs banked six feet high with snow, pedestrians creeping slowly through the narrow pathways carved along the sidewalks. There was a croissant shop in the lobby, inside which a few dazed customers perused glass cases under the unfriendly eye of a portly South Asian woman in a hairnet. I joined them, turning over in my mind the possibility of a second cup of coffee.

By the time I got back upstairs, the receptionist had arrived and was snapping on the lamps in the foyer, still in her long brown coat. A light shone, too, from the office directly opposite her desk.

"Oh, hi," she said, in a manner that wasn't exactly friendly. She unbuttoned her coat and slung it over her arm, then began walking down the hall, away from me.

"I'm the new assistant," I called. "Should I just, um, go to my desk? Or should I—"

"Hold on, let me hang up my coat," she said.

A few minutes later she reappeared, fluffing her short hair. "What's your name again? Joan?"

"Joanna," I told her.

"Right. Joanne," she said, seating herself heavily in her chair. She was a tall woman, with a figure my mother would have called statuesque, and she was dressed today in a turtleneck sweater and the sort of fitted pantsuit worn in the 1970s, with wide-legged trousers and wider lapels. Seated in her chair, she appeared not just to tower over but to fully preside over her desk and the room around it. Next to her phone sat a Rolodex of enormous magnitude. "Your boss isn't in yet. She gets in at ten." It was 9:30, the time I'd been told the workday started. "I guess you can wait out here." She sighed, as if I were causing her a great inconvenience, then twisted her full mouth in contemplation.

"Or you can go back to your desk. Do you know where it is?" I nodded. "Okay, I guess you can go back there. But don't touch anything. She'll be in soon."

"I can take her back," called a voice from the lit office. A tall young man strode through the doorway. "I'm James," he said, extending his hand. His head was covered in curly light brown hair, his eyes in gold-rimmed spectacles, as was the fashion that year, and his chin sprouted a thick reddish beard, all of which gave him the aspect of Mr. Tumnus, the noble faun in *The Lion, the Witch, and the Wardrobe*. I took his hand and shook it.

"Follow me," he said, and I trailed him down the main hallway, past a row of dark offices. As on the day before I longed to linger over the books lining the walls. My eye caught some thrillingly familiar names, like Pearl Buck and Langston Hughes, and some intriguingly foreign ones, like Ngaio Marsh, and my stomach began to flutter in the way it had on childhood trips to our local library: so many books, each enticing in its own specific way, and all mine for the taking. "Wow," I said, almost involuntarily. James stopped and turned. "I know," he said with a real smile. "I've been here six years and I still feel that way."

As predicted, my boss arrived at ten, swathed in a whiskey mink, her eyes covered with enormous dark glasses, her head with a silk scarf in an equestrian pattern. "Hello," I started to say, rising from my chair, as one might for royalty or clergy. But she swooped past me into her office, as if her glasses prevented peripheral vision.

Twenty minutes later her door opened and she emerged, having shed her coat, her enormous sunglasses now replaced by enormous glasses with clear lenses that covered half her pale face, exacerbating the corresponding paleness of her blue eyes. "Well," she said, lighting a cigarette and positioning herself at one end of my L-shaped desk. "You're here."

I smiled brightly. "I am," I said, rising from my chair, my feet sliding a little in boots I'd borrowed from Don's roommate, Leigh. My loafers had dried into a sad C shape on the radiator at Don's apartment. This, of course, was where I was really living: Don's apartment in Brooklyn.

"Well, we have a lot to do," she said, pushing a smooth lock of hair out of her face with one long finger. "Now, I know you can type." I nodded encouragingly. "But have you ever used a Dictaphone?"

"I haven't," I admitted. I had never even heard of such a thing. Had she mentioned it in the interview? I wasn't sure. It sounded like something out of Dr. Seuss. "But I'm sure I can pick it up quickly."

"I'm sure you can, too," she assured me, expelling a stream of smoke that seemed to contradict her statement of confidence. "Though it *can* be a little tricky." With one hand, she tugged a stiff, cloudy cover off the white plastic box sitting next to the typewriter. Exposed, it resembled a first-generation tape recorder, tricked out with an excess of wires and outsized headphones and lacking the customary tab buttons labeled "play," "rewind," "fast-forward," and "pause." There was a slot for the cassette, but that was it. As with so many tools of efficiency from the 1950s and 1960s, it looked both charmingly archaic and spookily futuristic.

"Well," she said, with an odd laugh. "This is it. There are pedals for playback and rewind. And I think you can control the speed." I nodded, though I saw no controls of any sort. "Hugh can show you if you're confused." I wasn't sure who Hugh was, nor was I sure that I understood what I would be doing with the Dictaphone, but I nodded again. "Well, I have a *lot* of typing, so I'll give you some tapes and you can get started. Then we'll have a little chat." She strode back into her office and returned with three cassette tapes, a fresh cigarette in hand, not yet lit. "Here you go," she said. "All yours!" And then she was gone, through the archway to the left of my desk, which led to the finance department, and beyond that the kitchen, and the other wing of the office, which held all the other agents' offices and the door to the outside world.

I couldn't actually type. I had lied about my typing skills at the urging of the lady at the placement agency. "No one your age can type," she'd told me, wrinkling her pretty face in a gesture of dismissal. "You grew up with computers! Tell her you can do sixty words a minute. You'll be up to speed in a week." As it happened, I'd once been able to type sixty words per minute. Like all New York middle school students, I'd taken a state-mandated typing class in eighth grade. For a few years afterward, I pounded out papers on the typewriter at my dad's office, never glancing down at the keys. Junior year, we acquired a Macintosh II, and my typing devolved into the loose, two-fingered, technique-free style of the digital age.

I pulled the dustcover off the Selectric. It was enormous, with more buttons and levers than I remembered from the machines on which I'd learned. And yet—and yet—there was one button I couldn't find: the one that would turn it on. I ran my fingers all over the front and sides and back. Nothing. I stood up and peered at it from all angles, contorting myself around the edges of my desk. Then I sat back down and tried again, reaching all around it, tilting it back, in case the switch was underneath. Sweat soaked the underarms of my green sweater and slicked my forehead, and my nose pinged with that awful pricking, the sign that tears were coming. Finally, thinking perhaps there simply was no on/off button, that the machine was actually unplugged, I crouched under the desk, feeling around in the dark for the cord.

"Do you need some help?" called a soft, tentative voice, as my hands traced a dusty wire up from the floor.

"Um, maybe," I said, unfolding myself as gracefully as I could. Next to my desk stood a man of indeterminate age who so resembled my boss he could have been her son: the same wolfish eyes and straight ash-brown hair, the same slack cheeks and painfully fair skin, his discolored with acne scars.

"Are you looking for the on button?" the man asked, miraculously.

"I am," I admitted. "I feel so silly."

He shook his head sympathetically. "It's hidden away, in a really strange place. No one can find it. And it's awkward to reach if you're sitting in front of the thing. Here." He joined me behind the desk, careful to keep a few feet between us, slipped his arm around the left side of the typewriter as if he were hugging it, and with an audible click flipped the switch. The machine let out a loud hum, like a sleeping cat, and began to vibrate, almost visibly.

"Thanks so much," I said, with perhaps too much emotion.

"Sure," he said. I pressed my back into the desk so he'd have room to climb out, which he did, gawkily, tripping over the plastic mat beneath my chair and an errant cord. He sighed and held out his hand, a plain gold wedding band around his ring finger, which surprised me. He seemed, somehow, *alone*. "I'm Hugh," he said. "You're Joanna."

"I am," I confirmed, taking his hand, which was warm and dry and very, very white.

"I'm right over there." He cocked his head toward the door directly opposite my desk, which I'd taken to be a closet. "If you need anything, just come get me. Sometimes your boss doesn't"—another heavy sigh—"explain things. So if there's anything you don't understand, just ask me." His face changed suddenly, his mouth turning up. "I've been here a long time, so I know all the ins and outs of the office. I know how everything works."

"How long?" I asked, before I thought better of it. "How long have you been here?"

"Let's see." He crossed his arms in front of his chest, compressing his brow in thought. His slow speech further slowed. "I started in 1977 as Dorothy's assistant"—I nodded, as if I knew who Dorothy was—"and I did that for four years"—his voice drifted off—"I left for a while. In 1986. Or 1987? But I came back." Once again, he sighed. "Twenty years, I guess. I've been here about twenty years."

"Wow," I said. I was twenty-three years old.

Hugh laughed. "I know, wow." He shrugged. "I like it here. I mean, there are things I don't like, but it suits me. What I do. Here."

I wanted to ask what exactly that might be but wasn't sure if this line of inquiry qualified as rude. My mother had instructed me never to inquire about a person's money or position. This was an agency, so presumably Hugh was an agent.

Alone again at my desk, the light from Hugh's office casting a reassuring glow on the carpet to my right, I picked up one of the cassette tapes and with some fumbling popped it into the Dictaphone, then began yet another search for an on button. *No,* I thought. There was nothing, no "pedals," nothing but an unmarked dial. I picked up the smooth plastic box and inspected it, but found nothing, not a thing.

Softly, I rapped on Hugh's half-open door. "Come in," he said, and I did. There he sat, behind an L-shaped desk similar to mine, covered with a mountain of paper, a pile high enough to obscure his chest and neck: opened and unopened envelopes, their ragged edges frilled and curled; letters still folded in triad or in the process of unfurling; yellow carbon copies and black sheets of the carbon paper that had created them; oversized pink and yellow and white index cards; paper upon paper upon paper, a mess so vast and unfathomable I shook my head to make sure it was real.

"I'm a little behind," he said. "Christmas."

"Oh," I said, nodding. "So, um, the Dictaphone—"

"*Foot* pedals," he said, sighing. "Under the desk. Like a sewing machine. There's one for play, one for rewind, one for fast-forward."

I spent the morning listening to my boss's low, patrician voice murmuring to me through the Dictaphone's ancient head-gear, a peculiarly intimate experience. Letters: I was typing letters on the Agency's letterhead—yellowish, undersized, thirty-pound stock—some several pages, some as brief as a line or two. "As discussed, attached are two copies of your contract with St. Martin's Press for *Two If by Blood*. Please sign both copies and return them to me at your earliest con-venience." The longest ones were addressed to publishers, requesting intricate and often inexplicable changes to con-tracts, the striking of words and clauses, particularly those having to do with "electronic rights," a term that meant noth-ing to me. These proved both unbearably tedious, requiring gymnastic feats of formatting and spacing, and oddly sooth-ing, for I understood so little of their content that the typing itself—my fingers on the keyboard, the sound of the keys striking the paper—hypnotized me. Typing was, as the place-ment agency lady had assured me, like riding a bike: my fingers remembered their places on the keyboard and flew across it as if by their own will. By noon, I had a neat stack of letters—the product of one dictation tape—addressed enve-lopes neatly clipped to them, as Hugh had instructed.

As I popped out the first tape and put in the second, my phone rang and I froze: I still wasn't sure of the appropriate greeting. "Hello," I said with false confidence, tucking the phone behind my ear. This was my first real phone call.

"Joanna!" a mirthful voice cried.

"Dad?" I asked.

"It is I," affirmed my father, in his Boris Karloff voice. My father, in his youth, had been an actor. His comedy group performed in the Catskills, at bungalow colonies and the occasional resort. The other members became famous: Tony Curtis, Jerry Stiller. My father became a dentist. A dentist who told jokes. "Dear old dad. How's your first day at work?"

"Okay." My parents had asked for my work number minutes after I told them I had a job. I hadn't thought they'd call my first day. "I've just been typing up letters."

"Well, you're a secretary now," said my dad, laughing. I came from a family of scientists, and my every move seemed to provide them with amusement. "Oh, sorry, an *assistant*."

"I think it's slightly different from being a secretary," I said, hating the solemn tone of my voice. This was another constant refrain in my family: Joanna takes everything too seriously. Joanna can't take a joke. *We're just teasing, Joanna! You don't need to get upset*. And yet I always did. "I'm going to be reading manuscripts." This was the only non-secretarial task that came to mind. My boss, as it happened, hadn't mentioned it, but everyone I'd spoken to in the weeks since accepting the job had emphasized that assisting an agent primarily involved reading manuscripts. No one had mentioned typing. "Stuff like that. They were looking for someone with a background like mine. In English."

"Yes, yes," cooed my dad. "Of course. Listen, I've been thinking. How much are they paying you again?"

I looked around to make sure I was alone. "Eighteen five."

"Eighteen thousand dollars?" my father cried. "I thought it was more." He made a guttural sound of disgust, the last remaining evidence that he'd been raised in a Yiddish-speaking household. "Eighteen thousand dollars a year?"

"Eighteen thousand *five hundred*." This sum struck me as huge. In college, I'd earned fifteen hundred dollars per semester as a writing tutor, and in grad school I'd scraped by on minimum wage, serving beer at a pub and fitting hiking boots at a camping store off Oxford Street. Eighteen thousand five hundred dollars was a vast and unimaginable amount of money to me, perhaps because I imagined it as a lump sum, handed over in stacks of crisp bills.

"You know, Jo, I don't think you can live on that. Do you think you could ask them for more?"

"Dad, I've already started the job."

"I know, but maybe you could tell them you've looked at your expenses and you just can't live on that little money. That's, let's see"—my father could do complex calculations in his head—"fifteen hundred dollars a month. After taxes, maybe eight hundred, nine hundred a month. Are they paying for your health insurance?"

"I don't know." I'd been told the Agency provided insurance, which would kick in three months after I started—or maybe six months—and which I assumed they covered. But I'd honestly not paid very much attention to the financial details. The fact that I had an actual job seemed to supersede any other concerns. This was 1996. The country was in the grips of a recession. Almost no one I knew was gainfully employed. My friends were in grad school—getting MFAs in fiction or PhDs in film theory—or working at coffee shops in Portland, or selling T-shirts in San Francisco, or living with their parents on the Upper West Side. A job, an actual nine-to-five job, was an almost alien concept, an abstraction.

"You should find out." I could see that his patience with me was running thin. "If they're not paying for your insurance, you're not going to be bringing much of anything home. How much are you paying Celeste in rent?"

I swallowed, hard. I had moved in with Don—albeit unofficially—before even paying Celeste the first agreed-upon month's rent, though Celeste's closet still held a few of my dresses and my one good coat. My parents knew nothing of Don, not even his name. As far as they knew, I was moments away from marriage with my college boyfriend, of whose handsomeness and kindness and intelligence they wholeheartedly approved. When my parents called Celeste's, I was never there, but they took this as another irksome symptom of youth.

"Three hundred fifty dollars," I told my father, though I had agreed to pay Celeste $375, fully half of her rent. As was so often the case with me, I'd submitted to these terms without thinking them over, and it had since occurred to me that they were less than fair. Paying half the rent on an apartment in which nothing was mine, in which I couldn't even extend my legs while sleeping, made no sense. I couldn't imagine living indefinitely without even a modicum of privacy. But Celeste seemed to crave such close quarters: She seemed, like Hugh, alone. Alone in her anxieties and insecurities, alone in the tyranny of her mind, but also simply, literally, physically alone, her only companion an oversized, paraplegic cat who dragged himself around the apartment like a mythological creature, his front half leonine and furry, his hindquarters shaved bald, for he no longer had the flexibility to groom them. One night, I got back to her place after meeting a friend downtown and found Celeste in bed, covered to the neck in a flower-sprigged flannel nightgown, watching reruns of a once-popular sitcom and stroking her strange cat, tears running down her face. "What's wrong?" I whispered, perching myself on the edge of the bed, as if she were an invalid. "Celeste, what is it?"

"I don't know," she said. Her round, freckled face—a face I thought of as the definition of wholesome—was red and raw from crying.

"What did you do tonight? Were you home? Did something happen?"

She shook her head. "I came home after work and made some spaghetti." I nodded. "And I thought I'd make the whole box, then eat it over the next few days." A lone tear rolled down her plump cheek. "So I ate some, and then I ate a little more, and then a little more." She looked up at me sadly. "And then, before I knew it, I'd eaten the whole thing. A whole pound of spaghetti. I ate a pound of spaghetti by myself."

In the year or so since we left school, she'd gained some weight, but I knew this wasn't what was bothering her, that pound of pasta translating into another pound on the scale. What terrified her was the set of circumstances that allowed her to eat a full pound of spaghetti, the unmoored, untethered quality of her life, in which no one—no mother, sister, room-mate, professor, boyfriend, anyone—was there to monitor her habits and behaviors, to say, "Haven't you had enough?" or "Can I share that with you?" or "Let's have dinner together tonight" or even "What are you doing for dinner?" She woke up, went to work, came home, alone.

"Three hundred fifty dollars?" my father cried. "To share a room? Aren't you sleeping on the sofa?"

"It's actually a really cheap apartment for that neighbor-hood."

"Your mother and I have talked about it," my father said, his patience now fully gone. "If you're going to take this job"—*I've already taken it,* I thought—"you need to live at home. You can take the bus into the city and save up the money for your own apartment. Maybe you can buy a place. Renting is just throwing money away."

"I can't live at home, Dad," I said, measuring my words. "The bus takes almost two hours. I'd have to leave the house at six thirty in the morning."

"So what? You're an early riser."

"Dad," I said quietly. "I just can't. I need to have a life." Through the archway, I saw my boss slowly making her way to our side of the office. "I have to go," I said. "I'm sorry."

"Everyone," said my dad, "doesn't get to have exactly what they want."

"I know," I said as quietly as I could. I loved my father fiercely, and a pang of longing for him, his physical presence, hit me in a sick wave. "You're right." But I was really thinking what all children think: *You didn't. But that doesn't mean I won't.*

The letters piled up on my desk and the hours clicked by. At 1:30, my boss put her coat back on and went out, returning with a small brown bag. When, I wondered, would she tell me to go to lunch? And was I meant to do the same? To buy my lunch and bring it back, eat at my desk? The outside world had come to seem like a dream. There was just me and the Dictaphone, typing letter after letter, adjusting the dial on its side to slow down my boss's voice so that it turned from alto to bass and I spent less time replaying bits. I was starving and my fingers ached, but not as much as my head. A steady stream of smoke drifted from my boss's office out toward my desk. My eyes itched and burned as they did after a night at a bar.

Around 2:30, as I made my way through the final dictation tape, my boss came over to my desk. She'd walked by several times without acknowledging me, an odd sensation, as if I'd been turned into a piece of furniture.

"Well, you look like you've made some headway," she said. "Let me take a look." She grabbed the letters off my desk and retreated to her office.

A moment later, Hugh poked his head out of his office. "Have you had lunch?" he asked. I shook my head. He sighed. "Somebody should have told you. You can go to lunch whenever you like. Your boss usually goes a little earlier. I go later, but I often bring my lunch." Somehow, this didn't surprise me. He was the sort of person I could imagine eating a neat peanut butter and jelly sandwich, sliced into triangles and wrapped in wax paper. "Go now. You must be starving."

"Are you sure?" I asked. "She"—I gestured toward my boss's office—"just took the letters I was typing."

"They can wait," he said. "Those tapes have been sitting around here for a month. Go get a sandwich."

Out on Madison, I found myself gazing through the windows of a chain sandwich shop, its wares too much for me, because everything was too much for me: I had nothing. A few dollars my father had slipped me, meant to last until my first paycheck, which I presumed would come at the end of the week. I didn't even have a bank account in New York yet. I had so little money there seemed no point. My account in London was still open and there was some cash in it, but I wasn't sure how much or how to access it, in this pre-electronic era. My wallet held two credit cards, but these I reserved for emergencies, and it didn't occur to me that I might use them for anything but, that I might use them for something as unnecessary as lunch, no matter how hungry I was.

I would, I decided, simply buy a cup of coffee and an apple. A couple of dollars, at most. On the west side of Madison, I turned in to a deli and inspected a vast pile of overripe bananas. "What you like?" called the white-clad man behind the sandwich counter, smiling.

"Turkey on a hard roll," I said, without really intending to, my heart beating with the recklessness of this gesture. "Provolone, lettuce, tomato, and a little mayo. Just a little. And mustard."

At the register, I handed over a ten and was given two dollars and two quarters back, several dollars more than I'd expected to spend on so humble a sandwich. My pulse quickened with regret. Five dollars was lunch. Seven fifty? Seven fifty was dinner.

Back at my desk, I set down my sandwich and slipped off my coat. As I pulled out my chair to sit down, my boss appeared in the doorway to her office. "Oh, good, you're back," she said. "Come in and have a seat. We have some things to talk about."

Glancing sadly at my sandwich, wrapped tightly in white butcher paper, I walked into her office and sat down in one of the straight-backed chairs that faced her desk.

"So," she said, settling in her own chair, behind the vast expanse of her desk. "We need to talk about Jerry."

I nodded, though I had no idea who Jerry was. "People are going to call and ask for his address, his phone number. They're going to ask you to put them in touch with him. Or *me*." She laughed at the ridiculousness of this. "Reporters will call. Students. *Graduate* students." She rolled her eyes. "They'll say they want to interview him or give him a prize or an honorary degree or who knows what. Producers will call about the film rights. They'll try to get around you. They may be very persuasive, very manipulative. But you must never"—behind those huge, heavy glasses her eyes narrowed and she leaned across the desk, like a caricature of a gangster, her voice taking on a frightening edge—"*never, never, never* give out his address or phone number. Don't tell them anything. Don't answer their questions. Just get off the phone as quickly as possible. Do you understand?"

I nodded.

"Never, ever, ever are you to give out his address or phone number."

"I understand," I told her, though I wasn't sure I did, as I didn't know who Jerry was. This was 1996 and the first Jerry that came to mind was Seinfeld, who presumably wasn't a client of the Agency, though one never knew, I supposed.

"Okay," she said, sitting back in her chair. "You understand. Now go. I'm going to take a look at your correspondence." She gestured to the pile of letters I'd typed, neatly stacked on her desk. Seeing them, oddly, gave me a little rush of pride. They were so beautiful, that heavy yellow bond crowded with letters in inky black.

As I left her office, smoothing my skirt, I happened to glance at the bookcases directly to the right of her doorway, on the wall opposite the side of my desk that held the type-writer. I'd been staring at that bookcase all day, staring at it without seeing it, so focused was I on my typing. The case held books in corresponding hues: mustard, maroon, tur-quoise, imprinted with bold black type. I'd seen these books countless times—in my parents' bookcase and the English department closet at my high school, at every bookstore and library I'd ever visited, and, of course, in the hands of friends. I'd never read them myself, due at first purely to happen-stance, then to conscious choice. Books so ubiquitous on the contemporary bookshelf I barely noticed them: *The Catcher in the Rye, Franny and Zooey, Nine Stories.*

Salinger. The Agency represented J. D. Salinger.

I'd reached my desk before it hit me.

Oh, I thought, *that Jerry.*

Don lived in a large, dilapidated apartment at the intersec-tion of two large, dilapidated thoroughfares—Grand and Union—in the Williamsburg section of Brooklyn. The apart-ment had three bedrooms: a small one, with a door leading directly to the common room, where Don slept; a large one, with two exposures, claimed by Leigh, Don's roommate, who held the lease; and a central one, the door to which was tightly closed on my first visits to the place, like something out of du Maurier or a Greek myth. I assumed, at first, that a third roommate lived therein—space being the most valu-able commodity in New York—but one evening in the late fall, I found the door open and saw that the room contained nothing but a vast pile of clothing—a *mountain* of clothing—all of it twisted and wrinkled and knotted and balled so that shapes could barely be discerned: a slip here, a skirt there, the sleeve of a sweater dangling onto the floor. This clothing was old—from the 1940s and 1950s, based on the prints and colors—and I asked Don if it had come with the house, found in a trunk or the attic, abandoned by a dead tenant.

"It's Leigh's," he said, rolling his eyes. "She can't find the energy to put it away, so she just throws it on the floor. Every once in a while, she decides to pick it all up and take it to the cleaners." Laughing, he shook his head. "But she usually gives up after an hour."

Leigh was tall and thin, so thin that her veins stood out from her pale skin like a topographical map, and her blond hair fell to her shoulders in greasy clumps. No matter what time I arrived at the apartment, she appeared to just be waking up, sleepily wandering out into the common room in a wrinkled silk kimono or a pair of faded men's pajamas, her large blue eyes magnified by the thick lenses of her glasses, their frames so hideously unfashionable as to qualify as cool. Rarely did she leave the apartment, other than to grab a pack of cigarettes or a pint of milk, throwing on an old men's coat over her pajamas. How she paid for these things—with bills crumpled in various pockets and ancient purses—was a mystery, for she had no visible means of income. According to Don, she came from wealth, true wealth, but her father had grown tired of supporting her shortly before I first walked through the door of their apartment in October. "He told her to get a fucking job," Don explained, laughing, though this struck me as sad, rather than funny, as though Leigh were a character out of Wharton, constitutionally incapable of handling the demands of the postindustrial era.

No job had materialized, though I had seen her, on occasion, circling ads in the *Voice*, and now Leigh subsisted purely on coffee—thick and black, made from cheap espresso grounds in an old drip machine—and cigarettes, and the occasional box of generic-brand macaroni and cheese. "It's a perfect food, if you think about," she explained to me. "It's got protein and carbohydrates"—she ticked these nutritional components off on her fingers—"and if you add a pack of frozen spinach, you've got a complete meal." Her genteel background manifested itself largely in the form of advice. Where to drink real absinthe? Repair a cashmere sweater? Get one's hair cut to perfection? Leigh knew, though she could no longer do such things herself. She drank cheap wine—usually purchased by someone else, like me—wore ragged sweaters, and hadn't had a haircut in what looked like years.

Sometime in the middle of December, just before my interview at the Agency, I blew out my knee—an old injury, exacerbated by walking—so badly that I could barely move and was given a prescription for painkillers. I took one pill, which didn't touch the pain in my knee but made my stomach churn and crept insidiously into my brain so that I couldn't read, couldn't think, could do nothing but sleep, as if in a coma, with dark, murky, horrible dreams, in which I was endlessly being chased by some nameless, faceless menace. When I woke, my throat was sore and I could barely move, not even to shift my body and sit up. I called for Don, but Leigh came instead.

"Are you okay?" she asked, putting one icy white hand on my forehead.

"I took this painkiller," I croaked. "It was horrible."

And then, as I watched, her face changed from friendly concern to calculation. "What painkiller?" she asked coolly.

"The bottle's over there," I told her.

"Vicodin," she said reverently, picking it up and cradling it in her palm. "That's what I thought." She paused for a second, rattling the white pills in their amber bottle. "If you're not going to take the rest, can I have them?"

My heart, already palpitating, began to beat faster. Why would she want the pills my orthopedist had given me for my knee? What on earth would she do with them? "Um, I should keep them," I said. "I may need them."

"Just one?" she asked, in a pleading tone that scared me.

"Maybe," I said. "Let me think about it." Reluctantly, she put the bottle down and left, petulantly. "I might need them," I called.

A few hours later I woke to the sound of glass shattering and, a moment later, screams. In the hallway, a gust of freezing air shocked me out of my drugged fog. At the opposite end of the loft, I found Leigh sitting under a broken window, staring at her hand, which was covered in blood, jagged shards of glass sticking out of it. "Oh my God," I cried, tamping down a wave of nausea.

"I'm okay," she said dreamily. "It doesn't hurt at all." She looked up at me, but seemed to see through me or past me or at another me five yards behind me. "I only screamed because of the sound. The sound of the glass." She pointed to the window. "The window broke."

I looked from her face to her hand to the window, shivering in the cold air. "What happened?" I asked, incredulous. For I truly couldn't fathom the scene before me.

"I put my hand through the window," she said, still looking at her hand as if it were a specimen, as if marveling that it was attached to her own body.

"How?" I asked. "Why?" It occurred to me then that we needed to stop talking and get her to a hospital. The amount of blood on and around her was terrifying. I wondered if we were alone in the apartment building, if I should call an ambulance. Where was Don?

"I just wanted to. It looked so beautiful. I knew it wouldn't hurt and it didn't."

Just then, there was a quick rap on the door, followed by the knob turning—Leigh had left it unlocked, yet again—and in walked a tall, handsome man of South Asian extraction—his black hair curling luxuriously around his ears, dusted white with snow—ridiculously underdressed for the weather in a cotton army jacket. We'd met once before, just for a moment, and I knew he was a friend of Leigh's from Antioch, now a grad student in biology at Princeton. Pausing by the front door, he looked toward the kitchen, then toward Leigh's bedroom, where I stood watching him, unable to speak. "Where is she?" he asked.

"Here," I said. "She's bleeding."

"Leigh," he cried, more exasperated than worried, walking past me, into the bedroom. "What did you—" Before he reached her, at the window, his eye went to her bureau, and mine followed it: to an amber bottle. *That can't be mine,* I thought, as he grabbed it. *She wouldn't have.* "Vicodin?" he asked, wearily. "Where did you get these?"

Leigh looked at me and smiled. "From Joanna," she said. "She gave them to me." She smiled wider. "Thank you, Joanna. You're such a good kid." Her smile turned into a grimace. "Don is such a little shit. You should dump him. You're so pretty."

Her friend, whose name, I remembered now, was Pankaj, was shaking the bottle. He cracked it open and counted the pills in his palm. "How many did you take?" he asked Leigh. She held up three bloody fingers. "Three?" he said. "*Three?*" She nodded. He looked at me. "How many were in here?"

I wasn't entirely sure. "Ten?" I said. "I took only one. This morning. I hurt my knee. I didn't—" I paused here, unsure of whether I should take the time to explain that I absolutely hadn't given her the pills. "Why would she take them?" Counting the pills back into the bottle, he looked at me strangely. "They made me sick," I told him. "I threw up. All I could do was sleep. I couldn't read. I had the worst dreams."

"It's fun," called Leigh.

Her friend shook his lovely head and sighed. "You're just lucky she didn't sell them," he said. Then he turned his attention to Leigh. "Okay, let's get to the hospital."

Later, when they returned with Leigh's hand wrapped

in pristine white gauze and sat down at the kitchen table with cold beers, Pankaj explained that Leigh had called him, sounding very strange, and he'd known something was wrong. He'd borrowed a car and driven to Brooklyn from Princeton in the snow. "I had," he said, "an instinct." I nodded. Don was still not home.

At five, my phone rang, startling me out of this sad reverie. "Hey, lady, what's shaking?" came Don's low voice from the receiver. "How's work?" He pronounced this last word with quotes around it, as if I were merely playing at having a job. To Don, "work" meant laying bricks or mopping floors or stamping metal in a factory. Don was a socialist.

On our first date, we'd met at a clock-themed Italian restaurant on Avenue A, chosen—he explained, as he slid into the seat across from me—because of its proximity to the socialist bookstore up the street, where he had just finished a shift. "So, wait," I asked Don, as we waited for plates of pasta. "Do you—do, um, contemporary socialists—really think you're going to overthrow the federal government?"

He swirled his wine, then took a small sip, a little shudder passing through him. "No. I mean, yes, there are some people who do. But most don't."

"Then what's the purpose of the party?" I really wanted to know. In the 1930s, my grandmother had been asked to run for Senate on the Socialist Party ticket. My great-uncle had been shot in a union rally at the Forward Building on East Broadway. My father, when he enlisted during the Korean War, was investigated by the FBI. But no one in my family would talk about politics. The 1950s had scared the impulse out of them. "What do you do? Other than sell books?"

"We educate. We try to raise class awareness. We combat materialism. We work with unions and help laborers organize." And then, suddenly, he took my hand, and his voice—already low, a gravelly bass—became lower. "We offer an alternative," he said. "To everything else. We offer a different way of thinking about the world."

Now his voice came through the phone at me, gravelly and droll. He had a smoker's rasp, though he abhorred smoking. "Listen," he said. "Why don't you meet me at the L after work." The L was the one café in Williamsburg. Don often installed himself there in the evenings, writing in his journal and drinking so much coffee that his leg jumped up and down. "I talked to this realtor who may have a place for us."

"For *us*?" I asked. We'd known each other for just a few months. I had a boyfriend in California. Whom I would be joining. At some distant point in the future. "An apartment for *us*?"

"Us," he said. "You've heard this word before. It means you"—he spoke with exaggerated slowness—"and me."

My boss left at five on the nose, breezing by with a little wave. "Don't stay too late!" she called. I was still typing, Dictaphone still whirring. A few minutes later, Hugh came by, a down coat over his sweater. "Go home," he said. "You've done enough." There was a brief surge of laughter—a rustling of bags and coats—as the bookkeepers and the messenger went home, and then the office fell quiet and dark, the only light in our wing of the office the one on my desk. I finished the letter I was typing and pulled it out of the Selectric, then slipped my coat off the back of my chair and made my way toward the door.

For a moment, I paused in front of the wall of Salinger books and looked at the titles, the familiar spines. My parents owned most of these: paperbacks of *The Catcher in the Rye* and *Raise High the Roof Beam, Carpenters and Seymour—an Introduction;* a pristine hardback of *Franny and Zooey.* But I had read around them. Why? Why had I skipped Salinger? Partly due to happenstance. My high school English teacher never assigned *Catcher.* No older sibling put a copy in my fourteen-year-old hands and said, "You have to read this." And then my Salinger moment—the window between twelve and twenty, when everyone in the literate universe seems to go crazy over *The Catcher in the Rye*—had passed. Now I was interested in difficult, gritty fictions, in large, expansive novels, in social realism. I was interested in Pynchon, Amis, Dos Passos. I was interested in Faulkner and Didion and Bowles, writers whose bleak, relentless styles stood in stark opposition to what I imagined Salinger to be: insufferably cute, aggressively quirky, precious. I had no interest in Salinger's fairy tales of Old New York, in precocious children expounding on Zen koans or fainting on sofas, exhausted by the tyranny of the material world. I was not interested in characters with names like Boo Boo and Zooey. I was not interested in hyper-articulate seven-year-olds who quoted from the Bhagavad Gita. Even the names of the stories seemed juvenile and too clever-clever: "A Perfect Day for Bananafish." "Uncle Wiggily in Connecticut."

I didn't want to be entertained. I wanted to be provoked.

The realtor led us to a pretty row house on North Eighth Street, a block from the train, next to a large Polish bakery, leafless trees casting shadows onto the snow from the streetlights' glow. "It's back here," he said, unlocking the front door and walking past the graceful staircase, past the doors to the first-floor apartments, and out a door at the back of the building. *Where on earth are we going?* I thought, trailing the two men. We were going to an interior courtyard, covered in snow, at the end of which stood a tiny, three-story house, dilapidated and neglected, but also like something out of a storybook, a secret.

The apartment itself was small and strange, its wooden floors freshly painted an odd brick red—the fumes still filled the place—its doorways arched and lacking in actual doors. The living room held a closet and a tiny strip of kitchen, a miniature stove and fridge; the small bedroom overlooked the cement courtyard and the rear windows of the front house; the bathroom was tiled in lurid pink. The floor slanted visibly to one side.

"How much is it?" Don asked the realtor. "Five hundred?"

"Five forty," said the realtor.

"We'll take it," said Don.

Incredulous, I widened my eyes at him. "We might need a day to talk it over. We might want to look at a few other places."

"No," said Don, laughing. "We'll take it. How much is the deposit?"

Outside, the cold air felt delicious on my cheeks. *We're not really taking it*, I thought. And yet just the thought of going back to Celeste's—even to collect my things—made me stiffen with anxiety. The pasta. The overstuffed sofa. The paraplegic cat.

A moment later, we were in the realtor's office, filling out forms.

"It's going to be in her name," said Don, and I shot him a look of alarm, my heart beating faster. If the apartment was in my name, it meant that responsibility for the rent lay with me, that Don was not culpable at all. This seemed terribly scary considering $540 represented more than half my paycheck.

"You're the one with the job," Don explained, taking my arm, as we walked back toward his old apartment. "You're the one with good credit."

"How do you know I have good credit?" I asked.

"I just know," he said, stopping and pulling a pair of worn leather gloves out of his pocket. "Besides, it has to be better than mine."

"What do you mean?"

He took in a deep breath of frigid air. "I defaulted on my student loans," he said.

"You *defaulted* on your student loans?"

"That's what I just said." Shaking his head, he smiled brilliantly. "It's no big deal. The banks are evil, anyway. They're just preying on eighteen-year-olds. What do they care if they lose my twenty grand?" He planted a cold kiss on my right cheek. "You're so bourgeois. Seriously, Buba, it's no big deal. I had a novel to write. I didn't have time to worry about student loans."

I wasn't sure what to say about this, what to think.

"It was stupid, though." He took my arm again, and we continued walking across North Ninth Street toward Macri Triangle, a grubby patch of grass overrun with rats that was somehow considered, by the City of New York, an official public park. "I couldn't make the payments, so I deferred. You can keep deferring. You just have to do all this paperwork every six months. I got sick of doing the paperwork."

I was thinking about the rent. The truth was I didn't really understand how Don made a living. He seemed to spend most of his time at the gym—he was a boxer, "like Mailer," as he said, "but better"—or in cafés, working on a novel that was, he said, nearly done. In the past, he'd taught English as a second language to adults—immigrants from Russia and Latin American housewives—but now he had just a few private students. He always seemed to have money for wine or coffee, but he also—I was noticing—doled out cash with strict discipline. He didn't use credit cards. And now I knew why.

"I mean, college should be free anyway," he was saying. "In Europe nobody pays twenty grand a year for a BA.

All my European friends think Americans are *crazy*." Don's
European friends occasionally came up in conversation, but
they'd yet to materialize in real life. The friends we saw regularly were largely from New York and Hartford, where Don
grew up, and San Francisco, where he'd lived until a year
or so prior. Most had indeed attended colleges where tuition
exceeded twenty grand per year. His friend Allison had grown
up in a town house on the Upper East Side—the daughter
of a famous writer and a powerful editor—and gone to Ben-
nington with Marc, his best friend from Hartford, the child
of academics. Like Don, they strove to shake the trappings
of their privileged childhoods: Allison lived in a garret-like
studio on Morton Street and complained of poverty but ate
out every night. Marc had abandoned his expensive education to train as a cabinetmaker. Now he ran a high-end
contracting business out of his loft on Fourteenth Street, a
not-insubstantial piece of real estate.

"Was there something strange about that apartment?" I
asked.

"The floor tilted a little." He shrugged, then put his arm
around me and drew me close. "But who cares. We're not
going to find another apartment for five hundred bucks a
month. Right by the train. Right by everything. And that's a
beautiful block, North Eighth. All the trees."

"The trees," I repeated, smiling, though all I could recall
about them was the dusty shadows they'd thrown on the
snow.

When we got home, we found Leigh and Pankaj sitting at the
table drinking beer with Allison and Marc, whom Don had
apparently invited over and forgotten about—or forgotten to
tell *me* about. I liked both of them—far more than most of
Don's friends—but I was exhausted. "Donald!" Leigh cried.
The hand she raised in greeting was still bandaged. "Joanna!

Come have a beer with us. We're celebrating." Rising from her chair, she placed her warm cheek on my cold one. She was wearing one of her beautiful dresses—a deep maroon crepe with tiny covered buttons down the front—and a full face of makeup: foundation, which smoothed the pits and ruts on her chin, and mascara, which gave her actual eyelashes, and a deep red lipstick. Her hair, too, had been washed and blown into shiny waves. She looked not just presentable but gorgeous. "I have a job."

"Wow," I said. I'd not actually thought her capable of finding employment. "What kind of job?"

"Who cares?" called Allison gleefully, clinking beers with Pankaj, who merely smiled. He was still wearing his unlined army coat, a scarf wrapped around his neck, though the apartment was stifling at the moment. I tried to catch his eye. We'd been through something together, I thought, we had a special understanding. But he looked down at the table, at his lap, the beer. "Hey, man," he finally said to Don. "How's the party?"

A few minutes later, he and Leigh disappeared. First him, then her. "I'm going to change," she said. "I've been in these clothes all day."

"Hey," I called after her. "Guess who's a client of my Agency?"

"Thomas Pynchon," answered Allison, sipping wine out of a large blue goblet. It was the only vessel in the apartment resembling an actual wineglass, and Allison always claimed it when she came to visit.

"Close," I said. "J. D. Salinger."

The room fell into stunned silence. Allison, Marc, and Don stared at me, openmouthed. "Here," Marc said finally, pushing a beer in my direction.

"*J. D. Salinger?*" asked Don, finally, shaking his head in disbelief. "For real?"

I nodded. "He's my boss's client."

Suddenly everyone was talking at once.

"Did you speak to him?" asked Marc. "Did he call?"

"Is he working on a new novel?" asked Allison, her lips ghoulishly purple with wine. "I've heard stories—"

"How *old* is your boss?" asked Don. "Didn't Salinger start writing stories in, like, the '40s?"

"Was he nice?" asked Allison. "People get so angry about him, but I always got the feeling that he was really nice, that he truly just wanted to be left alone."

"He's a fucking phony," said Don with a smile.

Marc narrowed his eyes, annoyed. "You're kidding, right?" he said, taking a swig of beer. "Just because he wants to be left alone doesn't mean he's some kind of fraud." Like Don, Marc was short and muscular and possessed of a certain intensity. He had the looks of a 1970s film star: blue eyes, chiseled jaw, long nose, wavy blond hair. Looks so stunning that even men commented on them. His fiancée, Lisa, was oddly plain—unusually plain—and as silent and reserved as Marc was garrulous and open. These were just a few of the grounds on which Don objected to her. He was convinced Marc would call off the wedding.

"My friend Jess worked at Little, Brown a few years ago"— Allison looked at Marc—"Salinger's publisher you know?" Marc nodded. "She was just an assistant and she had nothing to do with Salinger, with the Salinger books. But her desk was near the reception area, and one night she was working late and the main phone line just kept ringing and ringing and ringing. It was like nine thirty at night. Who calls an office at nine thirty, right? So finally she picked it up and there was someone screaming—like *screaming*—on the other end. Screaming, 'THE MANUSCRIPT IS OKAY! I SAVED THE MANUSCRIPT!' And something about a fire, and other stuff that she couldn't understand. Just *screaming*. So she thought this was a crazy person, right?" We nodded. "The next day, she got to work and it turns out—"

"It was Salinger," said Don.

"It was Salinger," confirmed Allison, her cheeks hollowing in annoyance. "There'd been a fire at his house. His whole house had burned down. Or half his house. Anyway, his house was actually *on fire* when he called, but somehow he thought the most important thing was to call his publisher and let them know that his new book was okay. Like before even saving his family or calling the fire department."

"How do you know he didn't save his family or call the fire department first?" asked Don.

"Jess told me," said Allison.

"Why is it crazy to call your publisher and let them know your manuscript hasn't been destroyed in a fire?" Don persisted.

"That's not the crazy part, Don," Allison groaned. "He called in the middle of the night, when no one was there. He assumed that the people at Little, Brown *knew* that there was a fire in some small town in New Hampshire—"

"You know what?" Don's gravelly voice had grown raspier with drink. "This sounds like bullshit to me. Salinger's not working on another book. Why should he? What is he now, a millionaire how many times over? Your friend just made this all up."

"*Oh my God,* Don!" Allison shrieked, her dark eyes glassy, her cheeks flushed red. "Why would she make this up? *How* would she make this up? There was a fire. Everyone knew about it. I remember my mom talking about it. It was in the paper. I read about it. *She* read about it."

"Exactly," said Don, grinning.

"I read about it, too," said Marc, brushing back an errant lock of hair. "Or I read something. I'm trying to remember. Was it in the *Times?* He says he's writing but that he never wants to publish. That he writes for himself now. He doesn't need to publish."

Again, the room fell silent. Don's face had grown slack and earnest. He looked at me and smiled. I knew that this accorded with his own ideas about writing. "Writing makes you a writer," he'd told me. "If you get up every morning and write, then you're a writer. Publishing doesn't make you a writer. That's just commerce."

"Hey," came a voice from the hallway. We turned to find Leigh, alone, now clad in her usual bathrobe, a tattered, sateen affair in maroons and blues. Her makeup was still in place, but she seemed to be moving in slow motion. "What's going on?" she said, her speech ever so slightly slurred. *She's drunk,* I thought, with a sudden clarity. I'd seen her like this many times before, I realized, but I'd never thought about it. Or I'd thought her simply tired. *I* was tired. And hungry, very hungry. Though I'd drunk just half my beer—if that—my head suddenly began to spin. An irresistible urge to lie down came over me.

"I'll be right back," I said, carefully rising from my chair. I made my way down the hallway, past the room of sad, crumpled dresses, and opened the door to the bathroom, where I found Pankaj, sitting on the toilet. "Oh!" I cried. "I'm sorry." He looked at me strangely, blankly, and it was then that I saw his arm, which was wrapped with the sort of rubber tubing used in hospitals, a needle inserted in the crook below. His face, as I watched, arranged itself in an expression of both pain and the absence of pain. "Oh!" I cried again, stupidly.

For a moment we stared at each other, the blank remove on his face turning to sadness, then anger, until I left, returning not to the kitchen table, to Don and Leigh and the others, but to Don's room, where I sat down heavily on his bed, a futon without a frame, then lay back and stared at the ceiling.

When Don came in to check on me, I rolled to face him. "Okay," I said. "Let's take the apartment."

. . .

Late the next morning, I rapped softly on my boss's half-open door and handed over the rest of her dictation. She had come in, again, without so much as a hello. And she'd not yet mentioned my letters from the day before. They sat on her desk, still neatly piled, awaiting signature. "Sit down for a second," she said. I sat. Pulling a pack of cigarettes from her desk drawer, she began to slowly peel off the plastic. "Some people," she began, shooting me a significant look, "take this job thinking they're going to meet Jerry. Or even"—she smiled—"become friends with him. They think he's going to call every day." She peered at me over the tops of her glasses. "He's *not* going to call. And if he does, Pam will put the call directly through to me. If I'm not here and by some chance he gets put through to you, don't keep him on the phone. He's not calling to chat with you. Understand?" I nodded. "I don't want you thinking you're going to be on the phone with him every day or you're going to be"—she laughed—"*having lunch with him* or something. Some assistants have even made excuses to call him. Without checking with me, of course. That is something you can never, ever do. Our job is *not* to bother him. We take care of his business so he doesn't have to be bothered with it. Do you understand?"

"Absolutely."

"So, you're never, ever to call him. If something arises that you think needs his attention—though I can't imagine what that would be—you tell me, and I'll decide if he needs to know. You *never* call him. You *never* write to him. If he calls, you just say, 'Yes, Jerry. I'll let my boss know.' Got it?"

I nodded, trying not to smile. I would never have thought to needlessly keep J. D. Salinger on the phone, much less pick up the receiver and call him.

My boss looked at me seriously and emitted one of her

odd, low laughs. "He doesn't want to read your stories. Or hear how much you loved *The Catcher in the Rye*."

"I don't have any stories," I told her, half truthfully. I had stories. Just not finished ones.

"Good," she said. "Writers always make the worst assistants."

Everything was wrong. The two days of typing, the piles and piles of letters. Margins, tabs, proper names, everything. Every single letter had to be retyped. "You'll be more careful this time, won't you?" my boss said, and I smiled, holding back tears.

Trying now for competence rather than speed, I began again, checking my work after every line, as the phone in my boss's office rang and rang. "Happy New Year," she cried, again and again. "How was your holiday?" These one-sided conversations were somehow more distracting than plain old two-sided ones. I found myself filling in the other end of the dialogue and speculating on the parts I could hear. Motifs began to appear. My boss spoke frequently of someone named Daniel, who seemed to have been ill—perhaps gravely so—but was now doing better thanks to a change in medication. *Her husband?* I wondered. *Her brother?* Someone named Helen arose with slightly less frequency and less detail. But I couldn't figure out who this person might be. Regardless, her words began to insert themselves in the letters. "Thank you for sending on the countersigned sandwich," I typed. "I'll be in touch in two weeks to discuss the details of the upholstery." Again and again, I ripped a half-finished letter out and started all over. *Please close your door,* I silently begged my boss. *Please stop ringing,* I begged the phone. On cue, it rang again.

"Jerry," my boss shouted. Why was she shouting? Her

voice had grown louder as the day progressed. *Please stop shouting,* I thought. "Jerry, it's so good to hear from you. How are you?"

At precisely that moment, my wish came true: my boss got up and closed her door.

Boom. The door burst open and my boss was yelling. "Hugh," she called, appearing in the doorway, cigarette poised dramatically in one hand. "*Hugh! HUGH!*" She marched toward his door, more quickly than I'd previously seen her move. "Where *is* he?" she muttered. I was pretty certain he was in his office, but said nothing.

"One second," he called calmly.

"I don't have a second," said my boss, tittering with discomfort at her own testiness. "Oh, for heaven's sake, Hugh!"

"Okay." He appeared in the doorway. "You *rang*?"

"Oh, *Hugh,*" my boss said, laughing against her will. "Jerry just called."

"Jerry called?" Hugh's face immediately lost its levity. It was as if my boss had told him that his parole officer was sitting in the reception area.

"Yes." She nodded with satisfaction. "He wants to see his royalty statements"—she looked down at a slip of paper in her hand—"for *Nine Stories* and *Raise High the Roof Beam.* From 1979 through 1988."

"Okay." Hugh shuffled on his feet a little. "Paperback? Or hardback? Or trade paperback?"

My boss shook her head impatiently. "I don't know. Just pull them all. How quickly can you get the numbers together?"

For a moment, Hugh stared off into the middle distance, his mind presumably drifting to some better place, where he could sit eternally and sift his papers without being called to perform tedious tasks for an unseen master. My boss tapped her foot, which was surprisingly tiny, almost hooflike, and shod in a beige orthopedic-style shoe. "End of the day tomorrow," Hugh told her. "Maybe sooner. Why does he want them? What does he need them for?"

"Who knows?" my boss said. "He's always wanting to check up on Little, Brown. You know. He's convinced they're making mistakes. And they *do* make mistakes." Suddenly she noticed the cigarette in her hand, which had burned down to the filter. Just as the ash began to fall on the carpet, she dropped it into a small black ashtray on the credenza outside Hugh's office, specks of gray softly depositing themselves on her shoes and the carpet around them. "Darn it," she said quietly. "Just get them. Don't worry about why he needs them."

"Okay," said Hugh, glancing at me for the first time and offering a small smile. "Whatever Jerry wants."

Office Equipment

For weeks I typed and typed and typed. I typed so much that
I dreamed of typing. In my dreams, my fingers ran over the
keys and nothing happened, though my ribbon was intact
and my machine appeared to be functioning. Instead of letters imprinting on paper, birds flew out of the innards of my
typewriter, chirping and flapping, or swarms of white dusty
moths, some huge, some tiny, and took up roost around the
office. The hum of the machine filled my days, a backdrop to
every conversation, every word I read, so that when I shut the
Selectric off at the end of the day, and sheathed it in its plastic
cover, the ensuing silence filled me with immeasurable joy.

James had an affinity for the office hardware and was
often called upon to resolve technological issues, such as
malfunctions with the fax machine or clogs in the photocopier. Both were relatively new additions to the office. Only
a couple of years before my arrival, James told me, the agents
had still communicated with their sister agency in England
via an enormous telex machine. In the files, I found missives
from the late 1980s imprinted on long, columnar sheets of

telex paper, in that device's charmingly chunky lettering, a font I associated with a different era, with *Thin Man* movies and steamship travel. The Agency, it seemed, had held on to that era, fox stoles and all, as long as it could. It was still holding on, of course, but the modern age was encroaching, in manifold ways. A few years earlier, one of the agents—now retired—had convinced his colleagues that he needed a fax machine in order to properly look after their clients' film rights, as was his province. In Hollywood, communication via fax was de rigueur; deals happened too quickly for the U.S. Postal Service. And so a fax machine was installed by the coffeemaker, the telex machine retired, though it sat in the office for years, just in case such technology should be called into service again.

The photocopier was a relatively recent acquisition, too. Until just a few years prior, assistants had typed every letter in duplicate, inserting into their typewriters a paper sandwich consisting of a thick sheet of creamy letterhead, a slender black wisp of carbon, and a piece of soft, pulpy yellow paper, on which the carbon imprinted a copy of the note. Copies of all correspondence, even those notes that simply said, "Attached is a countersigned agreement for your records," were kept and eventually filed away in folders devoted to each of the Agency's authors. Now, though, we assistants didn't need to bother with carbons. We could simply type up our letters and Xerox them. How lucky we were! My boss, and Hugh, and James—and any number of others—reminded me of this from time to time. We were spoiled, my generation, by modern convenience!

James had started at the Agency six years earlier as assistant to Carolyn, who sold foreign rights and who had been there even longer than my boss, since the 1960s or earlier, no one knew for sure. Tiny as a child, Carolyn spoke in a low, sophisticated southern drawl and dyed her hair a rusty shade of red that—based on her freckled complexion—must have approximated its color in her youth, which was now gone, though it was not clear how long. I guessed she was about seventy, but she could have been older or younger, her diminutive size and smoker's wrinkles—like my boss, she smoked long, slender Mores—throwing off all guesses. Often, in the afternoons, she fell asleep at her desk, her head curled into her chest like a baby bird; the first time I'd happened upon her in this position—as I walked by her office on my way to the bathroom—I started, thinking she'd passed into a deeper state than sleep. Then she let out a long burp.

Though James now had his own lovely, book-lined office, he was still officially considered Carolyn's assistant. Or so I discovered one morning, when I walked by his office and found him typing, calmly and quickly, the Dictaphone headgear perched oddly atop his leonine head. He was thirty, the same age as Don, and married. And yet he was still someone's assistant, after six years of employment and with an Ivy League degree. With a *wife*.

Now that I understood this, I looked away in embarrassment when I encountered him typing or filing correspondence in the big metal cabinets behind the finance desks. But James didn't mind, really, typing letters for Carolyn, he told me one afternoon in February, the office already dark as midnight, though it was barely four o'clock. My boss had gone home early to take care of a matter involving the people I often heard her talking about or to: Daniel and Helen. I still didn't understand who they were and how they fit into her life, but it was clear that they took up much of her time. She also regularly left early to check in on Dorothy, who I now knew was the Agency's former president, a formidable and legendary agent, in her nineties and felled by a stroke. She'd never married, never had children. "She kind of married the Agency," James told me. And now the Agency—in the form of my boss, her successor—took care of her. She herself had been the successor to the Agency's founder, and the person who'd discovered Salinger, who'd sent his stories to *The New Yorker* over and over again, until finally William Maxwell accepted one, "Slight Rebellion off Madison," which would eventually become *The Catcher in the Rye*. "You can look at the card," Hugh told me excitedly. The Agency used a bizarre, overly complicated system for tracking submissions—of both books and stories, though there wasn't much business in the latter anymore—involving the oversized pink cards I'd found in my desk that first day, on which one recorded the various editors who had seen it, the days on which one called to check in on it, the sale and contractual terms when sold, and so on. These cards appeared to have been invented by the Agency's founder and were produced specifically for our use. It was the assistants, of course, who typed them up, squeezing impossible amounts of information into the network of grids and lines. "You know what else is neat?" Hugh said, an almost mischievous glint in his pale eyes. "Look up the card for *The Catcher in the Rye*." Dorothy had, of course, made that sale, too. The large, windowed area we now used as a conference room had once been her office. Hugh, when he first started at the Agency, as her assistant, had sat in there with her, taking live dictation. Perhaps we assistants *did* have it easy now, with our Xerox machine and our Dictaphones.

"Typing is sort of a mindless task," James opined, stretching his arms behind his head and hoisting his loafer-clad feet on his desk. "I spend so much time *thinking*. Or editing. Or, just, figuring out difficult things, so it's nice to turn on the machine"—he gave it a friendly pat—"and type for a while. It relaxes me." James sat up and smiled. He took himself, our work, so seriously. His smiles always took me by surprise. Hugh's, too. "Still. It's ridiculous that we don't have computers."

"You think?" I asked. This was the first I'd heard such an opinion expressed, and I was afraid that it was a trap.

"Um, yeah," he said, laughing. "Don't you?"

I did. Of course, I did. And yet I also, at that moment in time, didn't know what I thought. About anything. I had an inkling—a vague suspicion that I was afraid to articulate even to myself—that this had something to do with work, with my boss. That in order to become part of something—and I did, desperately, want to be part of the Agency, more than I had wanted anything in ages, and without really understanding why—I had to relinquish some semblance of myself, my own volition and inclinations.

We'd moved in just a box or two before I realized why the apartment looked off-kilter, strange, wrong: the kitchen had no sink. How had we not noticed this when we looked at it? "I noticed it," Don admitted. "But who cares? It's five hundred dollars a month. We can wash the dishes in the bathtub."

"I think we should ask the landlord to install a sink," I said. "It's just weird."

"Why should the landlord install a sink?" Don scoffed, shaking his head at my naïveté. "He can find someone else to take the apartment without one. Like that." He snapped his fingers for emphasis. "You can ask, but it's not going to happen. And then the landlord is going to hate us."

That night, a more pressing problem arose: we couldn't figure out how to turn on the heat. There were vents in the floor, but nothing came out of them. In the hallway outside our front door we found a thermostat and turned it up, but nothing happened.

It was cold. Unusually cold for New York in January. And the walls of the little building appeared to lack any insulation at all. Inside, the air was as cold as out. I put on my warmest pajamas, a heavy sweater, piled blankets on the bed, but I still froze.

"I'll turn on the oven and open the door," said Don.

"Is that safe?" I asked. "What if the pilot blows out? Couldn't we be gassed?"

Don shrugged. "It's fine. This apartment is so drafty. There's plenty of ventilation even if the windows are closed."

"Okay," I agreed, nervously. The next morning, we were still alive and the apartment was warm: it was so small that the oven could heat it entirely. As soon as I got to work, I called the realtor, who said he'd call the landlord. Her name, he told me, was Kristina. "She's a real character," he said.

That night, I arrived home to find Don talking to a squat woman with a platinum-blond bouffant and an excess of tanned flesh spilling out of a red tank top. "Hello," she said in a thick Polish accent. "You are the wife. I am Kristina. I am very happy to meet you. Very happy to have such a nice couple, a nice professional couple, in this apartment. You met the man downstairs?"

"Um, no," I said, taking off my coat. Don still had the oven on and the apartment was quite warm. Had he left it on all day? While we weren't here?

"He is Mexican. Nice man, but he drinks. Mexicans, they work hard, but they drink. Poles, they don't work hard, and they drink. The man upstairs, he is Polish, but he's okay. Old." Her eyes narrowed and her jaw began to protrude in an expression of distaste. "The man who lived in this apartment before you? He *destroyed* it. Holes in the walls. Gah." She pursed her lips, her jowls doubling into themselves, and shook her head in disgust. Suddenly she turned to Don, who was sitting at his desk, wearing his glasses—round, wire-rimmed—in a plaid shirt and jeans. My jeans, actually. We were about the same size. "You are Jewish?" she asked him, though it came out more as a statement than a question.

"Me?" he said, smiling. "No. I'm not Jewish."

"Of course you are!" she cried, throwing up her bare arms. "Look at you." She turned to me with a conspiratorial smile. "He thinks because I'm Polish I don't like Jews. But I do. I love Jews. Jews are good tenants. Pay the rent on time. Quiet. Reading books." She gestured to Don's desk, which was indeed littered with serious-looking tomes. "Jews are best tenants, yes?" She turned to me again and smiled, as if I, too, were a slumlord with fiercely held opinions on such matters. I smiled back. "He is Jewish, yes?"

"*She's* Jewish," said Don, laughing, waving his hand in my direction. *Oh my God,* I thought. *Really?*

"*She?*" Kristina scrunched up her face in contemplation. "No. Look at her. She's so beautiful." She gave Don a stern look. "You play joke. Stop."

"So, we were wondering how to turn on the heat in here," I interjected, before this line of discussion could go any further. "We noticed that there's a thermostat in the hallway, but turning it up didn't seem to have any effect."

Kristina was shaking her head vehemently. "That is from when this was one-family house. It does not work now. We disconnect."

"Oh, great," I said. I was still standing by the door, unsure if I should sit down. "So how do we turn on the heat?"

Kristina's blond head began shaking again, even more frenetically. "Heat? What you need heat for? It small apartment. It's warm in here. *Hot.*" She gestured to the round folds of her body. "Look at what I am wearing. And I'm hot. No heat. You don't need heat."

Don began laughing nervously. "Right, that's because the oven's on. We couldn't figure out how to turn on the heat, so we turned on the oven and opened the door."

Kristina's eyes narrowed in her fleshy face. She crossed her arms over her bosom and sighed, pursing her lips again into a forbidding line. We were no longer her friends, no longer her dream tenants.

"I'm gonna check for you. But what you need heat for?" She smiled broadly. "You have oven. Oven is fine. Oven is same as heater." She picked up a nylon track jacket, also red, with white stripes down the sleeves, slipped it on, and zipped it to her chin. "Jewish?" she said, looking at me and smiling. "You think I am stupid."

Salinger hadn't called since the day he'd requested the royalty statements—we still didn't know why he wanted them; James and Hugh chalked it up to yet another of his eccentricities—but others began to call *for* him, just as my boss had told me they would.

Some of the callers were simply old—Salinger's peers—and perhaps didn't understand the extent of Salinger's self-enforced isolation from the world. When last they'd checked, he'd been a tortured young writer, on the cover of *Time* magazine, the future of American literature writ large. These callers felt an enormous kinship with Salinger, for they, too, had served during World War II, or grown up on the Upper West Side in the 1930s. Often, they had a personal matter to discuss with Salinger: They thought a character in one of his stories was based on their cousin. Or they thought their cousin had done basic training with Salinger. Or they'd lived down the street from him in Westport in 1950. Now, at the dawn of their dotages, they wanted to be in touch with this man whose work had been so significant to them in their youth. Or they'd reread *Catcher* and only now realized the extent to which it was about Salinger's experiences during the war. Or they'd just turned back to "A Perfect Day for Bananafish" and found themselves sobbing with recognition, for they, too, had been suicidal after the Battle of the Bulge. No man should ever see what they saw.

Equally harmless were editors of textbooks and anthologies, guilelessly hoping to include "Teddy" in their collection of stories on marriage and divorce or an excerpt from *Catcher* in the new edition of *The Norton Anthology of American Litera-*

ture. "We can grant permission for *Catcher* to appear in the Norton anthology, right?" I'd asked Hugh.

"No!" Hugh cried. "We can't. You didn't tell them yes, did you?" His face was turning red with panic.

"No, of course not," I said. "But, we shouldn't ask him if he wants to be included?" This was, after all, the *Norton.* The anthology used on every campus in America.

"No." Hugh shook his head and sucked in his upper lip. "No anthologies. No excerpts. If you want to read Salinger, you have to buy his books."

I thought of the last category simply as the Crazies. This was, if not the largest genre of caller in sheer volume, then certainly the most consuming, in terms of time. Occasionally said craziness was clear from the moment I picked up the phone, and I quickly extricated myself, replacing my receiver with a satisfying little thud. Other times, I'd pick up the phone and find myself talking, say, with a polite man—"Oh, yes, hello! Thank you so much for taking my call!"—who explained that he was the dean of a community college in southern New Jersey. "We would be very honored if J. D. Salinger would serve as our commencement speaker this year. The ceremony is on May 28 and we can, of course, offer a small honorarium, as well as accommodations at a very fine inn." There was more—the history of the college, information about the current student body—but I interjected as soon as he took a breath.

"It's so lovely of you to think of Mr. Salinger, but I'm afraid Mr. Salinger isn't accepting speaking engagements at the moment."

"Yes, I *know.*" The dean's polite formality quickly devolved into testiness. "But I thought he might make an exception for our particular school because"—insert your reason here; in this case it was—"as I *mentioned,* our student body is largely comprised of veterans—from the Gulf War—and seeing as Mr. Salinger is a veteran himself and has written about

the experiences of veterans adjusting to life in civilian society . . ." There was more. Already, I realized that there was
always more.

"I completely understand. But Mr. Salinger isn't accepting any speaking engagements at all."

"Well, could you at least put me in touch with him so
I could extend our invitation directly? I'm sure if he let me
explain the situation, he'd be happy to come. We put all our
speakers up at a *lovely* inn—"

"I'm afraid I can't put you in touch with Mr. Salinger.
He's explicitly asked us not to give out his phone number or
address."

"Well, if I sent on a written invitation, could you forward it?"

I took a deep breath. It would be so much easier to lie. To
say, "Sure! Of course!" And just toss the thing in the garbage,
let them blame Salinger when they never got a reply. But I
stuck to the script. There was a perverse pleasure in it. "I'm
afraid that I can't. Mr. Salinger has asked us not to forward
any mail that arrives for him."

"So if I sent on an invitation, what exactly would happen
to it?" I could virtually hear the blood vessels bursting in this
man's face. This venture, I knew, was personal to him. It was
not about bringing glory to his tiny college but about the relationship he'd forged with Salinger in his mind. "Would you
just send it back to me? What would you do with it?"

Was I really supposed to tell him that his invite would
be either returned to him or thrown in the round trash can
below my boss's desk (if I dared pass it on to her) or lost in
Hugh's pile of papers?

Yes, I was.

"But isn't that illegal? Don't you have an obligation
to make sure Mr. Salinger receives all his mail? If it's sent
through the U.S. Postal Service?" This argument came up
from time to time.

"Mr. Salinger has hired us as his agents. He has hired us to act on his behalf. Our job is to carry out his wishes."

"But how do you know what his wishes are?" The dean was shouting by now, and I was sweating under the arms. "How do you know what he wants? Who *are* you anyway?"

"Mr. Salinger has detailed his wishes for us and we are simply carrying them out," I said smoothly. He had a point, though. How *did* we—how did *I*—know the confines of Salinger's wishes? What if he really did want to drive down to the Pine Barrens and stay at a very nice inn and talk to some veterans? Such a thing didn't seem outside the realm of possibility. "I'm so sorry, Dean Something"—I'd also discovered that remembering and using the callers' names helped defuse their anger—"but Mr. Salinger has explicitly instructed us to turn down all speaking engagements. It's been a pleasure talking with you and I'm sure you'll find a perfect speaker for your commencement."

I hung up the phone. My sweater was soaked through under the arms, though my boss had decided to air out her office: an icy wind was now snaking through her windows, swirling around my desk. My body convulsed, briefly, as the chill air insinuated itself into my hot points. Confrontation made me very, very anxious. Then it hit me: I wasn't anxious. I was ill. I had a fever. As a kid, sickness came upon me this way, out of nowhere: my head suddenly too heavy to keep up.

I stood up from my chair, my legs wobbling dangerously. Halfway across the office, I realized I was *running*, fueled by adrenaline. *Slow down*, I told myself, forcefully. Under the thin, anemic glare of the bathroom's fluorescents, I splashed water on my face—noting my forehead's coolness—then caught myself in the warped, peeling mirror: My cheeks were flushed pink, my eyes glistening brightly. This wasn't illness. This wasn't anxiety.

This was excitement.

Things were happening. I wasn't *becoming* part of something. I was *already* part of something.

My best friend from high school, Jenny, worked a few blocks away, in the McGraw-Hill Building, editing social studies textbooks. Or text*book*, for she spent the entirety of her tenure working on one enormous project, a fifth-grade social studies primer that was being adapted for the public schools of the state of Texas. Apparently, Texas was so enormously powerful—so large, with so many schools and students, so much money—that it could demand a textbook tailored specifically to its needs, with a whole chapter on the Alamo, and another on the history of the state, and—most distressingly—the chapter on the civil rights movement omitted entirely. Jenny made light of all this, but she was genuinely troubled by it, and yet she also loved her job, the cleanness and rigor of it, the meetings at which her presence was required. She had drifted through college, transferring twice and picking up a variety of prescriptions along the way, but now she had a purpose, a structure to her life. Now she had Texas.

"It's so nice just to be *normal*," she'd told me a few months earlier, when I returned from London. In high school, we'd not wanted to be normal. We'd made fun of the normal people. We'd hated them.

"I know," I said reflexively, but I didn't. I didn't want to be normal. I wanted to be extraordinary. I wanted to write novels and make films and speak ten languages and travel around the world. I wanted everything. So, I'd thought, had Jenny.

Perhaps as much as normalcy, she loved having money, her own money. She had a fraught relationship with her parents—more so than any of our friends—and she'd rushed into the trappings of grown-up life earlier than the rest of us. Editing textbooks paid far more than the literary jobs available to those who had recently graduated from Swarthmore with a degree in poetry—as had Jenny—and, thus, she'd made a calculated decision to toil in the less glamorous realm of educational publishing. At the time, this was unfathomable to me. As was her equally calculated decision to move to a remote, cultureless, suburban section of Staten Island, in a newly built complex of identical fiberboard apartments. The commute to midtown took her a full hour and a half—each way—and meant that she couldn't, for instance, meet after work to go to the Angelika for the new Hal Hartley movie, or for drinks at Von, or—certainly not—to see a band at Mercury Lounge. She had to join her fiancé, Brett, at the train and start the arduous journey home.

But Staten Island was cheaper, she said, than any of the neighborhoods to which my other friends were moving, most of them in Brooklyn: Carroll Gardens, Cobble Hill, the Fifth Avenue part of Park Slope, Fort Greene and Clinton Hill, a nebulous square off Flatbush that we would eventually learn to call Prospect Heights, and, more than anywhere else, my neighborhood, Williamsburg, and its neighbor to the north, Greenpoint, areas so densely populated with friends, and friends of friends, and distant acquaintances, or simply the loose network of Oberlin-Bard-Vassar-etc. that I couldn't buy a cup of coffee at the L without running into several people I knew. Often, when I went out for breakfast on Sunday morning, at the Mediterranean place around the corner, I was seated by a dancer who'd been a year ahead of me at school and waited on by a painter who'd been two years ahead. At night, Don and I could meet Lauren for Thai food, or Leigh and Allison for gin and tonics at the Rat Pack–era bar on Bedford and watch an alternative circus, which involved one college friend of mine eating fire, another clowning in the style of Jacques Lecoq, another riding a unicycle and playing trombone. For me, this was heaven, heaven that could only be improved by Jenny moving in down the street.

For Jenny, though, it turned out this was hell. She had cast off such childish things. Heaven was, she told me, eyes shining, driving to a large supermarket and unloading a week's worth of groceries directly into her apartment from her designated parking spot. Like me, Jenny was a child of the 1970s—her mother an Afro-sporting feminist who published poetry in *Lilith* and ran a women's shelter—but she seemed to be morphing into a housewife from the 1950s, by sheer force of will. Her wedding, at the Central Park Boathouse, was to be a royal affair.

One unseasonably warm day toward the end of March— the sort of day when you realize that spring might actually arrive at some point, that it won't be winter forever—I walked across Forty-Ninth Street, to Sixth Avenue, checked in with security, took the elevator up to the umpteenth floor, and met Jenny at her cubicle, which was large and white and newly constructed, at the center of an enormous open room filled with dozens and dozens of identical cubicles, their interior walls lined with pinned-up photos of boyfriends or husbands or smiling children, with postcards from faraway places. Jenny had a photo of Brett and one of her sister, Natalie, smiling goofily. But her cubicle was dominated by work: alongside the photos were printouts of e-mails. She gestured to these, made a monster face, and moaned, "BLARGH!"

"What?" I asked, laughing.

"My boss has decided that our office is going to be completely paperless," she explained.

"How is that possible?" Now this sounds like a ridiculous question. But in 1996 it truly did seem impossible to eliminate paper from an office. Especially an office devoted to the production of *books*.

"Well, we're going to do everything by e-mail. No more interoffice memos." She pointed to her desk. "It's driving me *insane*. Every two seconds I get ten new e-mails about NOTHING. She'll send out something that I need to look at while

I'm working—like updated style sheets—and I just have to print it out, but there's no printer on this floor, so I have to walk downstairs or upstairs to the printer, and half the time someone has taken my printouts accidentally, so I have to come back here and print them again, then go back downstairs and AGH!"

This didn't sound like such a big deal to me, but I said nothing. I worked in an office that considered the photocopier a newfangled invention. What did I know.

"But what's really driving me crazy is that *no one* talks to each other anymore. At all." She widened her lovely brown eyes and stretched out her mouth. "So, my boss is just right there"—she pointed across the room to an empty cubicle identical to her own—"but instead of getting up, walking the fifteen feet over to my desk, and saying, 'Hey, Jennifer, how close are we to being done on the Mexican immigration chapter,' she *e-mails* me, from *across the room*! And I then have to e-mail her back, from *across the room*." She smacked her hand into her head for emphasis.

"Could you just get up and answer her in person?" I asked.

"Apparently not! I tried that, and she looked at me like I was a complete weirdo and then said, 'I can't talk right now. Could you just e-mail me?'"

"That," I agreed, "is crazy."

Jenny put on her coat—a navy-blue duffle she'd worn for ages, in which she looked about twelve—and we headed out to the hallway and down so fast in the elevator that my ears popped. In the lobby, her mood shifted, her buoyancy gone. We had left her territory and were out in the world, where anything could happen. In high school, in college, we'd talked about everything, talked for hours and hours, through long road trips and whole nights, a unified front against the world. But we were no longer fully unified, and we didn't quite know how to face the world with these points of departure between us.

This is, I know, an old story.

In silence, Jenny and I walked across the southern end of Rockefeller Center, to the little Dean & DeLuca outpost, and scanned the prewrapped sandwiches in the refrigerated case. I refrained from looking at the prices—everything would be too much, so what did it matter—but chose mozzarella and tomato because I suspected it was the cheapest, being vegetarian. "Hmm," said Jenny, "should I have the *nine-dollar* bowl of soup or the *eight-dollar* sandwich?" She picked up the latter. "The extremely tiny eight-dollar sandwich." She raised her eyebrows. "Or maybe I should just have an enormous three-dollar doughnut." I loved her all over again, even though she was marrying a person who had told me that he "didn't really read fiction," because it was hard for him to get around the fact that "it's all lies."

"How's Don?" she asked in a falsely cheerful voice. She was fiercely loyal to my college boyfriend and baffled by my defection to Don. Brett had just sent off his law school applications. "How's his novel?"

"I think he's pretty much done." Jenny was ostensibly a writer herself. In high school, in college, her life began and ended with poetry. Her work was beautiful, brilliant, strange. But since meeting Brett, she rarely talked about poetry anymore. "He's just making final changes. He seems to be working over every sentence a thousand times."

"Mmm," said Jenny, resting her cheek on her hand. She looked tired, I noticed. Though her cheeks were rosy, as always, and her eyes bright, there was a drawn look to her face, dark circles under her eyes. "Have you read it?"

"He won't let me. He doesn't want anyone to look at it until it's completely done."

"I get that," she said, chewing thoughtfully. Her sandwich, on some kind of flat, oily bread, looked much better than mine. "Have you read *any* of his stuff?"

I hesitated. In fact, the previous week, he'd given me a story, for the first time. I'd come home from work to find him leafing through papers at his desk. Nervously, he clipped a few together and handed them to me, before I'd even taken my coat off, then put one hand on my shoulder, another on my hip, and folded me down onto the couch. "Sit," he said, laughing. "Stay." He stood, though, pacing lightly back and forth in front of me. "I wrote this a long time ago—two or three years ago—and it's very different from what I'm working on now. But it's maybe the only successful short story I've written." He paused, running his hands through his hair. Without pomade, it was thin and lank, a few white threads among the brown. "I'm not *really* a story person. I'm a novelist." He smiled. "I think big. Big picture. Big ideas. Stories are miniature."

I nodded. "You want me to read this?" I asked. "Now?"

He nodded. "You can take your coat off."

The story was very short, just a few pages, and written in such dense prose that the events were not altogether clear. But the narrative appeared to concern a short, dark-haired working-class young American man involved with a tall, gorgeous Swedish woman whose pale blond hair and "perfect ass" and odd passivity drive him into a sexual rage. Panties are ripped. Otherwise, not much else happens. The story seemed to me less an actual story—with a narrative arc, and a beginning, middle, and end—than a sketch or an exercise, an exploration of this character's mixed feelings of desire and disgust, of unworthiness and superiority. There was something about it that made me uncomfortable and it wasn't just the sex. There seemed, within the story, an unconscious desire to punish this perfect blonde. It was a mean story.

I wasn't sure what I'd expected from Don—Don who

quoted Hegel and Kant, who loved Proust—but it certainly wasn't this.

"Okay," I told him warily, when I finished, and handed the thin sheaf back to him. He'd had to force himself not to stand over me as I read.

"That's it?" he said. "Okay." He let out a strange cackle. "Did you like it?"

I shrugged. "I guess, well, this character seems kind of like a male fantasy. The blonde with the perfect body who says, 'Do anything you want to me.'"

"It's funny you say that," said Don, his face darkening, nostrils flaring. "It's really funny. Because this story is completely taken from my life. That character is based on one of my girlfriends in San Francisco. Grete."

"Greet?" I asked. This seemed a strange name, even for a Swedish girl. "Her name is *Greet*?"

"Grete," he said. "It's a softer *e* sound. From the back of the throat. It's hard to pronounce if you don't speak Swedish."

Don did not, to my knowledge, speak Swedish.

"He showed me a story last week," I told Jenny. "But it was something old and not really relevant to the novel. I think his style has changed a lot since then." For a moment, I considered my sandwich, which was chilled from the refrigerator, the bread tough and hard. "Do you show Brett your poetry?"

She started, then gave me a cold look. "No," she said. "I don't." Some small—infinitely small—victory was mine, but I wished it were otherwise. "But," she said, swallowing a bit of crust, "I'm not really writing poetry anymore."

I nodded. I suppose I had already known.

When I returned to my desk, overpriced and unremarkable cup of coffee in hand, Hugh came by and dropped a bundle of letters in front of me. I looked at him questioningly. I was getting used to the long silences of the office.

"These are the Salinger letters," he said.

"Oh?" I asked.

"Fan letters. To Salinger." He sighed and shifted the bundles in his arms. "We need to answer them."

"Okay." I took a sip of coffee. "Does it matter what I say?"

Tersely, Hugh nodded. "There's a form letter. Somewhere. I'll find it."

Hugh could, to my continual amazement, pull anything one needed from the mountain of paper on his desk. A few minutes later, he returned bearing a disintegrating sheet of the yellow paper used for carbon copies, its edges faded and frayed and soft with handling.

> Dear Miss So-and-So:
> Many thanks for your recent letter to J. D. Salinger. As you may know, Mr. Salinger does not wish to receive mail from his readers. Thus, we cannot pass your kind note on to him. We thank you for your interest in Mr. Salinger's books.
>
> Best,
> The Agency

The date at the top of the carbon: March 3, 1963.

"So I just send this, verbatim? I just retype it?"

Hugh nodded. "Yep. You don't need to keep a carbon"—the Xerox machine was still new enough that many Agency employees still referred to copies as "carbons"; I loved this—"and you can toss the letters, too."

"Really?" I asked, surprised. Nothing was tossed at the Agency. Every bit of correspondence was meticulously copied and filed. I couldn't believe they'd throw out anything to do with Salinger, in particular. "Just put them in the garbage?"

"Yeah, we can't keep them." Hugh smiled a little. "They'd take up the entire office. Or, we'd need a separate archive."

I nodded. "It's a lot," I admitted, gesturing toward the bundle, which still sat where Hugh had left it on the corner of my desk.

"And that's just what came in today," said Hugh.

I laughed. "Of course," I said.

"No," said Hugh. "That's really just what came in today."

"You're kidding. Where's the rest?"

Hugh resumed his habitual sigh. "In my office. Some-where. I tried to respond to some of it back in December."

"Does this much come in every day?" If so, I would henceforth spend my entire day, every day, retyping the letter in my hand.

"No. It ebbs and flows. We always get a lot right after the New Year."

"Okay," I said. "I'll start on this right now." I pulled the bundle toward me and began unwinding the rubber band.

"There's no rush." Hugh shrugged. "Just when you get to it. Maybe on Fridays, when your boss isn't here. If you have nothing to do." Sighing, he bent his neck awkwardly, trying to crack it. This was either a new nervous habit or one I'd not noticed before. "They're just fans. It's sort of the least important thing."

"Okay," I said again, but as soon as he returned to his office, I took the rubber band off one packet and sifted through the letters, which bore postmarks from all over the world: Sri Lanka, Malaysia, Japan, any number of Scandinavian countries, Germany, France, the Netherlands, everywhere. Quietly, I began slitting open the envelopes with my thumb, unfolding the letters inside. They were long, these letters, far longer than I expected, though what *had* I expected? I'd never written such a thing myself. What did I know? Some were typed on typewriters, in the style of the Agency. Some were modern missives, unfurled from laser printers on plain white paper. Many were written on stationery—pink, blue, fragile airmail, creamy white from Smythson, Hello Kitty, Snoopy, rainbows and clouds—the small, thick pages covered densely with words. One contained a friendship bracelet, woven of embroidery thread; another a photo of a small white dog. And yet another, inexplicably, some coins, taped to a sheet of ripped, dirty paper.

Over the next hour, I read and read and read, ignoring my typing and filing, impatient with the ringing phone. Many of the letters came from veterans—mostly but not entirely American—confiding in Salinger about their experiences during the war. Now, like Salinger, they were in their seventies and eighties, and they found themselves—they explained—thinking more and more about the friends who'd died in their arms, the cadaverous bodies at the death camps they'd liberated, the despair they'd felt when they returned home, the sense that no one understood what they'd undergone, no one except Salinger. Some, many, were turning to his stories again, they said, and finding that they loved them even more. They wanted Salinger to know, to understand, all this, they explained, with an urgency that made me slightly uncomfortable.

What else? Who else? There were what I came to think of as the Tragic Letters: missives from people whose loved ones had found solace in Salinger during their years-long struggles with cancer, who'd read *Franny and Zooey* to their dying grandfathers, who'd obsessively memorized *Nine Stories* in the year after losing their children or spouses or siblings. And there were the Crazies, of course, ranting about Holden Caulfield in smudged pencil, a dirty lock of hair falling out of the creased paper and onto my dark desk.

But probably the largest group of fans were teenagers, teenagers expressing a sentiment that could be summed up as "Holden Caulfield is the only character in literature who is truly like me. And you, Mr. Salinger, are surely the same per-

son as Holden Caulfield. Thus, you and I should be friends."
Schoolgirls professed their love for Holden. They understood
Holden, they explained, and they wished they could find a
boy like him, someone who understood the hypocrisies of the
world, someone who understood that people have *emotions*,
but all of the guys they knew were morons like Stradlater.
"My mother says you won't write back," wrote a Canadian
high school girl, "but I told her you would. I know you will,
because you understand what it's like to be surrounded by
phonies."

These young people deployed language that I knew
derived from *The Catcher in the Rye*. The repeated use of "goddam" and "crumby" and "as hell" and, of course, "phony."
The boys, I suppose, inclined more toward such imitation
than the girls, for the boys wanted to be Holden, while the
girls wanted to be *with* Holden.

One letter caught my eye:

> *I've read your book* The Catcher in the Rye *three times
> now. It's a masterpiece, and I hope that you're proud
> of it. You certainly should be. Most of the crap that
> is written today is so uncompelling it makes me sick.
> Not too many people have anything to write that even
> approaches sincerity.*

The flat-out nerve of this particular kid—who was, I checked,
from Winston-Salem, North Carolina—impressed me. Who
writes to possibly the most famous living American writer to
inform him that his beloved, best-selling book is a master-
piece and he should be proud? Amazing. But the boy's brio
came straight from Holden. He was hoping to impress Salinger with his likeness to Salinger's hero.

I was finishing this letter—eventually, he gets around to
seeking romantic advice from Salinger ("I used to get nervous as hell around girls")—when Hugh returned, materi-

alizing at my desk so silently that I started, as if he were a ghost. "I just realized," he began. "You should actually *read* them."

"The letters?" I asked, gesturing to my desk, which was covered with stationery.

"Yeah. Just in case." For a moment he stood up perfectly straight, as if he might balance a book on his head, then his normal slouch returned. "They're mostly harmless, but occasionally we'll get a death threat. Back in the '60s, Salinger got some pretty scary letters. Threatening him. And his kids." He grimaced.

"What should I do," I asked, "if I find something scary?"

He considered. "You can bring them to me. I'll decide if it's worth bothering your boss. We've been pretty careful since the Mark David Chapman thing." I nodded, knowingly, though it was only later that the significance of this name would come to me, with a shudder: Mark David Chapman, the man who'd shot John Lennon, then sat down on the steps of the Dakota and read *The Catcher in the Rye*. When the police confiscated the book, they found he'd scrawled "This is my statement" on the title page. Holden Caulfield, he said, had made him do it.

I gestured to my desk, the letters piled on it, robbed of their envelopes. "I've been reading them," I said. "I was curious."

"Great," said Hugh, but he didn't leave. Did my face, my tone, betray something? Some sentiment of which I wasn't even aware? "Don't get too caught up in them."

When I got home that night, the apartment was empty. Don was likely at the gym. He had a big match in a couple of weeks and had started running miles each day to get his weight down, training every night. I put on water for pasta and grabbed a book off his desk—Martin Amis's *London Fields*, which I'd taken out of the library the previous week, only to have Don claim it. Underneath I found a letter, in Don's cramped penmanship. For a brief moment, a flicker of a moment, I thought this letter was meant for me, that Don had left it under my book as a romantic gesture. "My dearest, mi amor," I read. *Oh God*, I thought, dropping it on the desk as if it were aflame. Those four words were enough. I knew, with utter certainty, that it was not at all meant for me. "Oh my God," I said aloud. A sick sensation, like vertigo or seasickness, began to overtake me. Slowly, I walked across the apartment and turned off the pot of water. Then I picked up the letter and read on. Whoever "mi amor" was, well, he missed her, he couldn't believe it had been two months since their days at the beach, he couldn't stop thinking about her beautiful brown shoulders—I stopped, for I was certain now that I was going to be sick. My skin, as Don often mentioned, was unusually pale. And we had never been to the beach together. Though we *had* been to his parents' house for Christmas, where I'd been awkwardly introduced to his extended family—awkwardly, since I barely knew him, was unsure of how or why I'd ended up there—and his oldest friends, a tight-knit group of guys who had mostly stayed in Hartford, doing pickup construction jobs or tending bar or living with their parents, still, at thirty. Only Don and Marc had left.

I checked the date on the letter. March 16, 1996. This was not a missive from Don's deepest past. This was a letter written five days ago. Three months ago, he'd been calling me every day, saying things like, "Let's just run away and get married." Then I realized: Los Angeles. In December, he'd gone to Los Angeles for a week, to do some final research for his novel. Had he met this person—her name, I discovered, from reading on, was Maria or Mariana—on the trip?

Was she someone he'd interviewed? Or—this seemed some-how worse—had he flown out to see her and spun the trip as research for my benefit?

I fell asleep before Don got home that night, but the next morning the letter was still there, partially obscured by the large black journal in which he recorded his thoughts and observations.

As the train raced me up to midtown to the Agency, I suddenly thought of Mark David Chapman. Had he written a fan letter—fan letters?—to Salinger? Had the 1980 or 1979 version of me methodically opened a plain white envelope and found a crazed rant? A plan for murder? A tirade against John Lennon? And sent back a crisp, formal dismissal in reply?

When I got to the office, I asked Hugh. He sighed, as usual. "Maybe," he said. "Probably. I don't know." He sighed again. "I guess that's why we usually keep all correspon-dence. It would be interesting to know, wouldn't it?"

I nodded.

"But I guess that's life, right?" he said. I nodded again, unsure of what I was agreeing with. "There's just a lot that we'll never, ever know."

Spring

The Cover, the Font, the Binding

How many times had I been told that Salinger would not call, would never call, that I would have no contact with him? More than I could count.

And yet one morning, a Friday, at the beginning of April, I picked up the phone and heard someone shouting at me. "HELLO? HELLO?" Then something incomprehensible. "HELLO? HELLO?" More gibberish. Slowly, as in a dream, the gibberish resolved into language. "It's Jerry," the caller was shouting. *Oh my God*, I thought. *It's him*. I began, slightly, to quiver with fear, not because I was talking to—or being shouted at by—the actual J. D. Salinger, but because I so feared doing something wrong and incurring my boss's wrath. My mind began to sift through all the Salinger-related instructions that had been imparted to me, but they had more to do with keeping others away from him, less to do with the man himself. There was no risk of my asking him to read my stories or gushing about *The Catcher in the Rye*. I still hadn't read it. "WHO IS THIS?" he asked, though it took me a few tries to understand. "It's Joanna," I told him, nine or ten times, yelling at the top of my lungs by the final three. "I'm the new assistant."

"Well, nice to meet you, Suzanne," he said, finally, in something akin to a normal voice. "I'm calling to speak to your boss." I had assumed as much. Why had Pam put him through to me, rather than taking a message? My boss was out for the day, it being Friday, her reading day.

I conveyed this to him, or hoped that I did. "I can call her at home and have her call you back today. Or she can give you a call when she gets in on Monday."

"Monday is fine," he said, his voice ratcheted down another notch. "Well, very nice to meet you, Suzanne. I hope we meet in person someday."

"Me, too," I said. "Have a great day." This was not a phrase I ever used. Where had it come from?

"YOU, TOO!" Ah, the shouting.

I put the phone down and took a deep breath, as I'd learned to do in ballet. My entire body, I realized, was shaking. I stood up and stretched.

"Jerry?" asked Hugh, stepping out of his office with a mug of coffee.

"Yes!" I said. "Wow."

"He's deaf. His wife set up this special phone for him, with an amplified receiver, but he refuses to use it." He sighed his trademark sigh. To be Hugh was to be let down by the world. "What did he want?"

"Just to talk to my boss." I shrugged. "I offered to call her at home and have her call him back, but he said Monday was fine."

Hugh wrinkled his face in thought. "Hmm, why don't you call her anyway. I think she'd want to know."

"Okay," I said, thumbing through my Rolodex.

She wasn't home and had no answering machine. She didn't believe in them. Just as she didn't believe in computers or voice mail, another newfangled invention not employed by the Agency. If you called during business hours, you reached Pam, the receptionist. If you called outside business hours, the phone just rang and rang, as it did at my boss's apartment, twenty blocks north of the office. I tried again, every hour or so, until the end of the day, to no avail. It would have to be Monday.

I'd been at the Agency for a few months now, and my boss had not yet asked me to read anything. Minus this task, my job did indeed seem to resemble that of a secretary, as my father had said, mildly bolstered by the proximity to great works of literature. Without really intending to, I found myself lying when questioned about my responsibilities. "So much reading," I would say at parties. "I'm always carrying a manuscript around with me. I can't keep up."

There was another assistant at the Agency, Olivia, who was indeed overburdened with reading, and it was her complaints that I mimicked. A beauty in the Pre-Raphaelite vein—ethereally pale, ashy ringlets, tubercular figure—Olivia was a truly terrible assistant, forever losing contracts and packages, misfiling correspondence, and simply not answering her phone. She had a handsome Italian boyfriend with whom she fought constantly—it was not uncommon to walk by her desk as she screamed at him and slammed down the phone—and who sometimes arrived at the office to pick her up, embracing her in a mildly inappropriate way. Hugh couldn't utter her name without rolling his eyes. I desperately wanted to know her, or at least wanted to absorb some modicum of her slender, languorous charms.

The following Monday, the burble of the coffeemaker informed me of her arrival. I had been saving a question for Hugh—regarding those complicated pink cards—and decided to use this as an excuse to say hello. "Oh, I always do that wrong," she answered nonchalantly, cupping her mug of black coffee in two hands and seating herself on her desk, a gesture that shocked me, for I knew that my boss would be horrified by such overfamiliarity with the office furniture. Today, she had on a black chiffon blouse covered in large white dots and a slim-cut black skirt, which hung loosely on her narrow hips, bunching up above her knees when she sat; on her feet, red ballet slippers that barely rustled when she traipsed across the carpet. "Maybe you just shouldn't bother. Will anyone know?" She yawned extravagantly. "Do you want coffee? I need more." As I followed her to the coffeemaker, she explained that she was a painter, and—like me—she'd ended up at the Agency through happenstance. "Basically, I have no interest," she said with a shrug. "I have to get out of here."

"But the reading must be great?" I asked, trailing her back to her desk, which she again leaped atop. "Some of it? My boss doesn't ask me to read anything."

"Not really," she said, rolling her large blue eyes. "Most of it's terrible. You read a few pages, you can tell."

Just then, as I'd feared, my boss came by, cigarette in hand. Every so often, she surprised me—surprised everyone—by coming in the back entrance, which led directly into our little suite. "Olivia, what on earth are you doing? Get down from there immediately." She raised her eyebrows at me, as if to say, *I told you not to fraternize with that good-for-nothing.*

Olivia worked for two different agents, Max and Lucy, who were often referred to as a unified entity—"MaxandLucy"—for they were the closest of friends and spent their days racing in and out of each others' offices, laughing throatily at each other's jokes, and lighting each other's cigarettes. Lucy oversaw film rights for all Agency clients and represented a host of children's book authors, as well as a few well-reviewed novelists. She'd started her career at the Agency, as an assistant, and though she was perhaps forty, at most, she embodied the best of the Agency's archaic charms: she smoked cigarettes through an ivory holder, her hand held dramatically in the air, dressed solely in elegantly draped black crepe shifts, and effortlessly emitted Parker-ish quips in her low Bacall-ish voice. Max had been brought in a few years earlier to—it was no secret—rejuvenate the Agency. He was a star, one of the best-known agents of the moment, and represented a host of writers I loved—Mary Gaitskill, Kelly Dwyer, Melanie Thernstrom—and just as many that I'd long wanted to read, like Jim Carroll and Richard Bausch. His writers published in magazines I read—*Granta, Harper's, The Atlantic*—and seemed always to be reading at KGB or Limbo, and his life was an endless succession of book parties. Every week, his circulating folder arrived thick with deal memos, and when he came to our side of the office to talk to my boss, it was usually to get her take on an enviable problem: three differ-ent editors were fighting over the same book and the author was losing her mind trying to decide which house to choose.

They were impossibly glamorous, Max and Lucy, and I loved merely to be in their proximity, listening to them ban-ter, cigarettes held aloft. Max was short, with a ring of curly hair surrounding a bald pate, and Lucy squat, her skin dulled by nicotine, but their intelligence and wit—and the passion with which they threw themselves into their work, their books, their authors—made them as attractive, as thrilling, as film stars. Also, they were kind: they treated both Olivia and me less like furniture than did the older agents—Lucy asking me about my dresses, Max about my books. And an idea struck me as I sat chatting with Olivia: I could read for them. My boss had no reading for me. They had an assistant with no interest in reading. I trotted directly to Hugh's office. "That makes sense," he said. "So long as it doesn't interfere with your work for your boss."

"It won't," I promised. "I'd do it at home. At night."

"Okay," he said. "Go talk to Max. I'm sure he'll be thrilled. I'll clear it with your boss."

"Great!" I said. "Thank you. So much."

Before I could walk over to Max's office, my boss appeared in the doorway, glowering. "Did Jerry call on Friday?" I nodded. Hugh, too, looked frozen. "Why didn't you tell me?"

"I tried to. I called all day on Friday, but you weren't home. I must have called ten times."

"She did," said Hugh, and I looked to him gratefully.

"He said not to, though," I clarified. My boss glared at Hugh, opening her mouth to shout. "*Jerry* said not to. Jerry said not to call you at home. That it could wait until Monday."

"Well, it's Monday now! Why haven't you told me?"

An hour later, the shouting began, and Hugh came out to watch my boss's door with me. "She's just going to yell for me the minute she gets off the phone," he said. "I may as well wait out here."

"Are you sure, Jerry?" we heard her shout. "Well, of course, if that's what you want. We'll take care of it."

"So good to talk to you," she shouted. "As always."

When the door opened, she emerged quietly, thoughtfully. "I need to talk to Carolyn . . ." Her voice trailed off. "Maybe I should talk to Max." She drifted toward the front of the office, then thought better of it, turned on her heel, and trod back to us. "Salinger wants to publish a new book," she said, in the same dreamy tone of voice. "Or an old book. An old story. 'Hapworth.' A publisher approached him about putting it out as a stand-alone volume. And he wants to do it."

"'Hapworth'?" asked Hugh, his voice choked with surprise. "He wants to publish '*Hapworth*' as a book?"

"Well, it *is* very long," said my boss. "It's really a novella. It *could* be a book."

"I think a novella is ninety pages, minimum," said Hugh stiffly, with a particularly sharp sigh. "'Hapworth' is maybe

sixty. With very wide margins, I *suppose* it could be a book."
He pursed his lips. "Just because it *can* be a book doesn't
mean it *should* be a book."

"Well," said my boss, emitting her own sigh. "He seems
pretty keen on doing this."

"Really?" asked Hugh. "Are you sure this isn't some
whim? He's not going to change his mind tomorrow?"

"Well, I'd say not," my boss said, laughing. "He's been
thinking it over for eight years."

Hugh and I looked at each other. "Eight years?" he said.

"Yesiree. The publisher first approached him eight years
ago. In 1988."

"The publisher approached him directly?" Hugh shook
his head in amazement.

"Yup," my boss said, swinging her arms back and forth.
It was hard to tell if she was delighted or horrified by this
turn of events. "They, or he—it seems like this press might
be a one-man show—wrote him a letter." She raised one finger in the air and smiled. "On a typewriter! Jerry was very
impressed by that."

It had not, until that moment, occurred to me that the
Agency's typewriters-only policy had anything to do with
Salinger. Was it possible that Salinger had somehow man-
dated our lack of modern office machinery? This seemed
crazy, but possible. Or was it simply that the Agency—like
an aging star of the high school football team—had simply
stopped developing during its glory days? That instead of
growing and changing and adapting, it had retreated into
the business of *being* the Agency. Which meant following
the same rituals and procedures it'd followed in 1942, when
Dorothy Olding first signed Salinger.

"How did the publisher get his address?" I asked. Hugh
had told me that an assistant had been fired, a few years back,
for giving out Salinger's address to a reporter.

"He just sent it to J. D. Salinger, Cornish, New Hampshire." She made a clucking sound with her teeth. "And the mailman delivered it. Can you believe it?"

"No," I said. I was impressed.

"Why has no one else thought of that?" asked Hugh.

"I don't know," said my boss, pulling a pack of cigarettes out of her jacket pocket and peeling off the plastic wrapper. "I don't know. Maybe someone has."

Hugh looked a bit as if he were going to throw up. "Which publisher is it? Why didn't they contact us?"

My boss began to laugh. "I don't even know. Some small press in Virginia. Orchid Press? Something like that. Tiny. I mean, tiny. Like I said, it might just be one man, it seems like."

"Orchises Press?" I asked hesitantly. Orchises published some poets I liked. But I knew nothing about it. I wasn't even sure how to pronounce its name.

"That's it!" my boss cried. She narrowed her brows in surprise. "You've actually heard of them?"

"They publish poetry," I told her. "Contemporary poetry. I like a few of their poets."

"A small press," said Hugh, unbelieving. "A small press in *Virginia*. A one-man press? For J. D. Salinger? How could this guy even meet the demand? Does he know what he's getting into? Salinger is pretty different from publishing poetry."

"You can say that again," said my boss, with a low chortle. Slowly, she pulled a cigarette out of the pack and lit it with the tiny lighter she always kept on her person, hidden in some pleat or fold. She took a long draw and smiled. She was enjoying this. "We have a lot to find out. For starters, whether this Orchises Press fellow"—she looked at a Post-it in her hand and read a name aloud—"Roger Lathbury. We need to find out whether this Roger Lathbury fellow still even wants to do this. It's been eight years. He's going to think I'm crazy when

I call him." Her face compressed in contemplation. "We need to go very slowly on this one. Very slowly and very carefully. I need to think for a minute."

When she was safely ensconced in her office, murmuring into the phone, I asked Hugh, in a low voice, "What's 'Hapworth'?" It sounded mysterious. Like a secret agent's code name.

"Salinger's last published story," Hugh told me, brushing imaginary flecks of dust off his sweater. "It ran in *The New Yorker* in 1965. It took up almost the whole magazine."

"Really," I said. "The *whole* magazine?" I could not imagine this.

"It wasn't that strange then," explained Hugh. "You know *Esquire* once serialized a whole Mailer novel?" I shook my head no, though I had actually known this. Don was a huge Mailer fan. "Every magazine ran stories. All the women's magazines. Salinger published stories in all of them. *Cosmo* ran a novella of his. A real novella."

"*Cosmopolitan*?" I asked, incredulous.

"I think *Mademoiselle*, too. And one other. *Ladies' Home Journal*? *Good Housekeeping*? One of those . . ." His voice faded to nothing and his hand moved in a circle, seemingly of its own accord, signifying I knew not what.

I'd known, of course, that glossy magazines had once run stories, largely because I'd written my master's thesis on Sylvia Plath, who had been obsessed with selling stories to what she called "the slicks." But somehow the idea of J. D. Salinger letting *Good Housekeeping* run one of his stories—or *Cosmo*, with its advisories on multiple orgasms—was absurd to the point of hilarity.

"You know that's what your boss did, right?" he asked, his voice suddenly growing sharper.

I shook my head in confusion.

"First serial." He nodded, as if agreeing with himself.

"She was hired as the first serial agent. To sell stories to magazines. So she sold stories for all the Agency's clients. For years. She worked at a magazine before she came here, as the assistant to the fiction editor."

"What magazine?" I asked.

Hugh raised his eyebrows and smiled. "*Playboy*."

"*Playboy*?" I whispered. I was sure he was joking. My boss, in her turtlenecks and slacks, at a girlie magazine?

But he nodded solemnly. "They ran serious fiction. Still do." He cleared his throat uncomfortably. "People always say 'I read it for the articles,' and you think it's a joke. But they pay well, so they get good writers."

"Did my boss sell 'Hapworth'?" I asked. For some reason my heart raced a little at the thought of this. "To *The New Yorker*?"

Hugh shook his head. "No, that was before her time. Dorothy would have handled that. Though I think, by that point, Salinger just gave all his stories directly to *The New Yorker*." He sighed and shook his head as if to clear it. "The story is a letter home from camp," he explained, his voice strangled and strange. Angry, I realized, he's angry. "Seymour Glass, at age seven, writing to his parents from camp. Sixty pages. A *sixty-page letter home from camp*."

"That sounds kind of postmodern," I said, smiling.

Hugh sighed and raised his eyebrows at me. "People consider this his *worst* story. I'm not sure why he'd want to publish it as a stand-alone." Shaking his head, he gestured toward the wall of Salinger books. "He says he doesn't want attention. This is going to get a *lot* of attention. I don't understand."

"Yes," I said, nodding, but I thought maybe, just maybe, I understood. *Maybe he's dying*, I thought. *Maybe he's lonely. Maybe he wants the attention now. Maybe he realized that what he thought he wanted wasn't what he wanted at all.*

. . .

The next morning, my boss stopped at my desk before heading into her office. "Call this Orchids Press and ask for a catalog and a sample of their books."

I nodded, but she'd already glided off across the thick carpet. From my shelf, I pulled down the *LMP—Literary Market Place*, an enormous, dictionary-sized tome, which lists the name and address of every publisher in the country, along with its staff—and sure enough, there it was: Orchises Press, Alexandria, Virginia. Publisher: Roger Lathbury, the Man Who Conquered Salinger. No other staff was listed. I took a deep breath and dialed. "Hello," a brisk voice chirped midway through the first ring. Was this the man himself, Roger Lathbury? Suddenly I felt silly, unsure of what to say. When I identified myself as an employee of the Agency, would he not immediately realize I was calling on behalf of Salinger? For once, I wished my boss had dictated a letter. "Yes, hello," I said finally. "Is this Orchises Press?"

"It is," said the voice.

"I'm calling from the Agency." Simply uttering the Agency's name allowed me to regain my composure. "We're expanding our submission base, and we'd love to see your most recent catalog, as well as a sample of current books."

"Well," the man said, "it would be my pleasure to send those materials on to you!" If he recognized the name of the Agency, he gave no indication of it. Or maybe he simply didn't know that the Agency represented Salinger? After all, he'd written directly to Jerry.

"You did it?" my boss called the minute I hung up. I hadn't realized that she could hear my phone conversations from her office and flushed a little, thinking what else she might have overheard over the past few months.

"Done," I called back. There was a rustling as she got up

from her chair and walked over to my desk. And another as Hugh joined her.

"Let's see who they are," she said. "We need to see what kinds of books they do, what kind of company Jerry will be in. And what the books look like. You know that will matter a lot to Jerry."

"Really?" I asked. I'd assumed the homogeneous—and singular—style of his books had been purely Little, Brown's choice. Publishers, I thought, took care of designing books. Writers wrote them.

"Oh boy!" cried my boss. Hugh actually laughed. "You didn't know that? Jerry has very strong feelings about how a book should look. Not just the cover. The font. The paper. The margins. The *binding*. No illustrations on his covers. Just text. It's all stipulated in his contracts."

"No author photo," added Hugh. "He almost sued his British publisher over the cover of *Nine Stories*."

"That's an exaggeration," my boss cried. "He did *not* sue them. He just was unhappy about it."

The original cover of *The Catcher in the Rye* bore an illustration, a strange and beautiful—lyrical, really—drawing of a rearing carousel horse. I could see it out of the corner of my eye while seated at my desk. But that was his first book, predating, I supposed, his ban on images, as well as the sort of fame that allows an author to dictate his covers. In truth, I understood his objection. He wanted his readers to come to his work utterly fresh, utterly free. This, too, was noble. Lovely. But it was also, I suddenly realized, impossible. For J. D. Salinger, that is. No one, *no one* could come to his books without preconceived notions about them. About *him*. Myself included.

In the weeks that followed, my lies became true: My shoulder quickly began to ache from toting manuscripts. In reading for Max and Lucy, the texture of my life changed, the fabric of my days growing more and more complex and thrilling. Many of the novels—for they were novels, all novels—that I brought home were indeed bad, as Olivia had promised, but many were good or almost good or at least evidenced a strong and strange voice, and even if I knew that Max or Lucy wasn't going to take on the writer, there was a certain frisson to being part of the making of a book, however far down the line, of a career, a life. Each time Max or Lucy took on a book I'd recommended, I walked around stunned for days. Reading manuscripts was the exact opposite of reading for grad school: it was pure instinct, with some emotion and intelligence thrown in. Does this novel work? Or can it be made to work? Does it move me? Does it grip me?

At night, I read, happy to have a break from the endless rounds of drinks and parties, a reason to get off the phone with my mother, an excuse to ignore my own imperfect poems—and stories, for I was, ironically, now working on some. I didn't mention these ventures to anyone, least of all Don.

One afternoon in April, Max came over to my desk, a rarity. He was too busy to come to our wing of the office unless he had pressing business for my boss. Sometimes he asked her advice on contracts, and now, it seemed, he—and Lucy, too—were being made partners, so there were all sorts of complicated legal and financial things to work out. "Hey," he said, "what are you doing tonight? One of my clients is reading at KGB. I think you might really like his novel. It's this fantastic coming-of-age story set in New Jersey. And New York, in the '80s. I really think you might like it. I just have a feeling. Come along. We'll all have dinner afterward."

My boss cleared her throat noisily—we were, somehow, disturbing her—and closed her door.

But another, with my name on it, had swung open.

. . .

And yet my boss—and all the older agents—still regarded me as something akin to a piece of furniture, perhaps even more so than when I'd first started. Parked in front of my desk, Carolyn and my boss could while away an hour discussing the quotidian details of their lives: the roasted chicken at such and such restaurant; Carolyn's attempts to quit smoking by putting her cigarettes in the freezer so they wouldn't taste as good; the rerouting of the bus that ran through their neighborhood; the perennial troubles of Daniel, who was still adjusting to some new medication. One day in the middle of May—I'd turned twenty-four the week before with little fanfare—as I typed and typed, Carolyn began talking about friends of hers named Joan and John, and their daughter, who had an odd name, an odd name that sounded oddly familiar to me. I'd heard her discuss Joan and John before, but now I realized, with a jolt, that she was talking about Joan Didion and John Gregory Dunne. These were Carolyn's intimates, the people whose pedestrian travails—bathroom renovations and missed flights—she chattered about. "Who is she?" I asked James the next day. "What's her story?"

He shrugged. "I don't know. She's very tight-lipped. I have this idea that she's from money and that she had a sort of wild youth." I looked at him. "Why don't you ask her? She's really nice."

For the next few weeks, I lingered in Carolyn's doorway after dropping off the circulating folders and on Fridays, when the staff gathered for scotch in the reception area, made sure to sit near her. But I couldn't bring myself to talk to her. I knew exactly why: She didn't see me. I was simply part of the landscape of the office. In the entire year I worked there, she spoke not one word to me. When I deposited the folders on her desk, she merely nodded in my direction. At first, I took this personally. Then I saw it as a quirk of her personality, her genteel reticence. But eventually I realized that I was a position to her, rather than an individual: How many like me had she seen over her decades there? Dozens? We were disposable, interchangeable, in our wool skirts and college ties, our eyes shiny with puppyish excitement about books. She had no use for us. In a year, we'd be gone.

One Saturday in May, I took the bus home for a belated birthday celebration with my parents. After dinner, my dad called me into his study and handed me three short envelopes. "I'm passing these over to you," he said. "Since you have a job now, it seems like the right time."

I glanced down at the top envelope. Citibank.

"They're bills," my father explained, taking them back from me and scanning the return addresses. He separated two out and held them up for my inspection, like an offering. "These two are from your credit cards." I must have looked baffled, because he continued. "You have two credit cards, right?" I nodded. Smoothing his white hair, he arranged his face into the mollifying expression he adopted before doling out bad news. I remembered it well from my teen years. "You may recall"—he had taken on the fake British accent he used sometimes at moments of intense discomfort, mastered while playing a butler at an Actors Studio production of some ossified drawing room mystery—"we gave you those two cards when you went to college. The idea was that you would use them for books or"—he threw up his hands—"anything. Plane tickets. Shoes." I nodded again, though my palms were beginning to sweat. "Well, I've been paying the interest while you've been in school. But now you're done, so you can take them over." I looked at him, too stunned to nod. All through college and grad school, I'd worked two jobs at a time, to pay for incidentals and small luxuries, under the impression that my parents were happy to cover my basic expenses. I had been under this impression because, well, they had told me that this was the case. My mother, in fact, had fought me about working. "You have your whole life to work," she'd said endlessly. "Just concentrate on school now."

My father held up the third envelope. "These are your student loans." The saliva disappeared from my mouth. My father had more to say—low interest rates, consolidation, federal blah blah, Pell Grant—but I couldn't focus on what he was saying. Student loans? As far as I knew, I'd gone to school on a National Merit Scholarship.

"I don't remember filling out the paperwork for loans," I said, my tongue sticking drily to the back of my teeth.

"Oh, I did it for you." My father waved his hands impatiently. "I forged your signature. I do it all the time."

"My scholarship . . ." But my voice trailed off. I didn't need to ask, I supposed. What did it matter?

"It didn't cover everything, every year. And we thought it would be good for you to have student loans. It's good debt and you can deduct the interest from your taxes." This meant absolutely nothing to me, but I resumed my nodding, aiming for brightness. "And it helps you build good credit. So when you want to buy a house, you'll be in good shape. Same with the credit cards. You have great credit right now."

"Great," I said, forcing myself to smile. With a theatrical flourish, he handed me the envelopes. "When I want to buy a house. Yes."

"The bills will start coming directly to you next month."

"Great," I croaked, then turned on my heel and left the room so he wouldn't witness my tears. The minute I lay down on my childhood bed they arrived, hot and heavy, and I buried my face in my old pillow, the feathers turned to dust.

Finally, I wiped my eyes and slit open the envelopes. The balance on one credit card was $5,643. The other $6,011. I owed Chase and Citibank $11,000. Almost two-thirds of my salary. How had I spent $11,000 in five years? On what? Books, I knew, and plane tickets home. In London, there had been food, and phone calls—my parents had asked me to call twice a week and instructed me to use the cards for this purpose. There had also been, yes, a few pairs of shoes. A backpack or two. And surely other things I could have lived without. I wished, now, that I could take it all back. I'd not, by any means, frittered away money recklessly, but I'd certainly spent more than I would have if I'd not thought the bills would be magically taken care of. How stupid I'd been.

The student loan bill was far more frightening. It didn't state how much I owed in total—ominously—but merely indicated I needed to send my payment for May within the next ten days: a payment of $473. Or, almost two weeks' salary. After rent, I'd have pretty much nothing left. Never mind the immediate problem, which was that I didn't have $473 to send them and likely wouldn't obtain such a sum in the next ten days. That I could barely pay for rent and food, as it was.

"Jo?" my mother called from the living room, but I couldn't bring myself to answer.

Perhaps ten days later, a package from Orchises arrived, the Agency's name handwritten on the front of the padded mailer. That afternoon, my boss leafed through the materials, over and over, trying, I supposed, to compose her thoughts on the matter. At the end of the day, she handed them back to me. It was cool and rainy, as it had been for a few days, and she didn't complain when Hugh dashed into her office and closed the windows. "Okay," she said wearily. "I guess we better get these off to Jerry. I'll dictate a cover letter. Tomorrow's fine, though."

"Okay," I replied, surprised. She was not a tomorrow's-fine person. She was a do-it-now person. She wanted, I supposed, the "Hapworth" situation to dissolve into thin air, to simply go away. If we waited until tomorrow to send the books, maybe Salinger would come to his senses. Maybe he'd call and say, "That guy's a phony. What was I thinking?" This deal would be a huge amount of work, which would net the Agency a minuscule amount of money, if any. But now that we had the press's books in hand, it was beginning to seem less abstract.

The next morning arrived—cold, rainy again—and I typed the sort of tiny letter that mystified me: *Dear Jerry, Enclosed are a few of Orchises Press's recent releases, as well as a copy of its most current catalog, for your perusal. I look forward to hearing your thoughts.* And off they went to Cornish. We would wait again.

While she waited, my boss found it hard to focus on any-thing else, and I found myself, for the first time since I'd started, without a backlog of typing. I sat at my desk and read manuscripts. I fended off the usual calls for Salinger. I pored over contracts for my boss, as she'd trained me to do, seeking out errant clauses and words: a tedious task but one I loved, for I could lose myself in it, so fully did it require my concen-tration. And when I was done, when I finally had nothing else to do, I turned to the Salinger letters.

They had been sitting on my desk for months now, the pile growing larger and larger until my desk began to resem-ble Hugh's. The previous week, I'd stuffed them into the large—and largely empty—filing cabinet at the lower right-hand corner of my desk. Every day more letters trickled in, and every week or two a large bundle arrived, courtesy of Salinger's publisher, where someone very much like me pre-sumably spent hours each week crossing out its address and writing in ours.

One day, as we waited to hear from Salinger, I pulled open the drawer to add a few more letters and found it filled to capacity. *One at a time*, I told myself. *You don't have to do it all today.* Taking a deep breath, I grabbed a few letters off the top. Ah, there he was: the boy from Winston-Salem.

> *I think about Holden a lot. He just pops into my mind's*
> *eye and I get to thinking about him dancing with old*
> *Phoebe or horsing around in front of the bathroom*
> *mirror at Pencey. When I first think about him I*
> *usually get a big stupid grin on my face. You know,*
> *thinking about what a funny guy he is and all. But then*
> *I usually get depressed as hell. I guess I get depressed*
> *because I only think about Holden when I'm feeling*
> *very emotional. I can get quiet emotional . . . Most*
> *people don't give a flying hoot about what you think and*
> *feel most of the time, I guess. And if they see a weakness,*
> *why for God's sake showing emotion is a weakness, boy,*
> *do they jump all over you!*

Rolling a piece of paper into the typewriter, I began tapping out the form letter. "Thank you for your recent letter to J. D. Salinger. As you may know, Mr. Salinger does not wish to see his fan mail, so we cannot send your kind letter—" *Kind letter?* I stopped there, thinking. Could I at least bring the form letter into the modern era? Give this kid a bit of hope? "Quiet emotional?" With a rip, I pulled my letter out of the Selectric and tossed it in the trash can. Then I pushed the letter aside and grabbed another, which turned out to be a Tragic Letter, from a woman in Illinois whose daughter—an aspiring writer whose favorite author was Salinger—had died of leukemia at twenty-two. Now she wanted to start a literary magazine in memory of her daughter and name it *Bananafish,* after the daughter's favorite story. Would Mr. Salinger grant her permission to do so?

This was not so simple either. Letter in hand, I ambled over to Hugh's office and explained the situation. "Can we let her call the magazine *Bananafish*?" I asked, "She doesn't seem crazy." I held up the letter: white paper, Times New Roman. "Is it possible that Salinger would approve of . . . this?"

"Who knows?" said Hugh with a sigh. "We can't ask him about it, if that's what you're wondering." I nodded, disappointed. "And we can't give her permission to use the title."

"So I should just send her the form letter?" My chest tightened at the thought of this.

"Yes," said Hugh, nodding.

As I left, he called after me, "You know that titles can't be copyrighted, right?"

I stopped. "What do you mean?"

"A title can't be copyrighted," he explained. "So if I want to write a book and call it *The Great Gatsby*, I can. As long as none of the actual text is lifted from *The Great Gatsby*." I didn't fully understand. "So she can call her magazine *Bananafish*. It's perfectly legal. You can't copyright a title. And you can't copyright a word."

"Oh!" I cried. "Thanks."

"But you'll send her the form letter, right?" Hugh asked, in overly loud tones, smiling impishly.

"Of course!" I was already halfway to my desk. *As you may know,* I typed, *Mr. Salinger has asked us not to forward his mail, so I cannot send on your kind letter. With regard to your question about entitling your magazine* Bananafish, *we cannot grant you permission to do so, because Mr. Salinger holds no claim over the term. Titles cannot be copyrighted. Words cannot be copyrighted. You are free,* I typed, *to do as you wish.*

That is where I should have stopped, but I went on. *We are so very sorry to hear of your loss. We hope that your new venture provides some consolation. Surely, a literary magazine is a worthy vehicle for honoring your daughter's memory. We wish you the best of luck with it.*

Before I could back down, I signed it and sent it off. The

original letter, I knew, was supposed to go in the bin, but I couldn't bring myself to put it there. I thought of the boy from Winston-Salem: *Most people don't give a flying hoot about what you think and feel.* I grabbed the Bananafish letter and stashed it in my file drawer in a manila folder that had previously been empty, purposeless.

Back in January, the Agency had held a large, formal retirement party for an agent named Claire Smith. By my first day, Claire had cleaned out her office, but she stopped in once or twice before the party, her bellowing laugh echoing through the hallways. She was tiny and energetic and not terribly old—perhaps in her early sixties—and I wondered why she was retiring. She didn't at all seem the type to move to Florida and take up golf. Hugh, of course, supplied the answer: She had cancer. Lung cancer. Advanced. On her visits to the office, she'd worn a turban, but I'd thought it mere fashion. My boss's mode of dress—enormous rings and necklaces, nebulous flowing garments—was one step away from turbans. "But, um," I began, telling myself not to continue, "wasn't she smoking? When she was here?"

"Yes," sighed Hugh. "She was. She says there's no point in giving it up now."

Claire had been a true grande dame of publishing, in the bygone style of martini-soaked lunches. "She was an important agent," James told me somberly. She was also, I saw, important to my boss: her confidante and adviser, her friend. My boss was a stoic person, a Teutonic midwesterner who didn't believe in unseemly displays of emotion. Her favorite counsel was "Pull your socks up!" So it had taken this long to realize that I was working for a person in mourning. In mourning for the Agency as it had been before Claire's departure and perhaps prematurely in mourning for Claire herself.

It didn't occur to me, in January, to ask what happened to

Claire's clients after her retirement. But as the months wore on, I slowly began to understand: They were passed on to my boss. And some were leaving. Every few days, the phone rang in my boss's office—Pam had put someone directly through to her, which meant the person was a major client or editor—and she greeted the caller with genuine cheer. "Stuart, it's so great to hear from you! How've you been?" The door quickly closed. Ten minutes later—or sometimes much, much less—it swung abruptly open, and she emerged, yelling for Hugh. "Well, another one down," she'd say when he popped out of his office.

My boss was a fine agent, but her expertise lay more in selling first serial rights—placing short stories and articles and excerpts in magazines—and overseeing estates, and, of course, contracts, at which she was something of a savant. Her style and tastes were very different than Claire's. My boss had few of her own clients: a health writer, who pitched her own stories to women's magazines, then sent the contracts to us for a working over; an environmental writer of some repute, who did the same, but also had a few books under his belt; a writer of strange, hybrid speculative fiction, with an intense, rabid cult following; and the writer I thought of as my boss's Other Client, for he was the only one in her ranks to possess even a fraction of Salinger's fame. A well-known poet who taught at a prestigious MFA program, he had also published a few well-received literary novels—one, in the absurdist vein, was, here again, something of a cult favorite—and a series of high-toned, meditative mystery novels. "He can do anything," my boss once said, with an awe I rarely heard in her voice.

"Things are changing," she told me one afternoon, lingering by my typewriter with cigarette, as always, in hand. She'd just returned from lunch with a friend at the InterContinental. It was nearly four. Later, it would occur to me that she was perhaps a bit tipsy. We were still waiting to hear from Salinger about the "Hapworth" deal. "Literary agencies used to be honorable. Business was personal. You had lunch with an editor. You showed him a manuscript you thought he might like. He bought it. And then he'd work with that writer for *years*. For that writer's whole career!" I nodded, thinking of Maxwell Perkins and Thomas Wolfe. "Now people just jump around. You sell a book to an editor, the editor leaves. The writer gets passed around to three different editors before the book comes out." She shook her head in exasperation, a smooth wave of ash brown falling in her face. Her hair was beautiful—shiny, smooth, ungrayed—though cut in an odd style, almost a bowl cut. "Then the publisher says the book didn't sell well enough and they don't want the next one."

I nodded my head in sympathy.

"And agents used to be *upstanding*. None of these multiple submissions"—she wrinkled her nose with distaste at this term—"no auctions, with publishers bidding against each other. It's uncouth. That's not the Agency way. We send things out to one editor at a time. We match writers with editors. We have *morals*."

I knew Max held auctions for his books—and knew that my boss knew this—but I simply nodded. In truth, I didn't fully comprehend her objection to auctions. The idea, as I understood it, was to get the most money for the author. Why was that bad? She answered my question without my having to ask it.

"No good comes of it, anyway. They say it's good for the writers, but"—she waved her hand dismissively—"it just creates these inflated advances that never earn out."

Taking off her glasses, she rubbed the inside corners of her eyes with one slender thumb and forefinger. Until that moment, I'd never seen her without her glasses. She looked at least ten years younger, her pale eyes twice as large when not dwarfed by the massive frames. They were green, I saw now, not blue. I'd thought her my mother's age—sixty-five or so—but now I wondered if she wasn't younger, perhaps even much younger, got up in the garb of the elderly: the orthopedic shoes, the caftans, the dinner rings. Was this all some sort of costume? To what end? "Listen. You give a writer money, he's going to spend it. That's just how writers are. If you give him a *lot* of money up front, he's just going to spend it all. Better to give the writer a little money up front. Enough to live on, but not enough to think he's rich. Enough so that he won't take forever to write his next book."

For my boss, the Agency was not just a business, it was a way of life, a culture, a community, a home. It had more in common with an Ivy League secret society or—though it would take me time to see the extent of this—a *religion*, with its practices defined and its gods to worship, Salinger being the first and foremost; Fitzgerald as a sort of demigod; Dylan Thomas, Faulkner, Langston Hughes, and Agatha Christie, lesser deities. The agents, of course, were mere priests, there to serve the gods, which meant that they were interchangeable. And which, in turn, meant that my boss—it seemed to me—felt herself to be as qualified as Claire to represent Claire's clients. But more important, it seemed to me that she believed that those clients saw the world from her perch: that their loyalty was to the Agency first, to Claire second.

She seemed truly shocked that their loyalties were, first, to themselves, to their work. I couldn't tell her much—I was twenty-four—but I could have told her that.

Don was tired. Tired of working menial jobs, tired of having no—or little—money. He was determined to finish his novel by the summer, to get it out to agents. Now, when I got home from work, I found him not at the gym but sitting at his desk, staring at the screen and chewing on his nails or frantically typing, barely able to tear himself away and say hello to me.

"I can't change gears just because you're home," he explained testily. "I'm working." I understood this and I appreciated the freedom, too, that it gave me to work or read. Though it still smarted, somehow, that he didn't *want* to rip himself from his novel and kiss me, to sit down on the couch with me and hear about my day.

One night in May, the phone rang as I left the office. "Meet me at the L," he said. "I have to get out of the house. Maybe we can just sit and work?"

"That would be great," I said. An hour later, I walked through the café's creaky wooden door and found him sitting at one of its small, round tables, his head bent over his laptop, hair falling in his face, journal splayed open on his lap. "Buba," he said, standing up and taking me in his arms. "You're all flushed from the rain."

We drank coffee and ate bagels with cream cheese and roasted peppers—the L's culinary specialty—Don as always staring at his screen, occasionally typing a word or two; me, trying to figure the bones of a poem on a legal pad. Every so often, he took my hand and gave it a squeeze across the small table. His hands were no bigger than mine; no longer in finger and thumb, but wider and always warm, like a child's. For a moment, I thought of my college boyfriend's hands, which were long and elegant and cool; I had loved watching him turn the pages of a book or slice an apple, loved feeling them on my ribs, my neck. My breath slowed with desire. *Stop,* I told myself, taking a bracing sip of coffee. I had not imagined life with Don. There was no time for that: he had entered my life like a gale force, making me question all the small assumptions I'd held to be true without ever quite knowing it. That it was important to pay one's taxes and sleep eight hours each night and fold one's sweaters with tissue. But if I'd considered what drew me to Don, it would be this: that for him a night spent in a café working on a novel was the greatest pleasure. We wanted the same thing, I thought. And we wanted it more than anything. The life of the writer.

A few minutes later—my poem somewhat complete—I looked up from my legal pad to see Don staring off into what appeared to be the middle distance. Turning, I followed his gaze to the counter, where a woman stood ordering coffee. Williamsburg was small and I'd seen this woman here before. She was tall and thin, with striking features: a large, hawkish nose; small, deep-set eyes; a long, curving slash of a mouth. Her hair was black and straight, but with dramatic streaks of yellow at her temples. She had the look of a gallery girl: fashionable and severe, her legs long in slim-cut pants. "Do you know her?" I asked Don.

"No, but I kind of want to," he said. "Looking at her, I was just thinking about how plenty of ugly men are sexy. When you're a man, you can be, objectively, ugly, but also be really sexy. Like Gérard Depardieu. But most ugly women are just, well, ugly." He laughed, folding his hands behind his head and stretching. "But then there are the few who aren't."

"Like her," I said slowly. I couldn't quite believe that Don—my boyfriend, ostensibly—was assessing the attractiveness of the woman standing behind me. But he was.

"Yeah, look at her." He leaned in across the table toward me. "She has an amazing body but her nose is *huge* and yet it somehow makes her more attractive."

"Hmm," I said, hastily sliding my legal pad into my bag. "I'm going home."

Don looked at me. "I'll come with you."

"No, you stay. There's a lot"—I splayed my arms open— "to interest you here. I'll see you later."

I was in bed, reading, when he came in, an hour or so later, the quilt tucked tightly around me. He sat down on the edge of the bed, rubbing my arm through the cotton. "You know, Buba, men like to look at women. That's what they do."

"Really?" I said, keeping my eyes on my book, Laurie Colwin's *Family Happiness*, in which an Upper East Side matron discovers her family's equilibrium depends on her maintaining her long-running affair.

"Really," he said. "I wasn't attracted to that woman. I just thought it was interesting that she could, objectively, be so unattractive and yet—"

"I know, I know." I didn't want to hear anymore. "I understand."

"You don't understand," he said, not unkindly. "You think that life is a fairy tale and when a man falls in love with a woman he never looks at anyone else again. But that's not true." With a sigh, I put my book down and turned to face him. "Maybe your Buddhist boyfriend at Oberlin thought you were the end all and be all of womanhood. Or had taken so many women's studies classes that he was afraid to look at some chick and think 'she's hot,' that it would make him a bad person or something." His voice had taken on a hard, angry edge. "But I have news for you, every guy in the world is looking at every woman in the world and deciding whether he would sleep with her or not."

"Right." Throwing off the covers, I scooted past him and into the bathroom to brush my teeth.

"It's part of being a man," he called. I heard the thud as he took off one boot and then the other. "You can't shut it off. Any guy who tells you different is lying. Even your fucking Oberlin boyfriend."

Did Salinger love the books of Orchises Press? Their content? Their design? We did not know. All we knew was that one day, a couple of weeks after we'd sent them on, I picked up my phone and someone shouted, "HELLO? HELLO?" followed by my boss's name. This time, I recognized Salinger's voice and volume. "IT'S JOANNA," I yelled, wondering if I should have identified myself as "Suzanne," just to expedite things. "Is that Suzanne?" Salinger asked, lowering his voice to something closer to a normal speaking level.

"Yes, Mr. Salinger," I replied, smiling. I could be Suzanne. Why not?

"Well, then let me ask you something," he said.

"Sure," I said, but my heart immediately began to beat faster. My boss's warnings with regard to Salinger had focused on not initiating a conversation with him. There had been no stipulations, no guidelines, regarding what to do if *he* initiated a conversation with me. Presumably, such situations hadn't arisen in many years. Decades even. The "Hapworth" deal had thrust us into new territory. A Wild West of Salinger etiquette.

"You saw those books from that fellow in Virginia?" he asked. Though his voice was just slightly louder than it needed to be, his speech, I realized, had the mildly garbled quality of those who've long lost their hearing.

"I did," I confirmed.

"What did you think of them?" he asked.

"I thought they were nice." *Nice?* Where did this word come from? "I liked some more than others. The design, you mean?"

"The books," he said gently.

"Yes." I tried to gather my thoughts, but they would not gather. "I liked some of them more than others," I said again. "But I've seen their books before. They publish a lot of poetry. Some very good poets."

"You read poetry?" he asked, his words more focused now, more sharp.

My heart beat faster. I was certain that if my boss walked in at this moment, she would be extremely displeased. "I do," I said.

"Do you write poetry?"

"I do," I said, desperately hoping he wouldn't ask me to

repeat myself, wouldn't put me in the position of having to utter the word "poetry" aloud when my boss could walk in at any moment.

"Well, that's great," he said. "I'm really glad to hear that." I did not know then, would not know for months and months—when I finally read "Seymour—an Introduction"— that Salinger equated poetry with spirituality. Poetry, for Salinger, represented communion with God. What I knew then was that I was somehow betraying my boss—if not expressly, then in spirit.

Just then I spied her crossing through the finance wing, into our section of the office. "Would you like to speak to her?" I asked. "She's just getting back to her desk."

"Yes, thank you, Suzanne," he said almost quietly. "You have a good day. Nice to talk to you."

"It's Jerry," I whispered as she neared my desk.

"Oh!" she cried and trotted into her office.

The requisite shouting began, followed by the requisite closing of the door. After a period of quiet, my boss wandered out of her office, a stunned look in her eyes. Her cheeks were flushed.

"Well, he wants to go through with it," she said, lighting a cigarette. Though her words were designed to express resignation, she seemed, I thought, *excited*. The truth was there had not been much going on. Now things were happening. This was a small deal, yes, but it was big news in the world, or it would be, if anyone found out about it. Salinger had, of course, said that he wanted no announcement of the book, no write-up in *Publishers Weekly*, no piece in the *Times* about his coming out of his seclusion, nothing. We were to tell no one and neither was Roger Lathbury, not even his wife. We could talk about it in the office with restraint and caution—by which she meant "don't talk to Olivia"—but we were not to breathe a word of it in the outside world.

An hour later, she handed me a dictation tape, which

confirmed the height of her spirits. "Dear Mr. Lathbury," the letter began, "You might want to sit down before you read this . . ."

She signed it with a flourish. That night, I was the last to leave, which meant I brought the mail down to the box on the corner of Forty-Eighth Street. *Okay, Jerry, here goes nothing*, I thought, and slipped the letter in the box, where it fell softly, without a rustle. Just, I supposed, as he would have wanted.

2

The Obscure Bookcase

One morning, as May drew to a close, my boss once again raced out of her office, calling for Hugh. This time, he came right out, alarmed—as was I—by the true panic in her voice. "Judy just called," she said wearily. "She's coming in. I need you to pull all her royalty statements and get me all her books and, well"—she waved her hands up and down in a gesture of frustration—"just anything you can. Clips, anything."

"Okay," said Hugh.

"Judy?" I whispered.

"Oh, right," said Hugh. "Judy Blume."

My jaw fell open. "Judy *Blume*?" I asked.

"Yes," he replied impassively. "The children's book writer. Have you heard of her?"

"I've heard of her," I told him, trying not to laugh.

"She was Claire's client. So now she'll be passed on to your boss. Or Max, I guess."

Dutifully, I gathered copies of *Tales of a Fourth Grade Nothing*, *Freckle Juice*, *Blubber*, *Forever . . .* , and my favorite, *Starring Sally J. Freedman as Herself*—which I found, with some difficulty, on an out-of-the-way shelf in the finance wing, a strange place for the work of an author so well known—and piled them neatly on one corner of my boss's desk. There they sat, for several days. On Tuesday, I dropped off some correspondence and found my boss scrutinizing the cover of *Deenie*. On Wednesday, I found her peeking at the first pages of *Forever . . .* , as if afraid of breaking the spine. It was the same edition I'd had on my bookshelf as a kid. The cover embossed with a gold locket.

On Thursday, I arrived at work to find my boss already ensconced at her desk. The books were gone. "Oh, good, you're here," she called as I took off my coat.

"I'm here!" I called back with exaggerated cheer. I had been looking forward to that half hour in the office alone. Lately, I'd been coming in earlier and earlier to bask in the cool quiet of the office. Sometimes I caught up on work. Sometimes I just sat at my desk and read, drinking coffee and slowly unpeeling a sticky bun from the ersatz Italian market in Grand Central. Sometimes I worked on poems, typing them up on my Selectric.

"Now," said my boss, making her way to my desk, "how would you like to read something? A manuscript? I'd need it read very quickly. Tonight."

"I'd love to," I said evenly, trying not to smile. I had been waiting for this moment.

"You've heard of Judy Blume?" asked my boss, her brow furrowed.

How was I having this conversation again? "Yes," I said. "I've heard of her."

"Well, this is her new novel. I don't quite know what to make of it."

"Great!" This didn't surprise me. My boss, as far as I knew, had no children, and she—like a certain breed of adult—appeared to have never been a child herself, but rather to have materialized on earth fully formed, in a taupe-hued pantsuit, cigarette in hand.

"Can you read it tonight?"

I could.

That night, I arrived home at twilight, my coat under my arm—the days getting longer, the air warmer, though still not warm—and found a letter waiting for me atop the radiator in the hallway of the building that fronted ours. My breath stopped at the sight of my college boyfriend's small, neat hand, the blue ink from his fountain pen, the fountain pen I had given him a year earlier.

Quickly, I stuffed the letter in my bag, a black leather carryall I'd bought in London, flat alongside the manuscript, and willed my heart to stop beating so loudly and quickly. I wanted terribly to rip it open, right in the hallway, and devour it—though I suspected it would not be the kindest of missives—but I also couldn't bear the thought of doing so, not with Don potentially waiting for me in the apartment, hunched over his laptop. It was not that I feared he'd be jealous. It was that I couldn't risk succumbing to the wave of emotion that would surely hit the moment I read the first line.

We were supposed to go to a party that night, Don and I. We were always supposed to go to a party. Parties at the fancy apartments of my college friends' parents or at the decrepit apartments in which my college friends actually lived. Parties in lofts: Marc's huge loft on Fourteenth Street that doubled as the offices of his contracting business, so one had to be careful not to get drunk and lean on a circular saw; lofts down by the water, enormous windows looking out on the Manhattan skyline, studios filled with half-finished paintings, kitchens salvaged from photo shoots; lofts in Dumbo, newly finished and pristine, the owners pleased that actual artists had come to their parties. Parties in East Village tenements, their kitchens floored in crumbling linoleum, which inevitably ended up on the roof, looking out over the water towers to Williamsburg across the river. There were parties at Don's old apartment, thrown by Leigh and her new roommate, and at my old friend Robin's apartment on Riverside, her enormous dog licking everyone's shoes, and parties in the back rooms of restaurants, where the bill always came to be more than anyone could afford.

In the courtyard, I saw that our light was indeed on, which meant Don was home. Inside, I found him not writing but lying on the couch, in boxer shorts and a sleeveless undershirt, listening to Arlo Guthrie and reading the third volume of *Remembrance of Things Past*, which he'd informed me was properly called *In Search of Lost Time*. He often quoted passages or recounted scenes from Proust, but when I asked directly if he'd read the seven volumes in their entirety—I knew no one who had—he said, "That's a silly question." His favorite passage had to do with the narrator's wondering why he loves Albertine most when she's sleeping.

Tonight's gathering was another loft party: the financial district, the launch of a magazine. And I didn't realize how much I'd dreaded going—changing my clothes, restoring my energy, getting back on the train—until I told him I couldn't. "I have a manuscript I need to read tonight," I said, and put on water for pasta, pleased by the urgency of my work and the prospect of a night at home alone in my pajamas. "By tomorrow."

"I'll stay home, too," said Don, shrugging. "I need to work." He had reached the stage where he appeared to be simply moving commas. "Sentences should be worked," he sometimes said. I agreed, but I also thought, privately, that they could be overworked and perhaps—based on the one story of his I'd read—he was exhausting the microstructure of his poor novel. That it might be time to give the thing some air.

"Oh, no! You should go." I peeled off my sweater and grabbed my old pajamas, maroon sateen things from the 1960s purchased in high school at Unique, the giant clothing repository on Broadway in which my friends and I had bought combat boots and army pants, worn Levi's and rusty black dresses, the accoutrements of alternative girlhood. It had long since closed.

He shrugged again. "Can you make pasta for me, too?"

Propped up in bed—or what passed for a bed in our apartment, a futon without a frame—with a bowl of spaghetti, I took the rubber band off the manuscript and stretched my legs. Don lay down beside me and plucked the title page from my lap. "Judy *Blume*?" He wasn't quite smirking. "Is she an Agency client?" I nodded.

"She's a good storyteller," he said. "She gets kids. I loved *Then Again, Maybe I Won't*. When I was eleven."

"You *did*?" I was less shocked that Don had read anything so pedestrian than I was surprised that he would admit it.

"Of course I did. I was a kid once, too. Hard as that is to believe. Now that I'm a million years old." He smiled. "But seriously, I loved that book. I was just like the hero, Tony. My parents were working-class, but then we moved to a more middle-class neighborhood and I didn't fit in. It's ultimately a book about class."

I nodded as he went on with his Marxist interpretation of Judy Blume's oeuvre, but my eyes turned back to the pages at hand, the pages I'd begun reading on the subway home. For the past five years, if not more so, I'd purely consumed literature—with a capital *L*, as my mother liked to say—of the sort defined by my professors and the sophisticated friends I acquired in college, the ones who'd graduated from private schools that offered semester-long classes focused exclusively on *The Waste Land* or the works of Beckett. And Don, of course. He was eternally amused by the gaps in my education, by the little I'd read of philosophy and political theory and works in translation. "You're so bourgeois!" he often cried, when he found me rereading *Persuasion* or *The Age of Innocence* or *Cranford*. "You just want to read these books about rich people getting married and having affairs. There's a whole other world out there, Buba."

He was right, but I wished that he weren't. I wished that I'd grown up not in the cultureless suburbs but in New York, as my parents had. I wished that in seventh grade I'd chosen French rather than Spanish. I wished I'd read more and widely. It pained me to think of all those years when I simply devoured whatever fell into my hands, whatever struck my fancy at the local library or on my parents' bookshelf: best sellers from the 1930s and 1940s, the names on the spines long forgotten; the comedic writers beloved by my father; and all those Agatha Christie and Stephen King novels, all that pulp. There had been good stuff, too, much of it by accident rather than design: Flannery O'Connor, Shakespeare, whose collected works I'd read in both Lamb précis and true form, the Brontës, Chekhov, and contemporary writers pulled from the "New Releases" shelf at the library, purely because I liked the titles or the covers. But when I thought about all the hours I'd spent lying on my bed or my parents' couch or our lawn or in the backs of cars on family vacations, all those hours that could have allowed me the collected works of Dickens, into which I'd barely delved, or Trollope, or Dostoyevsky. Or Proust. The list went on and on, all that I hadn't read, all that I didn't know.

My life appeared to be a project in catching up. Thus, it had been a long time since I'd read what Max referred to as "commercial fiction." I took the title page off the manuscript with something close to anxiety. What if I had outgrown Judy Blume?

But no one, I suppose, outgrows Judy Blume. When I

was a kid, her books had seemed to speak directly to my own experience, to the confusion and loneliness of an outsider. So why was I surprised to find her new heroine, Vix, ensconced in an office in midtown Manhattan, eating lunch at her desk? Not just lunch, but take-out salad from the deli around the corner?

By the final pages, when Vix says that her only regret is that her oldest friend, Caitlin, couldn't confide in her, couldn't explain the choices she'd made, I was quietly crying. It was past midnight and Don had fallen asleep, but he awoke, startled. "What's wrong?" he asked. "Buba, what happened?"

But I couldn't explain. "It's not a kids' book," I said, instead, through tears. He looked at me, bewildered. "My boss said she didn't get it. And I thought it was because she didn't understand kids' books or kids. But it's not a kids' book. It's a novel for grown-ups."

"Okay," said Don. "I think you might need to go to sleep." He yawned widely. "You can tell her in the morning."

I nodded. But the minute I put the manuscript down and closed my eyes, my thoughts began racing again. Why *couldn't* Caitlin confide in Vix? Because she knew Vix would judge her. Because she knew Vix would refuse to understand. Because it was easier simply to pretend everything was all right.

The next morning, I rose earlier than usual and dressed carefully in a sober brown knit shift with a matching jacket, purchased for me by my mother. The more closely I resembled a 1965 coed, the more seriously—and calmly—my boss regarded me, and I wanted her to take me seriously that morning when we discussed the Judy Blume novel.

I smoothed on foundation, dusted my nose with powder, and swiped my lips with lipstick, a futile gesture since it would be gone by the time I got to the office. Then I tucked the manuscript back in my bag and left, the flimsy door creaking shut behind me with an ineffectual little click.

Don had left hours earlier for his new job, watering plants in office buildings in the financial district—Marc had somehow arranged this for him, through a client—which paid ridiculously well considering how easy it was, but required leaving the house at four thirty in the morning so the plants would be watered by the time the employees of Deutsche Bank and Morgan Stanley arrived at their offices.

On Bedford Avenue, other people like me—young men and women in retro office wear, heading to jobs at film production companies and graphic design firms and recording studios—were sleepily converging on the sidewalk, blinking beneath their Navy safety glasses and round schoolboy frames, messenger bags slung across their chests. It was still cool out, oddly cold for May, and I shivered a little in my thin jacket, my legs breaking out in goose bumps, then ducked into the Polish bakery—my favorite of the three on this one block alone—for coffee and a Danish. It was only when I reached into my bag to pay that I remembered the letter from my college boyfriend, now crushed under the manuscript. A rush of longing hit me so hard that the room, ever so slightly, began to spin.

I'll read it on the subway, I thought, grabbing my coffee and taking a sticky bite of pastry. But both trains were so crowded I had to stand, clutching a pole, my coffee sloshing dangerously. *I'll read it when I get to the office,* I thought.

But I had underestimated the Judy situation: again, I found my boss waiting for me, this time pacing in front of my desk, cigarette in hand.

"Well, what did you think?" she asked, by way of a greeting.

"I liked it." I pulled the manuscript out of my bag, tapping it on the desk to straighten the pages. Surreptitiously, I ran my tongue around my mouth, wondering if black prune residue from my Danish was lodged in the crevices between my teeth.

"Really?" she asked. "But what did you *make* of it? It's not a kids' book, is it?"

"It's not a kids' book," I confirmed. "It's a novel for grown-ups. About kids. Or, teenagers. In part." I hadn't thought I'd be nervous, but I was, clearly.

My boss tapped her finger on my desk impatiently. "My concern is: Am I going to be able to sell this? Will adults really read a book about kids?"

The book's not about kids, I started to protest, but something in her tone of voice—impatience, resentment, exhaustion—stopped me. It struck me that she didn't want my opinion. Maybe she'd told herself that she did, that my thoughts, as part of Judy Blume's devoted audience, could be valuable. Or maybe Max or Lucy had told her I was a good reader, a helpful reader. Both had taken on clients based on my initial reads. But my boss was different. She didn't want input from a twenty-four-year-old. She wanted me to agree with her. That was my job.

"Lots of great novels have child protagonists," I began instead, knowing this was absolutely the wrong tack. "*Oliver Twist*—"

"This isn't *Oliver Twist*," she informed me, with a mirthless laugh. "But *you* would read it?"

I nodded. I was certain that I was not alone. "*Many* people would read this book. Would *buy* this book. Everyone who loved her as a kid."

She looked at me uncomprehendingly, not—I realized later—because she didn't understand the scope of Judy's fame, the way her books had reshaped the narrative of childhood, but because my boss's relationship to literature, to books, to stories, to writers themselves, was entirely different from mine. She'd never loved books in the way I'd loved

Starring Sally J. Freedman as Herself and *Deenie*. Or the way Don—I felt a strange pang of affection for him—had loved *Then Again, Maybe I Won't*. She'd never spent entire days lying on her bed reading, entire nights making up complicated stories in her head. She'd not dreamed of willing herself into *Anne of Green Gables* and *Jane Eyre* so that she might have real friends, friends who understood her thorny desires and dreams. How could she spend her days—her *life*—ushering books into publication but not love them in the way that I did, the way that they needed to be loved?

I glanced into her cool, intelligent eyes. Was I wrong? Was this all wrong? Had she once been just like me? And time—and publishing—had changed her?

"I just don't know if I can sell it," she told me. And there, I suppose, was my answer. She was a businessperson.

"There's a *built-in audience*," I said, with more passion than I'd anticipated. "All those kids who read her when they were little." I paused for a moment, unsure if I should go on. "But also, I just think women will relate to these characters. It's kind of a universal story. About female friendship." This sounded like some of the bad jacket material that crossed my desk, but it was also true.

My boss looked at me and smiled. "Hmm," she said. "Could be."

Was she really, *really* going to tell Judy Blume that she couldn't sell this novel? This eminently readable, enjoyable novel that surely many, many people would buy? As a parade of clients walked out her door, never to return?

"Well," she said, lighting another cigarette. "You've had your fun"—*Fun?* I thought as she ambled back into her office—"but now it's time to get to work. I've got a *lot* of dictation for you." She handed me a few tapes and some correspondence to which I would refer. "Let's take care of that this morning."

I'd barely popped the first tape in, a fresh cup of the

office's dark, bitter coffee on my desk, when the phone rang. It was just after nine o'clock. No one called this early. "Hello?" came a nervous, nasal voice. "Hello?"

"Yes, hello," I said smoothly. I had come to love answering the phone. The strange control of it, the anonymity. On the phone, I could be anyone. I could be Suzanne, subject of a Leonard Cohen song. On the phone, I had all the answers. Though the answers were frequently all too simple: No. Definitely not. I'm sorry, no.

"Is this ——?" The voice asked for my boss. This was, I suspected, a Salinger call. A crazy one.

"No, I'm her assistant. Can I help you?" There was a long pause, and I waited for an eruption. Sometimes these callers became enraged when they realized they'd been put through to an assistant, insisting their business was too important for a mere underling, that I couldn't possibly understand the complicated nature of their request.

"Well, I'm calling because—" The man broke off, clearing his throat. When he spoke again, his voice was lower and less hesitant. "This is Roger Lathbury. From Orchises Press. I'm calling about J. D. Salinger. I—" It was clear that my boss's letter—with its emphasis on secrecy—had terrified him. He had no idea how much I knew and was afraid of destroying this deal before it had even gotten off the ground. He was also just *afraid*. Afraid in the way most people become when they get what they've long wanted.

"Mr. Lathbury," I cried, interrupting him. "My boss has been looking forward to hearing from you. Let me see if she's in her office." She was, of course, in her office, but I had been instructed to say this to all callers before putting them through to her. I was always to check and make sure she wanted to talk or at least to warn her as to who was on the line. There was no intercom system, though, between my desk and hers—or there seemed to be, but I couldn't figure it out—so I simply rapped softly on her half-closed door.

"Ye-es," she called irritably without turning toward me.

"Um, Roger Lathbury is on the phone."

Jumping in her seat, she turned around, her face a mask of anger. "Well, for God's sake, put him through. And close the door." A wash of tears sprang into my eyes and I turned away quickly, running the few steps to my desk and pushing the appropriate buttons without a word.

An hour later, as I finished the last of my typing, a tanned, skinny woman in narrow-legged jeans and a close-fitting white T-shirt walked hesitantly through the finance wing, toward my desk. As she crossed the threshold into my domain, something caught her eye and she retreated back into the corner, crouching down in front of the obscure bookcase where I'd found Judy Blume's books. *Oh no,* I thought, as a frown arranged itself on the woman's face. *No. No, that can't be her.* She didn't look at all the way I'd pictured Judy Blume. How had I pictured her? More plump and smiley? I wasn't sure. Regardless, this had to be her. An overwhelming impulse to protect my boss, the Agency, overtook me, and I considered running out from behind my desk to greet her, explaining that we'd just renovated—true!—and the books were all out of order; we were in the process of reshelving them.

Before I could move, my boss cried, "Judy!" and raced out of her office. Pam must have warned her. Still frowning, Judy rose and allowed herself to be led away from the narrow bookcase. "It's *lovely* to see you!" Judy did little more than nod and followed my boss into her office.

A few minutes later, they left for lunch in grim silence— Judy glancing darkly back at the obscure bookcase—without even slowing as they passed me. I gathered my typing and placed it on the corner of my boss's desk for signature, put on my coat, and grabbed my bag. On the corner of Forty-Ninth Street, I decided to splurge, as I occasionally did, on a tray of gyoza at the Japanese restaurant on the ground floor of our building. The restaurant was always packed with suit-clad Japanese businessmen, and I tended to be both the only woman and the only Caucasian, which lent me a lovely anonymity. I was so out of place that I disappeared. Perched on a high stool at the bar, I ordered my gyoza—the cheapest thing on the menu and the only one I could afford—when I again remembered the letter. There it was, at the bottom of my bag, jostling with the Arts section of the newspaper and the previous week's *New Yorker*, which I'd intended to read at lunch. I pulled the letter out and, before I could think better of it, slit the envelope with my thumb. Inside lay two sheets of the thin, airmail-like paper my college boyfriend favored, both sides covered in his neat print. I read the salutation, "Dear Jo," and, without intending to, let out a great, gulping sob, for no one in my current life called me Jo. Just my family and my old friends. And my college boyfriend. I missed him so. Missed all of him, in every way. "Dear Jo." *Oh God,* I thought, *what have I done?* A moment later, my gyoza arrived, lightly charred, their green skins glistening with oil. I slipped the letter back into its envelope, and though I knew the dumplings were too hot, I pulled one off the neat row, biting into it. Hot oil and broth spurted everywhere and my eyes watered all over again. For days afterward, the roof of my mouth prickled with pain, but for a moment I relished the burning.

The next morning, the phone rang in my boss's office just after she arrived. "Judy, hello!" I heard her cry, with manic cheer. Her door closed. When it opened again, she was standing in the frame, blinking forlornly. "Hugh?" she called. He came running out of his office and looked at her expectantly. "Well, that's over," she said.

"Judy?" he asked. She nodded. "She's leaving?" It was more a statement than a question.

"Yep," said my boss, with a raise of her pale brows. "She's leaving."

"I won't ask for whom," said Hugh.

"Doesn't matter," said my boss.

I wondered what my boss had said to Judy about her new novel. But I kept my head down, my eyes focused on the contract in front of me, for my thoughts were utterly disloyal: if I were Judy, I would have left, too.

3

The World Wide Web

A week later, Jenny came by my office at the end of the day. I had succeeded in convincing her to stay in town for an early dinner, though I worried that my small victory was Pyrrhic, that she had agreed to this plan purely out of guilt or obligation. She'd not been excited about seeing the Agency for herself—though I'd been to her office quite a few times—and this, more than anything, distressed me: she no longer cared about the details of my life apart from her.

Still, she was trying, sort of, and she arrived at the Agency in her duffle coat, for though it was now June, the weather patterns appeared to be stuck in March: at 5:00 p.m., the skies outside Hugh's window—just barely visible from my desk—grew dark and ominous, a gray rain pelting down, fierce winds shaking the blinds. "Hello!" I cried, embracing her. Pam, at the reception desk, averted her eyes from this unseemly display of emotion.

"I'm here," said Jenny, smiling, though her eyes flashed discomfort.

"Let me take you back," I said, and gestured for her to follow me down the front hallway. "I have to get my coat. And you can see my desk."

"Okay," she said, in the sort of tone she used with her mother. "It's really dark," she whispered. "Are they trying to save money on electricity?"

I held my finger to my lips like a librarian. *Shhhhh!* And smiled. Other than the finance department, with its glaring fluorescents, the office was lit almost entirely by shaded lamps, which meant that its warren of rooms were indeed much more dim than a modern office, like Jenny's, with walls of windows and bright overheads. But this was part of what I loved about it: the soft, consoling glow cast by the lamps; the hush of my co-workers' feet on the soft carpet, the leather armchairs and dark wood bookcases. It was like working in someone's apartment or a private library.

"Or a funeral home!" said Jenny as we walked across Forty-Ninth Street, back in the direction of her office. "Or a bar. I can't believe your boss really smokes. At her desk!" Jenny had been, actually, the first of my friends to take up smoking, her junior year of high school, the side effect of dating a college guy. This shocked me at the time. "Isn't it depressing, being in that office all day? Everyone looks so sad. It really does remind me of a funeral home. All those old-fashioned lamps. The rugs."

"Maybe a little," I conceded, though it didn't at all. I loved the lamps and rugs, loved that the office was hushed and softly lit. "Do you want to come back to Williamsburg for dinner? We could go to Planet Thailand." I had been contriving to get Jenny over to my neighborhood for dinner or coffee, to show her my apartment, my lovely block, hopeful that if she came for the afternoon, she'd fall in love and move there.

"I don't think I can go all the way to Brooklyn," she said. "It'll take me forever to get on the ferry from there."

"It's not that far," I began. This was true: I was just one

stop in from Manhattan. Twenty minutes from where we stood. "But should we just get on the train and go downtown? We could go to the Grey Dog? Or John's Pizzeria?" Jenny loved John's.

She shifted uncomfortably on her Mary Janes. "Maybe we could just stop somewhere here? I should get on the ferry in an hour or so."

"Here?" We were on the West Side now, at the edge of the theater district, surrounded by overpriced restaurants designed for conventioneers and tourists, steak houses with laminated menus, chain Italian joints, loud Irish pubs. No one I knew would ever willingly eat in any such establishment.

"There's a place that my boss sometimes takes us to." She spoke now in mollifying tones. "It has a terrible name, but the food is actually really good."

"What's it called?" I asked.

"Pasta Pasta!" she said, smiling. "Pasta Pasta Exclamation Point!"

Ensconced in a booth, spearing quills of penne, I felt silly: Jenny was right. There had been no need to go downtown. The food was beside the point. We talked about Texas, about the latest installment of Jenny's wedding saga—her parents had deemed the boathouse too expensive—about Don's novel, which was still not done.

"How is Brett?" I finally asked. "Has he heard from all the schools?" His acceptance letters—and rejection letters—from law schools had started arriving back in March. I knew he'd been accepted to two in New York: Brooklyn Law and Cardozo. And he'd been wait-listed at a few places.

Jenny nodded. "He has. He got into Case Western off the wait list, and he's decided to go."

"Case Western?" I asked, my stomach dropping. "Why? He got into Cardozo."

"Well, he just thinks Case Western is the right place for

him. It's a really good school. And, you know, he's from the Midwest. He misses that area. He thinks law school in Cleveland will be a little bit less *intense*. Law students in New York have got to be crazy competitive."

I nodded. "And you'll stay here until he's done?"

She laughed. "No, I'll go with him." She rolled her eyes. "We're *engaged*."

"Oh, right! I'd forgotten." I took a bite of my cooling pasta. *Pasta!* I thought. *Exclamation point!* Did I have friends other than Jenny who would find that funny?

"I'm actually kind of excited about it. I've never lived anywhere other than New York. Cleveland is a cool city. The art museum is great. And it will be so cheap. We can get, like, a huge house for less than we're paying for our apartment."

I had gone to Oberlin. I knew all about Cleveland, but I just nodded, sipping the dregs of my house red. Jenny had not ordered wine, which made me feel like a lush. Everyone else I knew ordered wine with dinner by rote. What was the point of going to dinner—even at a cheesy, awful corporate restaurant in midtown—if you didn't order wine? For a few minutes, we sat in silence, then Jenny smiled goofily—her old smile, which I saw so rarely now—and said, "I think we should split the tiramisu. It's completely terrible. But also completely amazing."

"Sure," I said, as she signaled for the waiter.

"So what happened with Judy Blume?" she asked. A week or so ago, I'd told her that Judy was coming into the office. The old Jenny would have loved this turn of events, would have wanted to know everything. The new Jenny had waited until after dinner to ask about it. And though I wasn't sure that she even cared, I explained what had transpired.

"Of course she left!" Jenny cried.

"Because my boss maybe told her that she wasn't sure she could sell her new novel? And keeps her books in the least visible part of the office?" I smiled at her. "Or because the office looks like a funeral home?"

"All of that, obviously," she said, swirling a bit of cake in marsala. "But really because the Agency is like something out of Dickens. You step inside, and it's like you've time traveled back a hundred years." She gave me a funny look. "We were walking through the office and I was trying to figure out why it seemed so *weird*. And then, when we got to your desk, I realized, *There are no computers!*"

"I told you I typed everything. On a typewriter."

"I know," she said, shaking her head, dark waves bouncing glossily on her shoulders. "But I figured that was just some quirk of your boss. That she was old. I didn't realize there were *no computers at all*. It's 1996. How do they do any business? Everyone uses e-mail. How do they even communicate with the world?" She paused, cocking her head to the side. "If I were Judy Blume, I'm not sure that I would put my career in the hands of an agency that refuses to admit it's almost the twenty-first century."

Back in March, James had found the wherewithal to approach my boss about entering the digital age, if in the most minor, tentative manner possible. Not an office full of computers. No network. Just a few desktops, for the assistants, so that we might do our work more efficiently. Maybe without Internet connections even.

"Give me something in writing," my boss finally conceded, in April. "Price it out."

By the end of the day, he was back, rapping firmly on her office door. "Just wanted to give you this," he said, handing over a neatly typed sheaf of papers.

It was June, the week after the Judy incident, before she sent me to fetch him. "Come in, come in," she said as we approached. "Not you"—she tilted her head toward me—"just James." And she shut the door.

Half an hour later they emerged, chatting chummily. "Do they come in black?" my boss asked.

"It's possible," said James, nodding.

"All the computers I've seen are that awful putty color," she complained. "Yech. Why do they make them that color?"

"I'll see about black."

"Mind you, I'm not saying yes." My boss paused in front of my desk. "But you *have* intrigued me. It *could* help with Salinger."

"It could," James agreed. What might this mean? Were they talking about the fan letters? That a computer would save me the labor of typing that form letter over and over and over? I smiled just thinking about this. They weighed on me, the letters: all those Salinger fans waiting for responses. A computer would help.

"See if they come in black," my boss was saying, "and then we'll talk. And confirm the numbers."

"Okay." James allowed himself a small smile. I could see that he was trying to decide whether to say what he did indeed say next. "Thank you."

"Don't thank me," my boss said. "I'm not saying yes. And if I did say yes, it would only be for the Salinger stuff. I don't want people on the World Wide Web all day, doing whatever they do." She waved her hands around, to indicate the utter craziness that was the Internet. "I don't want people"—she glanced in my direction and gave James a knowing nod—"e-mailing their friends in Zimbabwe all day."

"I don't think," said James, with a wink at me, "that will be a problem."

The next day, Pam dropped on my desk a thick envelope bearing rows of colorful foreign postage. Inside, I found the Other

Client's new novel, his first literary venture in a decade. He was on leave from teaching at the moment, staying with his wife's family in New Zealand. "I just have a feeling about this," my boss told Hugh and me, bouncing excitedly on her toes, the thick manuscript clutched to her chest. "This is going to be huge," she told me the next morning. She'd read the entire thing in one night. "Prepare yourself for a multiple submission." I nodded, afraid to open my mouth. Multiple submissions, I'd thought, were not the Agency way. But veering from the Agency way could only be a good thing for the Agency.

"It's going to be a lot of work," she warned me. Perhaps, I thought, this was her problem with contemporary agenting, or contemporary publishing, in general: not that it was unscrupulous, but that it was too taxing. Thirty years earlier, she could have sold this book on a one-page proposal and a handshake.

For a week, my boss consulted with Max, working and reworking a list of editors to whom she'd send the novel, many of them younger and unknown to her, outside her network of cronies. The manuscript was handed to me to be sent out for xeroxing—our office machine couldn't handle twelve copies of a three-hundred-page tome—and while I waited for the messenger to arrive, I peeked at the front page. I'd been relieved, honestly, that my boss hadn't asked me to read the novel. It sounded gruesome and sensational and vaguely misogynist, the sort of violent thriller sold in airports. The first pages showed this to be absolutely true. The narrator excruciatingly details a Grand Guignol scene in which he finds the bodies of three dead girls in an attic, arranged in a sort of diorama. The writing, sure, was elegant and precise, the tone controlled and engaging—almost masterful—but there was still something about those pages—something beyond the grotesque subject matter—that turned my stomach.

In the end, my boss was right: the book sold for a large

amount of money, to a great editor, at the new literary imprint of a good publisher. A crossover literary thriller. Gold. "We did it!" my boss said, generously, to the group gathered near my desk. Had I ever seen her in such high spirits? I wasn't sure. But I was happy—as all assistants are, perhaps—to see my boss happy. Ecstatic.

"*You* did it," I said, smiling. It was true.

"I suppose," she said with a shrug. She was, I suddenly realized, an unlikely leader, a reluctant president. She disliked being at the center of attention, having us all at her beck and call. This was why she came and went with barely a word to me. Not out of hauteur. She was shy, quiet, retiring. "We're going for drinks tonight. All of us."

And so we filed out, at five, to the stark, 1980s-style restaurant around the corner and sat at the bar—birds on a wire—drinking cocktails. Outside the office, we had, somehow, nothing to say to one another, each of us too afraid of betraying allegiances. Only Carolyn and my boss made it past the first round. The rest of us filed out quickly, pulling on sweaters and light jackets. It was June, but still cold. The blizzard had set the tone for the rest of the year. At some point, things had to warm up.

The next week, a brown-suited deliveryman deposited a block of enormous boxes in the finance wing, across from the shelf that held Judy's books. From my desk I watched James hunched over a mass of cables, setting up a hulking desktop PC. Decidedly putty colored. I stopped by on my way to the bathroom. "No black?" I asked.

"Sony actually makes a black desktop," said James, smiling. "But it was a lot more expensive. Your boss decided it wasn't worth it. She thinks computers are just a passing fad."

"This is going to make form letters so much easier," I said, crouching down beside him. "The Salinger fan mail, especially. Oh my God." I wondered what would happen to my typewriter, the huge hulking mass of it. Perhaps they'd let me take it home. I'd come to love it, in a strange, Stockholm syndrome sort of way. And I imagined myself typing away the evening, seated at the blue schoolhouse desk I'd pulled in off the street, a stack of unblemished white paper to my left. Perhaps I would write a novel, the novel I'd been toying with, nervously plotting out, the typewriter's whir and hum coaxing me into a meditative state.

James stood up and stretched. "Not really," he said. I furrowed my brow in his direction. "This is the computer." With the back of his hand, he wiped a sheen of sweat off his forehead. "*The* computer." Uncomprehendingly, I looked from James to the partially installed monitor. "We're just getting one computer. Which we'll all share. We'll still type up correspondence on our Selectrics."

"But—" I asked, hoping that I'd misheard something. "*Why?*" I looked at him, a disproportionate sense of alarm filling me. "What's this for?"

"We'll use it to monitor copyright infringement. So, there are all these personal Web pages, right? And people are posting excerpts from Salinger and Fitzgerald and Dylan Thomas. We need to make sure that those excerpts are within the limits of fair usage. Which is eight hundred words or less for prose; five lines for poetry."

"Oh," I said, still stunned.

"Hugh can also use it for research so he doesn't have to go to the library as much." Hugh, I knew, would be deeply displeased by this suggestion. He loved going to the library. "And I think everyone else can use it, if they need to, just not for personal stuff."

A few days later, my boss walked around the office rounding everyone up, then brought the lot of us—Lucy and Max laughing like high school kids—over to the computer, pristine and beige, its monitor dark. "Well," she said. "We've done it." She cast her eyes around at us, meaningfully. "This is the office computer." She gestured to the keyboard. "Is it on?" she asked James. He shook his head no. "Okay, it's not on," she confirmed. Olivia looked at me and smirked. "We've put it here, right in the central part of the office, in full view, so that no one will be tempted to use it for personal e-mail or"— she paused, searching her mind for other activities in which one might engage with a computer—"*anything*. People waste a lot of time on computers and we're not going to have any of that. This computer is for research"—she nodded at Hugh, who nodded curtly back—"and for monitoring Agency business. If you need to use it for anything, just come to me and ask. But if I come out and see you sitting here, I'm going to assume you're doing something you shouldn't be doing." Surveying our faces, she shook her head with exasperation, as if we were a pack of mischievous children entrusted to her care. "Okay?"

"Okay!" cried Max, raising his fist in the air.

"Now, Max," said my boss, an edge rising in her voice. It was strange: Max generated pretty much all the Agency's new business. He'd just settled a deal for something in the sum of two million dollars. But my boss still regarded him as an interloper, a rebel without proper respect for the Agency's filing system. She did not, I suspected, consider him "an Agency person," like James and Hugh—and me. She'd quietly doled out this praise half a dozen times now. And though I relished it—I was nothing if not, as Don perpetually told me, the Obedient Child—it occurred to me that if these were my two potential futures, the choice was abundantly clear: I wanted to be Max, not my boss. To be Max was not just to broker big deals but to be utterly engaged with contemporary literature, as entangled with the ins and outs of narrative style as I'd been as a grad student, albeit in a far less rarefied way; to be in daily conversation with great writers and editors who cared deeply about words, language, story, which was another way of simply being engaged with the world, of trying to make *sense* of the world, rather than retreating from it, trying to place an artificial order on the messy stuff of life, preferring dead writers to living ones.

But then another, sobering thought occurred to me. Before I started this job, hadn't I wanted to count myself among the living ones?

That night, as I brushed my teeth in the bathroom, Don called to me from the couch. "Buba! Come here. I want to show you something." Inside me, something cracked and splintered into a million pieces. "Please stop calling me that," I shouted, storming into the living room. "I'm not a child." His large eyes grew larger and I thought, for a second—unbelievably—they might be filling with tears. "Do you know why I call you that?" he asked. I shook my head. And so he told me.

Don had a former student named Masha, with whom he'd remained friends. Masha emigrated from Russia in the early 1990s, and though he had enormous problems with communism—having not just experienced the philosophy in practice but been persecuted under it—Don was still thrilled to have found an actual Soviet with whom he could endlessly discuss socialism, even if those discussions turned into arguments. Masha lived with his wife—who had also been Don's student—in Washington Heights, in a large, dark apartment crammed with relics of Russian life and the toys of their three children, the youngest of whom they considered a miracle baby, for though both Masha and his wife were dark—blue-black hair, olive complexions, thick brows—through some trick of genetics, this last child had emerged from the womb with pale pink skin and blond curls and lovely gray-blue eyes. Her disposition, too, was extraordinarily sunny. "She's like a child of *light*," Don told me. "She's just so cute and sweet that no matter what she does you just want to pick her up and hug her." The child's name was Anna or Natalya, but everyone called her the Buba. "Why?" I asked. Don shrugged and laughed. A real laugh. Not his ironic, mean laugh, his default laugh, a sort of cackle. "She's just the *Buba*. There's just no other word for her. I can't explain it. You have to meet her and you'll understand. She's just all *light*." He stretched his arms above his head and yawned. We had seated ourselves on the gray couch in the tiny living room, a couch we'd pulled in off the street with the help of Don's friend Bart, an enormously tall poet, who composed his own verse around lines from famous poems. "So I was there, visiting Masha, this one afternoon, right after I met you, and the Buba was sitting on his lap, and it suddenly hit me. That you're like the Buba."

"*I'm* like the Buba?" I did not have blond curls or gray-blue eyes. And even during the years when I was an actual child, I had been told, frequently, that I lacked childlike qualities: My face was long and thin. I hated games. I preferred the company of adults.

"You are," Don said, delighted. "You're rosy and full of light. You walk through the world and it's as if you're filled with light. It was the first thing I noticed about you."

"That's not true," I objected, awkwardly. "I'm not rosy. I'm kind of pale."

"True?" asked Don. "There's no *true*. There's no one *truth*. That's a schoolgirl thing." He looked at me intently, his mouth pressed into a line, as if he were fighting off a wave of some undefined emotion. "The world is subjective. Experiential." Then his face turned slack and the ironic glint returned to his eyes. He shook his head professorially. "You need to read Kant."

It would not be an exaggeration to say that I'd always considered myself dark and heavy. A chubby child, burdened by sorrows: my own, those of my family, my plagued, storied race. But that instant, something shifted. Was it possible that Don was right? That the world perceived me in a manner entirely different from how I perceived myself? Was it possible, too, that one could be complicated, intellectual, awake to the world, that one could be an *artist*, and also be rosy and filled with light? Was it possible that one could be all those things and also be *happy*?

The next morning, the weather turned. The cold damp that had lingered well into the official start of summer evaporated overnight. I woke to a column of sunlight spilling through our kitchen window. From the back of the closet, I pulled my favorite dress, dark green and in a style alluding to the 1940s, with a collar and buttons up the front, an imitation of those dresses on Leigh's floor. It was wrinkled—crushed by the heavy wools of winter—but I pulled it on anyway, over a black slip, hoping it would uncrease on my way to the office, then raced out the door and into the fresh, warm air, turning onto Bedford, where the fig trees were in bloom, the tiny white flowers lining their slim gray branches, the street suddenly quaint and pretty, rather than industrial and ugly. Williamsburg's charms were not, *are* not, physical. Bedford, the main thoroughfare of the North Side, could be the high street in, say, Milwaukee, with its low storefronts and brick row houses. This was not the New York of Woody Allen, the New York of high-rises and doormen and big dreams and Hollywood montages. But it was my New York. Mine. And I loved it.

Most mornings, I took the 6 train to Fifty-First Street, emerging at the corner of Fiftieth and Lex in the shadow of the Waldorf-Astoria's wedding-cake glory. My boss, I knew, sometimes had lunch at the Waldorf's pub, the Bull and Bear, the entrance of which was at the back of the hotel—clubby and discreet—on the Lexington Avenue side, the southeast corner. I'd never been inside, of course, but I'd memorized its faded, genteel insignia, purely from walking in its proximity every morning. At night, as I traipsed back to the subway from my office, I encountered the Waldorf's grand front entrance, magically lit and reminiscent of the castle at the entrance to Disneyland.

On this particular morning, I skipped up the steps of the subway station, a warm breeze blowing the skirt of my dress. On Lex, I found a strange sight: a crowd of fire trucks racing down the avenue, their sirens off, the street strangely untrafficked. They were beautiful, those trucks, a brilliant red against the brilliant blue of the sky, and like the Agency they seemed like visitors from a different, pre-digital era, from the picture books my parents read to me in childhood.

I was early, as usual, and I stood on the corner, watching the trucks disappear down Lex. When I looked up, there was the Waldorf, looming in front of me. And before I could think better of it, I'd crossed to the northwest side of the avenue and pushed open the hotel's back doors, which led—I discovered—to a not particularly grand, shabby even, vestibule. To my left, the Bull and Bear, now closed; to my right, the hotel's other restaurant, Oscar's. In front of me, an escalator leading I knew not where. I stepped on.

The escalator dropped me in a hallway, carpeted in a pattern of dark red and gold, punctuated by large potted plants. I paused for a moment, unsure of where to go. If I walked straight, through the archway in front of me, surely I'd eventually reach the west side of the building, the main entrance, which opened onto Park. I could exit through that entrance, then walk a block over to my office on Madison. But before I made it through the archway, I noticed a tiny, dim storefront on my left: an antiquarian bookshop. My breath caught with delight. I had stayed at hotels of this sort as a child, with my parents: the King David in Tel Aviv; The Breakers in Palm Beach; Brown's in Denver. Before dinner, my mother and I would browse in the lobby shops, trying on sunglasses and pendants and scarves. Of course, I thought, a grand hotel in New York—the cultural capital of the country—would have a *book*shop.

I was close enough to the glass now to make out some of the titles: a beautiful, ornate copy of *Don Juan;* an oversized edition of *Peter Pan* with what appeared to be the original illustrations; the moss-green binding of *Alice in Wonderland*. And there, at the center—the window's most prominent spot—a book in blazing red, a book whose cover was so familiar I almost didn't see it, until I did, and gave a start, so strange was it to see this book out of context. It was, of course, a first edition of *The Catcher in the Rye,* its cover bearing an illustration of a carousel horse rearing in fury, or fright. I knew now—Hugh had told me—that Salinger's neighbor in Westport, a painter named Michael Mitchell, had drawn that horse specifically for Salinger, for *Catcher*. For the paperback, the publisher had chosen a more explicit image—Holden Caulfield in a red hunting cap—that Salinger, not surprisingly, had loathed. Out of alliance with Salinger, the Agency kept no copies of that maligned edition in the office.

But a few copies of this first edition, with its raging stallion, sat across from my desk. I had memorized the font on the spine. I saw it in my sleep. This copy was different in that it was slightly more pristine, the red more brilliant, the white more white. And that it had on it a price tag: twenty-five thousand dollars.

Around the corner from the bookshop, I found a ladies' room where I washed my hands in the water that came forth from heavy gold-toned faucets, drying them on paper towels as thick and soft as cloth, then smoothed down my hair and swiped my lips with gloss: a five-minute vacation from the dishes in the bathtub, the ramen dinners. For a moment, I indulged myself: imagined that my parents were in the lobby waiting for me, that we were going to the Met, would have lunch under the skylights, amid the Rodins, as we did when I was a child. Then I slung my bag back over my shoulder and walked out, past the bookshop, through the archway, and into the hotel's upper lobby, which was filled with business-men. *Men*, all of them men, with short hair and shiny shoes. They were young—some as young as I, their faces dewy and unlined, their smiles painfully open and warm, so different from Don's tight grin—and I wondered who they were and what they were doing here. Was it money that allowed them to smile that way? Money and security?

Nine thirty was approaching now, so I hurried down the wide, royal staircase that appeared in front of me—my shoes sinking into the deep carpet—and descended to the lower lobby, where I found even more men, checking in and out, affixing name badges, making calls on the house phones, talking to the concierge or the doorman; men laughing in crowds of three and four, or standing alone, flipping through dense binders of charts and graphs. They turned and glanced at me as I walked by, smiling and nodding as if I were part of their world, the realm of currency and privilege. "Good day, miss," the doorman said to me, tipping his hat. "Can I get you a cab?"

"Oh, no, thank you," I replied, in a voice that was not quite my own. "It's such a beautiful day. I'd rather walk. I'm just going a few blocks."

"It *is* a beautiful day," he agreed. "You enjoy it now."

"Thank you," I said in this alien voice—the voice of the me who stayed in suites at the Waldorf and took cabs across town in inclement weather—and walked through the door he held open for me, onto Park, where a battalion of tulips had commandeered the median strip. They swayed in the warm breeze, their heavy heads dipping south as one.

.   .   .

Now that the sun was finally out, the darkness of the Agency struck me as mildly oppressive, or perhaps *de*pressive. *It's spring*, I wanted to shout to Lucy, in her black shifts, nun-like and sober, and my boss, in her baggy brown suit, and even to the forest-green carpeting that muffled our footsteps, the deep brown wood that framed each room in bookcases. In the winter, the darkness had served as a cozy refuge, but now I counted the minutes until lunch, when I could walk in the warm sun, my arms bare. "Pretty frock," Lucy called as I passed her office. "Is it an antick-cue?" Before I could answer, she pushed herself up from her chair and joined me. "I've been wanting to ask," she said, her voice slightly below its normal throaty boom. "Are you eating?"

I looked at her uncomprehendingly. "Eating what?" I asked.

"Well," she began, then broke into nervous laughter and gestured theatrically at my dress. My eyes followed her hands, and I suddenly saw what she meant, or part of what she meant: my dress swam on me. "You're looking a bit"— she searched for the right word—"*wan*." Maddeningly, I felt as if I might cry. "I know it can be really hard to live on an assistant's salary." She laughed again. "If anyone knows, it's me."

"I'm eating," I told her, with a big smile. "I am." But was I? With my new bills, I could barely live. Every day, I called the bank to check my balance, and all too often I'd dipped into my overdraft, even though I budgeted every cent and painstakingly balanced my checkbook. I shopped for groceries once a week, on Saturday morning, carefully totaling up my cart before I approached the register, putting back anything too extravagant, like packaged cookies and cereal. For lunch, I limited myself to five dollars, which bought me a sad little Greek salad at the chain sandwich shop around the corner: limp romaine lettuce, sometimes turning brown at the edges; a pale winter tomato; a few translucent slices of tomato and pearly cucumber; and a crumble of feta, atop which sat one slim, salty olive. That olive made it all worth it.

That day, though, I did something I'd never, ever done: I walked directly and purposely to the elegant food shop on Forty-Ninth from which the agents obtained their lunches. Around me, the Masters of the Universe ordered frisée salads, rubbing elbows with their female counterparts, thin, tanned women with Cartier bangles dangling from their thin, tanned wrists. The sandwiches sat like pastries on silver cake stands. After much deliberation, I chose a slender flat of bread filled with some sort of pink cured meat. At the register, I grabbed a chocolate cookie, ordered a coffee, and handed over a crisp twenty. I was not, at that exact moment, overdrawn, but my heart still sped up as I placed my meager change in my wallet. Sandwich in hand, I walked over to Fifth, the sun warming my shoulders, sat down on the steps of St. Patrick's Cathedral with the tourists, and took a bite, a dense, salty, oily, warm bite. It was, there was no doubt, the most delicious sandwich I'd ever tasted. I ate half, planning to save the remainder for the next day, then went ahead and devoured that, too.

The next morning, I put on a spring dress I'd never worn before, a long-ago gift from my mother, red and shorter than anything else in my wardrobe, my knees pale beneath its bright hem. From the back of the closet, I pulled a pair of shoes, black leather sandals with a ladylike heel, yet another contribution from my mother. We had no mirror in the apartment, so I wasn't sure if this ensemble looked all right, but in my heels and close-cut dress I felt stronger, more erect, able to keep my head in line with my spine, as my acting teachers had always told me to do. I was a sloucher, a slumper, a huncher.

When I emerged from the subway that morning, I

crossed Fiftieth Street without a second thought and pulled open the back door of the Waldorf, gliding up the escalator and past the bookshop, with a glance at the window to make sure *Catcher* was still there. In the upper lobby, I again found clusters of freshly shaved bankers and consultants and who knew what, in their crisp suits, peering disinterestedly up at me from conference agendas and sales reports. Suddenly I longed to be one of them, among them, at home in this world, a shining card in my wallet that would allow me to sit down and order a five-dollar cup of coffee. My father and I—this memory came at me with brute force—had spent so many hours of my childhood in lobbies like this, making up stories about the people passing by. He had grown up in a sort of enforced poverty, my father, with his socialist parents, his activist mother—my grandmother, down on Grand Street, whom I owed a visit—and as an adult he'd relished even the smallest of luxuries, but none more so than the fancy hotel, that emblem of louche idleness.

I walked on through the men in their suits, my spine still neatly stacked, and continued down the stairs, smiling giddily. And then I looked up, way up, to the lobby's soaring, intricate ceiling, its borders painted in gold leaf, a pattern so complex and beautiful that for the first time I understood the true meaning of the phrase "took my breath away." For I did, truly, lose a breath as the patterns—leaves and vines and diamonds—revealed themselves to me, and as I under-stood the ceiling's true height, the magnitude of air and space between those gold vines and my small self. My shoe, with its narrow heel, caught on the thick carpet, and for a moment I thought—I knew, my heart beating faster—that I was going to trip and fall down that small flight of stairs, the world around me rotating, but then I simply laid my hand on the railing, steadied myself, and continued down.

Summer

The Pitch

They would be meeting. In person. Jerry and Roger Lathbury. This was big news. Jerry did not meet people. Jerry avoided people. Even people he'd known for decades. The two men had been corresponding on their own, circumventing my boss and the Agency. "It might be good to send me copies of your letters," I heard my boss say. But Jerry did not send copies of his letters. Nor did Roger. My boss described this as "highly irregular," shaking her head and laughing a little as she did when anxious or displeased. They bothered her, these letters. What if Jerry was agreeing to some strange terms? Or in some way putting himself at risk? Roger seemed, certainly, like the nicest, most genuine of fellows, but what if he were not? What if he were somehow manipulating Salinger into—what? My boss did not know.

And it didn't matter, for there was nothing we could do about it, about any of it. The situation now transcended the realm of business. Jerry and Roger were becoming friends.

Or at least Jerry was becoming friends with Roger. Roger was a bit too anxious, a bit too baffled by Salinger's enthusiasm, to truly reciprocate. He had started calling with more and more frequency. Every time he received a letter from Salinger, he called. Every time he sent a letter to Salinger, he called, worried that he had said the wrong thing.

And thus it was I who often ended up listening to Roger's concerns, his fears. Pam had been instructed, I gathered, to put Roger through to me first. "I've done some mock-ups," he told me in late June. "A couple. I think I understand what Jerry likes in a design and I think he's going to like these. Or, I think he'll like one better than the other."

"Oh?" I said, trying to hide the alarm in my voice. We'd yet to work out all the details of this deal. There was no contract. Not even a draft of a contract. It seemed to me that laying out a book before the contracts were signed did indeed qualify as highly irregular. It also struck me as bad luck.

"I retyped it," he told me, "so that I could mock up a design. I could have scanned it, but I thought Salinger would prefer it if I retyped it."

"Hmm," I murmured into the phone, wondering if Salinger would know the difference. It was Friday and my boss was at home, of course. Roger often called on Friday mornings, and I was beginning to think this a conscious choice, that he was using me as a sounding board. Or a therapist. Clearly, this deal, already, was causing him enormous anxiety. Or perhaps he was just an anxious, chatty person. He had told me all about his daughters, his syllabi, and his collection of literary relics.

"And it's a good thing, too. In typing up the story, I noticed that there are a few small typos." He seemed a bit pleased by this, to have caught *The New Yorker* in error.

"Really?" I asked, surprised. *The New Yorker*'s fact-checking and copyediting departments were legendary. Mistakes, I'd thought, simply didn't slip through.

"Oh yes," Roger affirmed. "Small typos, but typos still. I

went ahead and corrected them. Salinger is such a stickler for details, I'm assuming he'd want them corrected."

"I'm sure you're right," I said, discreetly rolling a piece of letterhead into my typewriter, though I couldn't type when on the phone—other than with Don, or my mother, or Jenny, or someone else who wouldn't be offended—as the Selectric made too much noise. Actually, I wasn't at all sure.

"I also considerably widened the margins to give the book some length. If it's too thin, I won't be able to fit the title on the spine horizontally. Jerry wants a horizontal title. He hates vertical titles. So I've made some really wide margins. But Salinger prefers that. Not too much text on the page. He wants the story to *breathe*."

"Vertical titles?" I'd never heard this term before and wondered if Roger—or Salinger—had invented it. It sounded like a Joy Division album. Or a collection of abstract poetry.

"Yes, yes!" In his overexcitement, Roger sometimes sounded like the White Rabbit. I pictured him as small and pudgy, his hair parted deeply on one side and combed over to the other. "Vertical titles. When the title is printed sideways along the spine of the book. So you have to turn your head sideways to read it. Most titles are printed that way, actually. Because you need a relatively thick spine to print a title horizontally. Look at Salinger's books." I glanced at the bookshelf in front of me. "All of them have horizontal titles." Squinting, I saw he was right. They did indeed. Each word of each title printed across each book's spine, the words stacked on top of one another.

The following Wednesday Salinger drove down to D.C. and met Roger for lunch at the National Gallery, a busy, public place if there ever was one, but Salinger was not—as Roger half expected—mobbed by fans or converged on by photographers. The two men sat and looked over Roger's designs, then parted ways at the little waterfall by the stairs leading up to the lobby.

"He insisted on paying for lunch," reported Roger, who seemed baffled by the fact that he, Roger Lathbury of Alexandria, Virginia—the kid who read *Nine Stories* in his suburban bedroom—had somehow ended up eating sandwiches with J. D. Salinger. He had, of course, called first thing Thursday morning to give me a postmortem. "The pub date will be January 1," he told me. "Jerry's birthday."

"January 1 of next year?" I asked. Producing and publishing a book usually took longer than six months. Could Roger really get this book in stores by the New Year?

"Yes, yes, of course. No need to wait," he confirmed. "There's not that much to do. Jerry chose the design I thought he would. And we decided against running the title at the top of each page. Because it's an epistolary story. You know. It's a letter. So it takes you out of the moment to have the title running across the top of the page. Jerry agrees."

The two men agreed on everything, it seemed, except for one. Salinger did not want the typos corrected. In fact, he'd bristled at Roger's correcting them without consulting him first.

"I don't understand it," said Roger. "He actually seemed put out that I'd fixed them"—he paused, unsure if he should even speak of the potential catastrophe—"I thought for a moment he was going to say, 'Let's just forget this whole thing.' Because I corrected some small mistakes. But okay. I'll put the typos back in."

"Did he say why?" I asked. I'd had a feeling—based on nothing—that Salinger would respond in this way. My suspicion was that with Jerry it was all about control: Had Roger asked him about correcting the typos in advance, he might have said, "Sure, correct them." But the fact that Roger had gone ahead and done so, without consulting him, just annoyed him.

"Sort of." Roger's voice was fading, the adrenaline rush of the lunch dissolving as he recounted its downside. "Not really. He just said he wanted it printed exactly as it had originally run in *The New Yorker*. It was almost as if he were saying the typos were intentional. Though he didn't exactly say that. But it made me realize . . ." He drifted off and I wondered, for a moment, if he'd hung up or the connection had been lost. Then he cleared his throat.

"Are you okay?" I asked. I liked him. I did. I wanted him to be okay. I wanted him to not mess this up. To not correct any more typos.

One night in early July, at a rooftop party, I spent hours talking to two young *New Yorker* editors. They were a few years my senior—and a few Don's junior—and dressed like caricatures of prep school types, like characters from a Whit Stillman movie. They were, in other words, exactly as I'd pictured *New Yorker* editors, if I'd actually had the wherewithal to even imagine the people behind the magazine that had so profoundly shaped my life, which I did not, nor did I ever imagine that I might really and truly find myself in the same room with such people, much less at the center of their orbit, as I did that night. I'd read *The New Yorker* religiously growing up, emulating my father's complicated, well-hewn reading system, which involved starting with the movie reviews, then turning to theater, then Talk of the Town, then features. But I'd not, somehow, understood the magazine's larger cultural significance until college. I'd thought it was a magazine for people who lived in New York, or were from New York, like my father. New Yorkers. I thought, too, that the magazine was a secret, something consumed only by my father and me. No one else read it in our small, conservative town, just as no one else read the *Times*.

The *New Yorker* editors knew the Agency, of course—the two entities having been founded around the same time, their histories intertwined—and so we talked about Fitzgerald and I answered the usual Salinger questions—no, I'd not met him; yes, reporters still called for him; no, I didn't know if he was working on a new novel—and recounted some of the more arcane Agency procedures and policies—the cards! the typewriters! the tumblers of "water" on Carolyn's desk—which made them laugh. Even *The New Yorker*, I learned—with its patina of old-timey fustiness—was fully computerized and Dictaphone-free. But they'd heard tales of the Agency's weirdness—as had many in certain publishing circles—and were hungry for more. And so I told them about the Salinger letters, of course, about the girl from Japan with her Hello Kitty stationery and the endless veterans and the woman whose daughter had died. And I told them about the crazy people who sent letters on dirty scraps of paper written with what seemed to be stubs of pencil, the lead smudged and smeared across the page. I told them, too, about the kids who wrote in the voice of Holden. "Dear Jerry, you old bastard," I cried, in imitation of these fans. "I'd sure get one helluva kick out of it if you'd find a goddam minute to write me back."

"No," said one editor. "Really?"

"Oh yes," I said.

"That's amazing," said the other, wiping a tear of laughter with one muscular thumb. "I didn't realize Salinger was still so popular. But I guess every teenager goes through a Salinger phase, right?"

"Definitely," I found myself saying, "but, you know, those stories really hold up." Where was this coming from? I'd not read Salinger as a teen, nor had I read him now. *Stop,* I told myself. "A lot of the letters we get are from Salinger's peers, who read *Catcher,* or the stories, when they first came out and are rereading them now—and seeing things they never saw the first time around. Like the war. All the stories, ultimately, are about the war."

"I should reread them," said one editor. "I loved *Nine Stories* in high school."

"Me too," said the other. "I loved *Catcher,* too. Though, I guess, who didn't?"

Finally, as the air grew cool, and the crowd thinned, I asked the question I'd wanted—and been afraid—to ask. "What's it like, working at *The New Yorker?*" My voice had fallen to almost a whisper and the wind picked up, whipping my hair and skirt around. I'd been to roof parties with Don, atop tenements in the East Village, five-story buildings from which one could catch a glimpse of our neighborhood across the river—the Domino sugar factory, the abandoned industrial buildings of the South Side—one's shoes sticking to the tar paper, if ever so slightly. But this was a roof garden atop a tall new office building, with pretty patio chairs and sleek gray tiles embedded in the floor, willowy plants emerging from square planters bent in the wind. A waiter stopped by, offering us fresh sloshes of icy white wine. We sipped deeply, the young editors contemplating my question. One was short and dark, with shiny hair that flopped into his eyes and an impish smile. The other was tall, with auburn hair and freckles and an extraordinarily direct gaze. They were both, it suddenly occurred to me, handsome. As if on cue, they turned to me and shrugged, smiling. There was, I saw, no answer to my question.

Don skittered at the edge of this scene. It was perhaps the first situation in which he'd struck me as ill at ease. Usually, at parties, he walked in and took stock of the room, then immediately engaged in his particular version of male territorial marking. We had been dating long enough that I could predict his behavior upon arrival at any gathering of more than, say, five people: First, he greeted every man he knew with half hugs and high fives and the intense and potent utilization of the sort of slang—"What's up, bro?"—he generally scorned. Next, he obtained a drink involving some sort of brown alcohol, ideally in a short tumbler, with ice cubes that could be rattled during lulls in conversation. Drink in hand, he staked out a spot that allowed him to survey the room so that—I now knew—he might both monitor the arrival of attractive women and further assess the attractiveness of the women already in attendance.

Regardless, tonight he'd been unaccountably subdued. Marc's wedding was approaching and he was, increasingly, brooding about it, retreating into himself. Usually, he took pains with his ablutions before any and every party—shower, shave, insertion of contact lenses. But tonight his dark stubble was in evidence and he wore his glasses—round, wire-rimmed—which made him look younger, and his white shirt was less than pristine. Don included *The New Yorker* in his list of bourgeois frippery, though he read it, of course, sometimes poring over issues in a way I rarely did. "The nonfiction is amazing," he said, when I'd mentioned this contradiction, some weeks back. "But the fiction is a joke. It's just atrocious. And that whole twee Talk of the Town thing, the flaneur in the top hat with the monocle. Blech. Doesn't it just make you want to throw up?" Cackling, he drew me to him in a hug, the way one might pull a child onto one's lap as a response to her blinding cuteness. "Of course it doesn't make *you* want to throw up. You love that shit. That"—here he adopted a high, warbling voice—"*Oh, we're all gathering for drinks at the Algonquin. I do wish you would join us* bullshit." I'd heard him air these opinions—and loudly—at all those parties on the roofs of East Village tenements and at the various dive bars he found "authentic" and romantic—the Holiday Cocktail Lounge and the International and Tile Bar and the Irish bar on Driggs—expounding on the corrupt, watered-down nature of contemporary fiction.

But tonight he stayed, literally, in my shadow, standing a step or two back from me in the dark double that stemmed from my feet, sipping a drink, his eyes wide. That night, as we left the party—"Come by the office," the taller editor said to me, pressing a card into my hand, "I'll show you around"— and walked to Fifty-Third and Lex, to catch the 6 down to Union Square, the air cool on my bare arms, I recalled something one of Max's clients had said to me, in passing, at a book party. "I judge a woman by her friends." At the time, this had seemed strange and harsh to me. But now I understood what he meant: that a person is only as good as those with whom he surrounds himself. All of Don's friends were, it was true, strange or damaged in some way or another: Allison and Marc and Leigh tragically hampered by their privileged upbringings, paralyzed by fear of failure. His friends in Hartford, stunted and angry.

Why didn't Don consort with writers? Successful writers, published writers, or even simply ambitious, interesting writers, published or no? Why hadn't he argued and bantered with the *New Yorker* editors? Why hadn't he made them his friends? Forged alliances? Told them about his novel? Why hadn't he talked about Gramsci or Proust with them? The answer sent a shiver through me: Don didn't want friends who worked at *The New Yorker*. He didn't want friends who dressed in creamy Brooks Brothers oxfords and college ties, friends who had health insurance and degrees from Harvard, friends who'd just published their first Talk of the Town pieces. He surrounded himself with fools—the broken, the failed or failing, the sad and confused—so that he might be their king. Which, obviously, made him nothing but the king of fools.

But what did that make me?

The next morning, I turned to the letters straightaway. There were the usual proclamations of love for Holden, the usual war stories, the usual stories of despair and redemption, the many, many letters from Japan and Denmark and the Netherlands. The Japanese *loved* Holden. I tapped out a few form responses and modified form responses, filed away a few Tragic Letters for another day, then slit open an envelope addressed in bubbly, girlish script. The letter was almost a novella unto itself, this girl's story unfolding over three pages of wrinkly, pencil-smudged notebook paper. She was a freshman in high school, she explained, and she hated school, particularly English class, which she was failing. Her English teacher was maybe an all right person, but she didn't understand what it meant to be young, and she assigned the class these stupid books that had nothing to do with their lives. The only book the girl had liked, over the course of the year, was *The Catcher in the Rye*. As things stood, she was going to have to go to summer school or repeat freshman English, which would be so embarrassing she wasn't sure if she could stand it, and her mother would *kill* her. The year was almost over, but she'd asked her teacher if she could do anything at all to bring her grade up, just enough so that she'd pass. "There *is* something you can do," the teacher told her. "Write a letter to J. D. Salinger and make it good enough that he'll write back. If he writes back, I'll give you an A."

Hmm, I thought, putting the letter down and staring, for the millionth time, at the wall of Salinger books. It was lunchtime and I had a neat stack of letters ready to be mailed. I ran them through the postal meter, threw on my coat, and slipped the girl's letter in my bag. On line to buy my salad, I read it again. Despite various misspellings and sloppy penmanship, this girl wasn't a terrible writer. She conveyed her story vividly and honestly, with passion and detail. And then there was the pure audacity—the ballsiness, the brattiness—of writing to J. D. Salinger and saying, "Please respond so I can get a free A." I kind of liked her. Salinger had been a terrible student himself. Perhaps he would like her, too. Perhaps he would—as the boy from Winston-Salem said—get a kick out of her letter. "I really need this A," I read, holding my plastic container of watery lettuce. "It will bring my entire GPA up to passing. My mother is mad at me all the time now. I know you understand."

And yet there was something that rankled me. What would Salinger say to her? I pondered this as I walked back to the office, across Forty-Ninth Street and down Madison, the sun warming my bare arms. He had failed out of schools himself. I knew this from Hugh and Roger and also the letters, many of which referred to incidents in Salinger's life. They could be informative, the letters. Holden, I knew, had also failed out of a few schools. Would either of them have attempted to maintain his place through this kind of trick? I hadn't read *Catcher*, so I wasn't sure about Holden, but I knew—*I knew*—that Salinger would not. He would have taken his failure as deserved.

Back at my desk, I ate my olive, then turned toward the Selectric and banged out a response to the girl, suggesting that it was decidedly *not* in the spirit of Holden—or Salinger—to be worrying about grades or her mother's anger. If she wanted to be like Holden—or Salinger—she should accept her failing grade, a grade she, by her own admission, deserved. Trying to trick herself into a grade she hadn't earned was a coward's way out, a *phony's* way out. "If you desire an A or at least a passing grade, there's only one way to earn it: you must study and do the work assigned to you. This might mean making up papers or tests. This might mean begging your teacher to give you another chance. This might mean apologizing or otherwise humbling yourself. But it is the only way. An A earned by trickery means absolutely nothing."

As I signed the letter with my name, my heart raced happily. I had done the right thing. I was mastering the art of What Would Salinger Say? But I had also crossed a line. The barely visible seam between bemused interest or compassionate engagement or plain sympathy and utter overinvolvement. *Why could I not leave these letters alone?* I asked myself as I walked over to the mail meter. *Why could I not just send on form letters to every single fan?* The answer was plain: I loved them. They were exciting. When I read them, sitting at my desk alone on, say, a Friday morning, I felt a strange charge, a mixture of anger and affection, disdain and empathy, admiration and disgust. These people were writing to me—or, well, no, to Salinger, care of me—about their marital frustrations, their dead children, their boredom and desperation; they wrote about their favorite songs and poems, about the trips they'd taken to the Grand Canyon and Hawaii, about their favorite dolls. They told me—*Salinger*—things I knew, for sure, they'd never told anyone else. Could I, over and over, respond to them in the most formal, impersonal manner possible? Could I just abandon them? Could I let them think that no one cared, no one was listening?

That Saturday, I was due home for my grandmother's birthday. My whole family would gather the following morning for breakfast: bagels and bialys, lox and sable. My grandmother was turning approximately ninety-six. No one knew her real age, not even my grandmother herself. She was born in the old country and had no birth certificate, no records. All she knew was that she arrived in the United States in 1906. Approximately.

"I have a present for you," said Don as I stashed some clothes in a bag. I looked at him quizzically. Don did not believe in presents, a principle he ascribed to communism, but which I suspected had more to do with poverty and stinginess. At Christmas, the previous year, he'd declined to bring gifts for his parents or his many brothers and sisters. My own birthday had come and gone two months earlier—I was now twenty-four—and he had likewise declined to celebrate with me. "It'll be more fun for your friends to take you out," he insisted. Indeed, my friends had been happy to take me out, and though I didn't necessarily miss Don, the strangeness of celebrating one's birthday without one's ostensible boyfriend clouded the night. When I got home, I explained this to Don, who explained, in turn, that birthdays were silly and, of course, bourgeois. "Hallmark invented birthdays," he said. "It's just another way of conning the masses into spending money, into thinking materialism is the answer."

Don had refused to come home with me for my grandmother's birthday, citing his opposition to the tradition, but—here again—I suspected that this alleged ideological stance might be simply a smoke screen for either poverty or cheapness, that he didn't want to spend the money on a bus ticket, not to mention a gift for my grandmother. In truth, I was pleased to be going home alone, if a bit stunned by my last visit: What might my parents spring on me this time? A preschool bill? Back pay for my childhood nanny?

Still, I was—perhaps foolishly—looking forward to the comforts of my parents' cool, spacious house: the puffs of central air wafting through the vents in my old room; my soft childhood bed with its pink-sprigged sheets; our green lawn and the enormous, sprawling trees that shaded it. Running out for bagels with my dad on Sunday morning. I was looking forward to being taken care of, if only a little.

"A present?" I asked Don warily.

"Something to take with you," he said, smiling. "Give me your bag." I held it open for him and he slipped a large, less-than-crisp manila envelope inside. "Don't open it until you get home."

I opened it on the bus. Inside, I found his novel, "Fellow Traveler." He'd told me the title on our first date. "It's a reference to the larger themes of the book," he explained, swirling the wine in his glass. I nodded. "You know the term, right? Fellow traveler." I didn't. "Your grandmother was a socialist," he cried. "And you don't know what a fellow traveler is?"

"My grandmother stopped talking about politics in the '50s," I explained. "For obvious reasons."

"Still!" Don shook his head, incredulous. "A fellow traveler is a friend of the party who isn't a card-carrying member."

"Is the novel about communism?" I asked. "Is it about the party? The present-day party?" This sounded strange and great to me.

"No, no. That would be deeply boring." He smiled at me, the sort of wide, joyous smile that makes one feel anything is possible. "But it *is* about class. And it's about how you can be part of something but also outside it. My hero—I mean, he's sort of an antihero, but anyway—participates in mainstream society, but he's not really part of it. And his girlfriend—his *ex*-girlfriend—is from this very, very wealthy background. She tried to kind of incorporate him into her world but it just didn't work." A little laugh escaped him, though his smile was gone. "Because he's working-class." That fictional girlfriend was based on his college love, who had grown up in Beverly Hills or suchlike, in what Don described as baronial splendor, but which sounded to me like simply upper-middle-class L.A. She'd broken up with him after college and he'd never quite forgiven her.

By the time the bus rolled into my hometown, I'd made it halfway through. The novel concerned a dark-haired young man from a working-class background who attended a fancy liberal arts college just outside New York City but for reasons never specified now works as a security guard at an office building, where he spends most of his time watching hot secretaries move around their offices. The first forty or so pages involve the protagonist watching one of these women masturbate on a desk. That night, while flipping channels, he pauses for a moment on a porno and realizes that the woman in the film is his college girlfriend, a wealthy, wholesome Los Angelen, with whom he'd parted ways because they simply could not bridge the class divide. In this pre-Google age, he sets off to figure out what happened to her.

Or that was what I gathered. Again, the prose was so dense—so purposefully opaque—that at times I couldn't even understand what was happening. This was not the opacity of, say, David Foster Wallace, whose stories I was reading just then. A few weeks earlier, I'd accompanied Max to Wallace's reading at KGB, which was so crowded I'd had to stand in a hallway—Wallace, sweaty and bandanna clad, had brushed past me when he arrived—and been transfixed by the force and energy of his language. The next day, when Max went to lunch, I filched his galley of *Infinite Jest* and read it at my desk, my pulse speeding up so that I barely remembered to fork bites of salad into my mouth. I'd returned it before Max got back and that night, on my way home, had picked up a used copy of *Girl with Curious Hair* at the Strand for a few dollars, hiding it from Don, who was scornful of all purchases—why couldn't I take books out of the library?—but also scornful of any writer who received too much attention. "How good could he be if his book's a best seller?" he'd said of Wallace. Very good, I saw now. Revolutionary, life-changingly good. Wallace's sentences thrummed with a strange kind of life, propelling the story forward and pushing the reader further and further into his characters' psyches, revealing and revealing, peeling back layers to get to the bone. They jumped off the page. Don's sentences seemed to bore further into the page. They obscured rather than revealed.

But there was intelligence underpinning the novel, certainly, and the bones of a cracking story. He needed to open that story up, to let it breathe, let it stand for itself.

As the passengers began to disembark, I was already making edits: trim the front section to get to the real story more quickly; streamline a good percentage of the sentences; more exposition, less description, so the actual story was more clear, so the reader wasn't distracted by confusion about what was actually, literally happening and could get lost in the story, the rhythm of the language. More scenes in the present, fewer flashbacks.

"Jo!" my father called from the curb, smiling. He wore a faded blue Lacoste golf shirt and navy pants that fell off his hips, in unconscious parody of gangster style. His white hair fluffed out from his forehead in the way my mother hated. Whatever anger I'd been harboring for him disappeared in a breath. "You look terrific," he said. "Very glamorous."

Seeing as I'd just spent two hours on a bus, this seemed unlikely. "Dad," I said and hugged him, breathing in his wonderful scent, of Old Spice and Ivory soap, with undertones of Pepto-Bismol and the medical-grade hand cleanser he used at his office. And then I burst into tears.

"Hey, hey," he said, startled, patting my back. My family was always startled by me, it seemed, as if I were an alien somehow dropped into their midst. Had I not resembled my mother to an uncanny degree—once, a high school friend had mistaken a photo of her, at eighteen, for one of me—I'd have harbored suspicions that I'd been adopted. "Stop," he said, "or you're going to make *me* cry. You don't want that. A grown man crying. Blech." He pulled me away from him and peered into my face.

"No," I agreed, my voice catching.

"Now, grandma's at the house. She can't wait to see you." He gestured toward the parking lot. "So let's go." He took my tote bag off my shoulder.

"I can carry that," I said.

"Nonsense," he replied.

As we drove along the parkway that led to our house, lush trees bowing over the black macadam, my father singing along to Benny Goodman, the world suddenly seemed to shift, to crack open. And a pang hit me—maybe I was wrong.

Maybe Don's novel was genius. Maybe it was *more* brilliant than *Infinite Jest*, made so by its very inscrutability. Maybe, I thought, maybe the problem was me.

That night, the phone rang. I picked up the extension in the kitchen, expecting my uncle Saul. "Jo?" a low voice asked. My college boyfriend.

"Oh my—" I said, then stopped myself. "How did you know I was here? *Did* you know I was here?"

"I called your apartment and your, um, boyfriend—" He paused. "Your boyfriend, right?" My face flamed, then crumpled to hear him say this. "Yeah, I heard about it from Joel—" This was Celeste's ex-boyfriend, whom she'd dropped a year or so after moving to the city, though they maintained a tortured contact.

"I, I—" I began, then stopped, because it seemed I was once again going to cry.

"Hey, it's okay," my college boyfriend said, his voice barely a whisper. He was a mumbler, even under the best circumstances. I loved this about him: when he spoke, in his low, rumbling tones—the words running together—he seemed to be speaking solely for me. "I get it. I understand. There was nothing for you out here. You wanted to be yourself. Not just my girlfriend." This was, I was astonished to realize, wholly true. "Did you get my letter?"

I nodded, unable to speak. "I did," I said, finally, looking around to see if my parents or my grandmother were nearby. They appeared to still be dressing, at the other end of the house. Stretching the cord into the den, I sat down in my mother's battered black recliner.

"I just wanted to apologize for, well, I was angry when I wrote it. There's a lot of stuff I didn't mean, things I said because I was angry."

"You don't need to apologize to me," I said. There they were, the tears, hot and fast. "Please. Don't. I deserve it. You should be angry."

"The letter—"

"I didn't read it," I confessed, before he could go any further. "It's been in my bag for a month."

"You didn't read it," he said, then began to laugh. I loved his laugh. "Why didn't you read it?"

"I was afraid," I said, a large, gulping sob escaping me.

"Well, you should have been. It's an angry letter." He laughed again. "That's why I'm calling. I'm not angry anymore. I guess I just needed to write the letter. You know you really hurt me. Deeply. It was horrible." Hearing him say this was too much. "I didn't want to live in this apartment alone. It's an awful apartment. It's depressing."

Suddenly I was laughing, too, for the first time in what felt like months. Months and months and months. "It *is* awful! Why did you choose it? You knew I would hate it. The catwalk! And it was so dark."

"I don't know, Jo, I don't know." He was laughing so much he could barely speak. "It's a good location. I thought I was being practical."

"I know," I said.

"So listen, the thing I want you to understand is I'm not angry anymore"—his voice cracked and for a moment we sat in silence—"I just want you back in my life. I don't want you to be afraid to call or write. Please call. Please write. I miss you. You were my best friend."

Just then, my father called, "Jo? I think we're ready."

"I miss you, too," I said, my own voice breaking, spent from tears. It was such a relief to say it, to admit it, even though the ramifications of this admission were too enormous for me to contemplate. And yet, strangely, as I leaned my head against the chair's cool leather, I found myself angry at him, as much as I was relieved. Why hadn't he railed at me? Screamed at me? Called me names?

"Jo?" His voice had fallen to a whisper.

"I'm here," I said. "I'll try not to be afraid." But I was afraid. Afraid that I didn't deserve him. Afraid of what I'd done. Afraid of myself.

On Monday, I knocked softly on James's door. He was typing intently, though without the Dictaphone headgear, which meant he was composing his own letter or memo. His workload, lately, had increased: two weeks earlier, Olivia had finally left—improbably, she'd accepted a job at an ultraconservative literary magazine, assisting a famously cantankerous editor—and James was handed a bit of Max's work for the Fitzgerald estate, to lighten Max's load until he could find a suitable new assistant. One had already come and gone, in a flurry of spilled coffee and botched phone calls and tantrums.

"Hey," said James, smiling, his fingers still on the keyboard. "What's up?"

"I'm not sure if I've ever told you this," I began, shifting my weight onto my left foot. I wore a blue cotton twinset selected for me by my mother the previous day and a pair of cream-colored, wide-legged trousers selected by my mother the previous fall. I suspected that I looked like a Jazz Age golfer. "Well, did you know that Don is actually a writer?"

"I suspected," said James with a smile.

"He's been working on a novel for years now. It's a literary thriller."

"Wow, cool. That sounds great." James and Don had met a few times and discovered—in a strange coincidence—that James represented one of Don's cousins, a Harvard guy who'd written a memoir about working on Wall Street in the 1980s.

Don's family was not quite as working-class as he liked to think. "Does he have representation?"

I shook my head. "He's just finished. He was about to start talking to agents."

"I'd love to take a look." James hoisted his feet, in their brown brogues, onto his desk. "Do you want to just bring me the manuscript tomorrow?"

"Sure." A strange weight seemed to have lifted from my shoulders. How had it been so easy? I had learned, I suppose, the first lesson of agenting: the pitch.

2

Sentimental Education

The next morning, I arrived at work slightly late—Don had kept me, fretting about small changes in the novel, printing and reprinting pages—and found the office strangely silent. Pam, from her perch, gave me a significant look. Carolyn was sitting in James's office. I slipped in, as unobtrusively as possible, and dropped Don's manuscript—in a manila envelope—on the desk. "Thanks," murmured James, with a lack of enthusiasm that made me nervous. At the coffee machine, Max and Lucy hunched in hushed conversation, but they stopped as I passed. My boss, I was surprised to see, was not yet in her office.

Before I'd even sat down, a messenger arrived with a thick padded envelope: the contracts for the Other Client's new book, for which we'd been waiting. I slit it open and began a cursory read, then pulled a sheaf of Salinger letters out of my desk. I was reading one from a woman in Sri Lanka—her handwriting enormous and slanting—and contemplating a cup of coffee, when Lucy appeared at my desk, clutching her own mug. "Can I talk to you for a sec?" She gestured with her head toward her office, hair falling in her eyes.

"Of course." I rose and followed her.

"Sit down," she said. I perched on the little couch opposite her desk. Lucy liked all things sleek and black, timeless.

"So you know Daniel?"

For a moment, I thought, *Who?* Then I realized, of course, that she was talking about my boss's . . . someone, something. The person my boss was always talking to or about on the phone. He wasn't her husband. He didn't seem to be her brother. There was never a title, a label, applied to him. And he was often mentioned in the same breath as someone named Helen, whose role in my boss's life I also didn't understand.

"Yes," I said. "I think so."

"Well." Lucy sighed and lit a cigarette. Then, to my amazement, tears began to fill her eyes and her face turned pink. She let out a little sob and buried her face in her hands. "I'm sorry."

"Oh!" I cried. "*Lucy.*" Lucy was normally so brisk and cheerful, so resilient and matter-of-fact.

She grabbed a handkerchief and wiped her eyes, then sniffed deeply. "Daniel," she said in a raspy voice. "Daniel died last night."

"Oh!" I cried again. "Oh no. Is my boss okay?"

Lucy shook her head no. No, my boss was not okay.

"I knew he was sick," I said. Suddenly everything seemed to make sense. All those phone calls. My boss's distractedness. "I mean, I didn't *know.* She talked about prescriptions. And she'd leave to—" Something in Lucy's demeanor made me stop.

"We don't know how long your boss is going to be out." Shakily, she stubbed out her cigarette, then immediately pulled another out of the pack on her desk and inserted it into her holder, like a character in film noir. "So if you can just hold things together. Is there anything pressing? Anything that needs to be done today? That you can't do yourself?"

I shook my head. There were the contracts, but they could wait.

"What about the 'Hapworth' thing?" She laughed a little, despite herself. The deal seemed to be providing consistent comic relief for the entire office.

"It's fine." I thought about Roger's odd tone at the end of our conversation. Was it fine? I wasn't sure.

"Okay, so just cover for her. Okay? If anyone calls, just say she's in a meeting or not in at the moment."

I nodded. I was her assistant. Covering for her was my job.

Later that day, Jerry called. The office was still strained and hushed. Carolyn had left to take care of my boss.

"JOANNE!" he cried. Somehow, he had figured out my name, or an approximation of it. I wondered, for a moment, if Roger had corrected him. Or Pam. "How's the poetry?"

I flushed. "Good," I said. "Good."

"You're writing every day?" he asked, lowering his voice. I flushed again. Suddenly I understood Roger's nervousness. It was strange to feel the force of a famous person's attention. "First thing in the morning."

"I am." This was mostly true.

"That's what you do," he said. "So, I have a question for you." *Oh no,* I thought, *not again.* "Have you met this Roger Lathbury fellow?"

"I haven't," I admitted. "But I've spoken to him on the phone many times."

"Yes, well, I went down to meet him last week. I don't know if you've gathered that. And I think he's a fine fellow. He showed me some designs for the book. One was terrible, but one was good. Very good."

"Hmm," I murmured, as I did with Roger.

"I'm inclined to go ahead and let him publish the book. The 'Hapworth' book. I gather you've heard about this."

"I have."

"And what do you make of this Roger Lathbury fellow?"

Ah, there was the question. How to answer it? "He seems like a good person. Like someone you can trust." I believed this.

"My feelings exactly," said Salinger, though these words were slightly more distorted, elongated, than usual and it took me a few extra seconds to decode them. "I don't know that your boss feels that way."

"Well," I said cautiously, "it's her job to look out for you."

"True." He sneezed, rather violently, then let out a little snuffle, and when he began talking again, his voice had risen in volume. Did his hearing drop in and out? "Is she in? Your boss? I'd love to talk to her."

"I'm afraid she's out at the moment. Shall I have her call you?" I wasn't sure when she would be returning calls, but my mouth formed these words almost automatically.

"Sure, sure, but no rush," he said. Where did these reports of his tyrannical behavior come from? He was never anything but kind and patient on the phone. More so than plenty of people who called the Agency. More so than plenty of his fans, for that matter.

The minute I put down the phone, Hugh came racing out of his office. "Jerry?" he asked.

I nodded.

"You told him that she was out of the office?"

I nodded again.

Hugh pressed his mouth into a thin, tense line. "You want to go get a sandwich?"

.   .   .

Outside, we found one of those grim New York summer days in which the sun hangs low behind a haze of gray and the air seems full to bursting with moisture. We both immediately began to sweat.

At the corner of Forty-Ninth and Park, Hugh stopped and turned to face me, his pale eyes steely with reserve. "Daniel killed himself," he said.

"Oh," I said, drawing in a sharp breath. "Oh."

"He had"—Hugh drew in his own breath—"psychological problems. He was bipolar. Your boss took care of him. Cared for him. It was a big job." We were stopped at a light on the corner of Park, the flowers still blazing in the median strip, the Waldorf in front of us. "I think it was very hard on her. Though she would never admit it. And she's taking care of Dorothy, too. Not in the same way." He sighed his trademark sigh. "Dorothy has full-time caregivers. But your boss is overseeing her care."

"Daniel was her—" I wasn't sure how to ask this, but Hugh saved me.

"Lover," he said tersely. It was not a word that fit comfortably in his mouth. "He was her lover. They'd been together for, oh gee, twenty years."

Lover? I thought, my mind spinning. *Twenty years.* Had she cared for him this whole time? Had she fallen in love with him first, discovered his problems, his difficulties, later? Had his illness only developed, emerged, later, after their lives were fully meshed? Or had she known everything from the start and accepted him as he was? *Lover,* I thought again. Why had they never married? Because of Daniel's illness?

We started across Park, me struggling a bit to match Hugh's long gait. It was strange to be out in the world with him. I thought of him as purely a creature of the Agency. Like the Wizard of Oz, barricaded in his strange castle. In reality, he was married—with two stepdaughters—and I had met his wife, a pretty, pleasant woman with long graying hair, but it was still impossible to picture him, say, eating dinner with her in their apartment in Brooklyn Heights or going to a movie or *anywhere* other than the Agency.

"How's she doing?" I asked, finally, though this didn't seem sufficient a question.

"I haven't talked to her. Carolyn says she seems to be doing okay. Keeping it together." Hugh touched his hand to his forehead, which was beaded with perspiration, and grimaced. "But I don't know how long that will last. It's just terrible, this."

At Third Avenue, we turned south, and Hugh led me to a narrow, ancient sandwich shop, so small, so tucked away that I would have never found it on my own. "How are you today?" he asked the man behind the counter. A large air conditioner rattled in the window, sending a stream of cold air in my direction, and I shivered a little, my perspiration drying. "I'll have an egg salad on whole wheat and"—he turned to me—"whatever she's having."

As we retraced our steps, Hugh carrying a small brown sack with our sandwiches inside, I asked him why they hadn't married.

Hugh's jaw tensed, a muscle twitching along its length. "Well, they couldn't, exactly," he said with a small sigh. "There was Helen."

"Who *is* Helen?" I asked.

"Helen?" said Hugh. He seemed, somehow, surprised that I didn't possess this information. "Helen is Daniel's wife. Was."

This was enough to stop me in my tracks. "His *wife*? But I heard. Well, I mean, my boss was always on the phone with her, or talking about her. It sounded like they were friends."

To my surprise, Hugh turned to me and smiled. "They *were* friends. They are friends. It's an unusual situation." I looked at him. "Daniel lived with Helen part of the week and your boss the rest of it. They shared his care. They shared *him*, I guess."

"Oh," I said, stunned. My boss, with her nunlike aspect, her pantsuits and caftans, her devotion to the Agency, her pull-your-socks-up attitude, had *shared* her lover with his wife. No wonder she didn't have the energy to seek out new clients.

"But he, um, did it in your boss's apartment. While she was there." Hugh's face had become flushed from the effort of discussing this.

"What?" I asked. "What do you mean?" We had resumed walking and were once again approaching Park. *How nice it would be,* I thought, *to just go in and sit down for lunch, to be waited on. To have a drink.*

"Shot himself. In the head." Hugh was nodding, like a wounded child, and I realized he was holding back tears. He had worked with my boss for twenty years. "Your boss was in the other room. I think he was in the bedroom and she was in the living room. But I might have misunderstood. It might have been the opposite—"

"*Oh my God.*" We had reached our building, but I couldn't stand the thought of going up. I couldn't stand the thought of my boss in her apartment twenty blocks north, her apartment where, the night before, her lover of twenty years had taken a gun, pointed it at his head, and pulled the trigger. How does one get over that? How does one go on?

"Yeah," said Hugh. "So you can see. She might be out awhile."

She was out awhile. Days passed, days in which I repeatedly explained that my boss was not in the office, never specifying if it was for the day or the hour. My boss didn't receive a large variety of callers, but the same few callers phoned over and over again: Salinger, amiable and chatty; Roger, nervous and chatty, more so with each passing day; the Other Client, sometimes smooth and charming, sometimes ill-tempered and impatient, his voice crackling and strange, due to bad connections. "I can receive contracts here whenever they're ready," he told me tersely. "And the advance money should be wired into my account. You have all the information."

Days became a week and then two. One morning during the first week, my boss arrived in a voluminous raincoat and dark glasses—her feet, heartbreakingly, clad in the sort of narrow white canvas sneakers worn by children—silently crossed the threshold into our wing, ducked into her office and grabbed something, then ducked back out without a word to anyone. She was, not unexpectedly, selling her apartment.

Midway through the second week, the editor of the Other Client's new book called to check in. We'd not yet gotten the contracts back to her. "What should I do?" I asked Hugh. "Should I call her?"

Hugh shook his head. "You've been doing contracts all this time. She trusts you. Just do the contract. Negotiate. It'll be fine."

Nervously, checking my work over and over, I did as he instructed. As it happened, the Agency rarely did deals with this particular publisher, and I had no recent contracts to draw on for models. I pulled every possible agreement I could think of, comparing clauses on royalties, first and second serial, on reprints and electronic rights, on everything, and checking, of course, the deal memo to see what rights we'd agreed to sell and which we'd retain to peddle in-house. Finally, after two days of this, checking and rechecking everything, I drafted the sort of long, laborious note my boss often dictated. Lately, those notes had been based on my preliminary work. Many changes needed to be made to this contract before the author could sign it. The publisher was not familiar with the Agency's standards, the standards of another era.

Without my boss, the office was oddly quiet. I hadn't realized how much life, how much urgency, she brought to each day. In her absence, everyone seemed to come in a bit later, to linger longer over lunch, to stay at home on Friday, when we closed early anyway. Summer Fridays, that great tradition of the publishing industry, a gentleman's business, at its inception at least.

Without dictation, my days were surprisingly free, and surprisingly pleasant. Once again, I caught up on my permissions and filing, and then I turned to the Salinger letters. The letter from the boy in Winston-Salem had remained at the top of the pile, unanswered, for months now. *Just send him the form letter,* I told myself as I unfolded the missive.

> *I think about Holden a lot. He just pops into my mind's eye and I get to thinking about him dancing with old Phoebe or horsing around in front of the bathroom mirror at Pencey. When I first think about him I usually get a big stupid grin on my face. You know, thinking about what a funny guy he is and all. But then I usually get depressed as hell. I guess I get depressed because I only think about Holden when I'm feeling very emotional. I can get quiet emotional.*

Yes, "quiet" not "quite." I assumed this was just a typo, and a beautiful, felicitous one, which I suspected Salinger would appreciate. Salinger who made typos himself. Which were reprinted in *The New Yorker,* apparently.

> *Don't worry, though. I've learned that, as phony as it may be, you can't go around revealing your goddam emotions to the world. Most people don't give a flying hoot about what you think and feel most of the time,*

I guess. And if they see a weakness, why for God's sake showing emotion is a weakness, boy, do they jump all over you! They seem to get right in your goddam face and revel in the fact that you are actually feeling something.

Oh God. I sighed a Hugh-worthy sigh. What could I say to him? *Dear Boy from Winston-Salem, I too can get quiet emotional. You're right, you can't go around revealing your emotions to the world. I've been trying to take your advice and I think I'm succeeding. My boss's lover killed himself and we're all pretending nothing happened. I left the man I love in California and he's pretending he's not angry with me and I'm pretending I'm not lost without him. I don't have enough money to pay my bills but I'm pretending I can go out to dinner and do all the things people in New York seem to do. So we're all doing a pretty good job not revealing our emotions, right? But if you can't reveal your emotions, how do you go on? What do you do with them? Because, you see, I keep crying at odd moments. Please advise. Yours, Joanna Rakoff.*

No, I would not be sending a form letter to the boy from Winston-Salem. I folded up the letter and set it aside.

Gathering my strength, I grabbed another letter from the pile. The shaky, lacy handwriting of the elderly. The writer of this letter was a man with a Nebraska address. His was one of the war letters. "Like you, I served in the armed forces during World War II," he wrote. "I lost many friends. Some died in my arms. Luckily, I had a wonderful wife waiting at home for me. If I hadn't, I'm not sure what would have happened to me when I got back home from the war. I was able to go on with life, to run my business, and raise my children. Now that I'm retired, I find myself thinking about the war. I read *The Catcher in the Rye* in those years after I came home and I loved it then. Holden Caulfield seemed to fully capture the anger I felt and the isolation. It may have helped save me.

Just last week, I read it again, and I found myself moved to tears."

As always, I sat too long with this letter, reading it over and over, trying to formulate an appropriate response. There were many war letters. But some—like this one—were so heartfelt, so true, it was—as always—difficult to simply send a form letter back. With this man, I found middle ground: I explained, as gently as I could, that Salinger had asked us not to send on his fan mail, so I couldn't, unfortunately, pass on his letter. But I told him that under a different set of circumstances Mr. Salinger would have likely been very glad to read his letter and particularly glad to hear that *Catcher* had played some small part in his recovery following the war. As he knew, Mr. Salinger himself had suffered considerably during the war. He, too, had held friends in his arms as they shuddered through their last breaths. Warmest regards, Joanna Rakoff.

Quickly, as if ripping off a Band-Aid, I typed up an envelope, folded the letter, and placed it inside, then grabbed another letter. *No*, I thought, *you can't go around revealing your goddam emotions to the world.*

Don was not, he said, nervous about James's verdict on his novel. He was not, he said, anxiously waiting to hear back. "James is not the only agent in the world," he told me, laughing, as he so often did whenever we discussed anything even vaguely serious. "If he turns it down, then it just wasn't for him. I can find someone else."

And yet he still sat, at night, reading over the novel again and again, grimacing at this word or that, as if an imperfect modifier would make or break the whole venture. He was training a couple of nights per week now, and he came home, lugging his bag of gear, in a manic state of exhaustion. Even punching an enormous vinyl bag—or a reedy Puerto

Rican kid—couldn't calm him down. Marc's wedding, too, was bothering him. Until now, it had been an abstraction, an idea, rather than an actual event that would transpire at some point in the space-time continuum, though I wasn't exactly sure when. Don would not be the best man—Marc's brother would play that role—but Marc had asked him to read a poem. Don was scouring our various anthologies, looking for something appropriate. "What kind of poem do you read when your friend marries someone completely boring and wrong for him?" he asked me, laughing.

"I don't know," I told him, "but maybe I could use it at Jenny's wedding." As far as I knew, I was to be a bridesmaid at Jenny's wedding, alongside her two best friends from college.

One Saturday night, as the skies ominously clouded over, Don and I dressed—Don silently, desultorily—and took the L a few stops to Marc's loft on Fourteenth Street for a party. The idea was a sort of pre-wedding blowout, but this being August in New York, no one was around. We found the loft populated with a few Marc-like guys—muscular, clad in Carhartts and Red Wing boots, self-consciously blue-collar gear, completely inappropriate for the weather—drinking beer out of bottles and nodding uncomfortably at each other.

Marc was leaning on the kitchen counter, talking to Allison, whom I'd not expected to see. Her parents kept a summerhouse on the Vineyard and she spent weekends there, though she had no shortage of invitations to Sag Harbor and Woodstock and various parts of Connecticut, the houses of her high school friends, alums of various uptown private schools, their lives funded by never-mentioned trust funds. Lately, she'd become my friend as much as—more than—Don's. We met for dinner and coffee; we lolled on the couch in her tiny studio; we ventured to the cheap Russian salon down the street to have our nails painted a deep, blackish maroon, then stared at our transformed hands, at glamorous odds with our jeans and T-shirts, our scuffed boots.

"I'm so glad you're here," I cried, throwing an arm around her. And I was. My life, lately, had narrowed to Don and work. Where had all my friends gone? They had receded from my life, as Don had advanced. Before I'd moved to New York, it seemed as though everyone was there, playing cockroaches in experimental plays, or making broody films at Columbia, or working at galleries, or teaching dance to the poor kids in Brownsville or the rich kids at St. Ann's. When I first returned, there had been parties and dinners and coffees and shopping trips—joyous cries of "You're back"—but now everyone seemed so busy, so involved with the minutiae of their own lives. And then: I had allowed myself to be subsumed by Don.

"I couldn't miss the pre-wedding party," she said with a roll of her dark eyes. According to Don, she'd long been in love with Marc, since undergrad, and I wondered now if this were true. She'd never mentioned it to me, certainly; yes, she avoided talking about the wedding, and about Lisa—whose charms, like Don, she found nonexistent, or at least unequal to Marc's, though she regarded the discrepancy with cool remove rather than vitriol. Now she seemed nervous, tense, irritable. Rather like Don. Suddenly I wished I'd stayed home.

"You ready for the big day?" Don asked Marc, patting him on the back. He was trying for cheer, for bonhomie, which gave him the aspect of an actor in a community theater production of *Our Town*.

"I don't know," said Marc, with an enormous smile. When he smiled, he seemed to radiate pure waves of goodwill and genuine happiness. This was, I supposed, the difference between Marc and Don: Marc was fully at home in the world, content with his life. He needed, he wanted, nothing more than what he had. Don wanted everything, everyone; Don wanted and wanted. "I guess I'd better be ready, right?"

"When *is* the wedding?" I asked. Allison raised an eyebrow at me. Marc's smile decreased slightly in wattage, and he looked at me strangely. Then he looked at Don, whose face had gone slack, blank. "Is it Columbus Day weekend? Or am I making that up?"

Marc had stopped smiling and was now glaring at Don. He took a swig of beer before replying. "It's next weekend," he said. "Next weekend. On Fisher's Island. You take the ferry. You—" He threw up his hands, beer sloshing in his bottle, and smiled again, this time wildly and without warmth. "Don," he said. "Did you make your reservation for the ferry? You're supposed to be there on Friday, for the rehearsal dinner."

Next weekend? I thought. How was it possible that I'd not known this? That I knew none of the details, nothing. My boyfriend's best friend's wedding. Fisher's Island. I wasn't even sure where that was. I'd thought the wedding would be held in Hartford, at Marc's parents' house, that we'd take the train, stay with Don's family. Why had I thought this? *Next weekend.*

Mentally, I began—vestiges of my mother—going through my closet, wondering what I'd wear not just to the wedding but to the rehearsal dinner.

"Yeah, yeah, of course," Don was saying. "Let's talk about it later." Where would we be staying? I wondered. A hotel? Had Don made reservations? Or were we being put up by friends? By Marc's family?

Just then Olivia arrived—I had invited her, in part so that I'd have someone to talk to—accompanied by a slender, bespectacled man in khakis and a polo shirt, looking very ill at ease. "This is Chris," she said. She'd told me, on the phone, that she had a new boyfriend, he did something at a bank, something involving computers, algorithms. Her previous boyfriend had been a painter, like Olivia, and this guy's exact opposite: tall and athletic, so classically handsome it was almost comical.

"Nice to meet you," I said, reaching over to shake his hand. They had met, it seemed, on a blind date.

The door to Marc's bedroom opened, and Lisa—Marc's fiancée—emerged, clad in loose jeans and a gray T-shirt, her hair pulled back in a ponytail. It suddenly occurred to me that she must live here, too. That perhaps she had lived here all this time—the whole time I'd known Don, through all the parties we'd attended, the times we'd stopped by for a drink on our way somewhere else—but Don had refused to acknowledge this. He referred to the place as "Marc's loft." And I did, too. Always. Marc's loft. How long had Marc and Lisa been dating? Likely years. *Marc's loft*. From across the room, I watched Don greet Lisa with a forced smile.

"How's your new job?" I asked Olivia.

"I quit," she said with a shrug. "It was awful. I'm just too old to be yelled at."

"She's going to focus on her painting," said Chris, with a close-mouthed smile. "We're converting the guest room into a studio for her. The light's not great, right?" Olivia shrugged. "But it's a pretty big room."

"Actually, we have news," said Olivia. She wore a pair of pale jeans—the most conventional clothing I'd ever seen on her body—and high-wedge sandals. Chris looked at her, blinking behind his glasses, as if he weren't quite sure he was implicated in said news. "We're actually getting married."

"Wow!" I cried. "How wonderful!" As if to undercut the seriousness of what she'd just told me, Olivia grimaced and shrugged, then held the bottle to her lips and took a long drink. On her left hand glinted a delicate gold engagement ring. I had not thought her the engagement-ring type. But I'd not thought Jenny the engagement-ring type. Maybe, I thought, *everyone* is the engagement-ring type.

"Pretty," said Allison, who had crept over to us. "It seems like everyone's getting married, right?"

"It does," I said. Did it?

"It does," agreed Olivia. "My sister's getting married, too, actually."

"Wow," said Allison, a strange glint in her dark eyes. "Maybe you should have a double wedding. Like on *The Brady Bunch*."

"Hey," I cried. "Should we get a drink? I think there's wine in the fridge."

Allison shook her head. "Just beer. *Lisa* doesn't drink, so Marc, being a guy, got only beer." She was Don's age, I suddenly realized, though I'd never thought about this before, had thought of us as equals, peers. No, she was *Marc's* age: two years older than Don. Thirty-three. How had I been so stupid? So utterly unaware. Of course. Everyone she knew probably *was* getting married. She seemed so content, her life so organized and productive: her little apartment, her little studio, her Good Job. "I think I'm going to head out," she said.

"We'll go with you," I said. "We can get a drink. A real drink."

She smiled limply. "Dearie, I'd love to see you, but I'm just not in the mood for Don's bullshit tonight. I've had enough for one evening." My jaw dropped open. I felt, strangely, as if I'd been slapped. "And you have people here"—she gestured to Olivia and Chris, whom I now had no desire to see—"we'll make a plan, okay? Breakfast tomorrow." I nodded mutely.

The party never really took off. It was barely eleven when Don and I walked through the hot rain to the Mee Noodle Shop on First Avenue for dumplings and dan dan noodles. I forced myself, as we ate, to say nothing about the wedding. To wait for Don to bring it up. But as we crossed the street to the Brooklyn-bound train, something in me dissolved. "Should I see if we can borrow my parents' car?" I asked.

"I don't know." Don shook his head impatiently. "You might need a car reservation for the ferry. It might be too late."

"Do you want to check?" I asked. We were descending the stairs to the L now, along with a stream of other people who looked rather like us: girls in sundresses from the 1950s; boys in jeans and boots too heavy for the weather.

"I can't think about this now," said Don sharply, almost shouting. A girl with hair dyed bright red turned to look at him, and he glared openly back at her. "Can we just talk about this another time?"

Silently, I nodded. When we reached the platform, I took a seat on the bench and pulled out my book, a novel by one of Max's clients, about a boy's obsessive, unrequited love for a much older woman. I was near the end and overcome with that sense of loss that comes with the close of a great novel. Soon, I would have to leave these characters. But for now, I read on, trying to ignore Don's tense, grumbling presence, his leg jumping up and down next to mine.

At home, I silently took off my dress and put on my nightgown, silently brushed my teeth, and got in bed, book in hand. "Listen," called Don from the other room, "I want to go to Marc's wedding alone."

I put down my book. "Alone?" I asked, as if I were unfamiliar with the word. "You don't want me to come with you?" Immediately, I thought of the letter, brown shoulders, Maria. "Why?"

"A lot of reasons," he said dismissively, as if this were an odd, unreasonable question. "It's too much to talk about it. I don't feel like explaining it all."

"You don't feel like explaining it?" I stared at him, incredulous.

"It's late," he said. "I'm tired. I just don't feel like talking about it now." He stretched his arms over his head, raising one hand higher, then the other. "Besides, I don't have to explain myself to you." He let out one of his cackle-like laughs. "Marc is *my* friend. If I want to go to his wedding alone, I think that's *my* business. Right?"

Maddeningly, my eyes filled with tears. I didn't care about this wedding. I didn't, really and truly, know Marc that well, and Lisa even less. But I cared about—or I'd thought I cared about—Don. Who not only didn't want to take me to his best friend's wedding—didn't want to share whatever joy, whatever catharsis, might come from that event—but didn't even feel he had an obligation to explain his inclinations to me. "*No,*" I said. "*No.* It's my business, too. You embarrassed me tonight. So that makes it my business. And everyone at the wedding will be wondering where I am. So that makes it my business. *And we live together, so that makes it my business.*"

He had dropped his aloofness and was smiling at me in a patient, conciliatory way, as if I were a child throwing a tantrum. "Buba," he said. "Come on. Don't be mad. It's not such a big deal. I made it sound like a bigger deal than it is. I just didn't want to talk about it, because I knew this would happen. It's just that, you know, all those guys will be there. Topher and Will and all those guys. My bros from Hartford. And I feel like, you know, Marc is getting married. It's like the end of an era. I just want to hang out with them by myself. Me and my boys."

"*Really?*" This explanation didn't seem so complicated as to warrant postponing it until the following day. I had no idea whether to believe it or not, but I was too angry from the conversation that preceded it to calm down. "*Really?* You want to hang out with your *boys*? This doesn't have to do with some girl who's going to be there? Let's see"—I was about to jump off a cliff—"the possibilities are endless. Maybe it's one of your million ex-girlfriends, whose picture or garter belt or whatever you're keeping in that box under the bookshelf? Or some woman you had a crush on in high school? Or maybe you're just hoping to meet someone who wants her panties ripped off? And you can write her letters next week, telling her how much you miss her brown shoulders?"

Now it was his turn to stare at me, incredulous. Then, as I watched, his wounded look turned into a smooth mask of cool amusement.

"Wow, Buba. I don't know what to say—"

"*Don't call me Buba,*" I shouted. "I'm not a child."

"I call you Buba," he said, "because I love you."

"You love me." My voice had slowed. I seemed to be talking through a stream of molasses. In all this time, he had never told me he loved me. Love, it seemed, was yet another bourgeois construct. Had I ever expected him to love me? "You love me, but you don't want to bring me to Marc's wedding?"

"That's right," he said. "That's right."

On Monday, my boss came in for an hour or so. She looked paler than usual but seemed heartbreakingly calm and composed for someone in the midst of a life-altering tragedy. As always, she walked past me without a word, seated herself in her office with a minimum of fuss, and began murmuring into her Dictaphone. The normalcy of this should have comforted me, but instead it brought tears to my eyes. I fled to the other wing of the office. "Hey," James called, as I passed the coffee machine. "I'm reading Don's novel and I like it." I stopped dead in my tracks.

"Really?" A mixture of surprise and relief washed over me, mixed with something else: that strange feeling I associated with getting an A on a paper on which I hadn't quite worked hard enough.

"Yeah," he said, pouring cream into his coffee. "I mean, it's *dense.*" I nodded. "But I like it." Raising his mug to his lips, he took a tentative sip. "So far. I'm about a third of the way through. After he sees his girlfriend in the, er, film"— his face turned red at this—"and he's remembering meeting her. All the sweaters she brings to school. Like a thousand sweaters." He laughed. "I remember going to girls' rooms in college and thinking, *How do they have so many sweaters?*" Before I could stop him, he'd pulled out a mug and poured coffee into it for me.

"Girls are crazy for sweaters," I agreed.

"Anyway"—he shrugged and handed me the carton of cream—"I'll finish it and see."

When I returned to my desk, I heard the telltale creak of my boss's chair. Slowly, she made her way toward me, her face curiously blank. "Here's some dictation for you," she said, in that same soft, sleepy way, though trying, I could see, for cheer. I stood up and took the tape from her.

"Great," I said. "I'll get right to it."

"Tomorrow's fine." One of her hands, with its long, slender fingers, rested lightly on my desk, but her gaze was on the far wall, the wall of Salinger books. Then, slowly, she turned to me. "You did an excellent job on those contracts." The Other Client. "That wasn't easy."

That afternoon, after she left—exhausted by this brief foray into the world, her eyes glazed, her forehead damp—the revised contracts came back and I looked them over. Most of the changes had been made, but the electronic rights clause had not been taken out, as I'd requested, per Agency policy. This clause had started showing up in contracts right around the time I started at the Agency and was the source of much consternation for my boss and the other agents, as it awarded the publisher rights to all digital offshoots of the book in question, including CD-ROMs and "forms not mentioned herein or as yet unknown." Any number of contracts had been held up this year as the Agency haggled with various publishers over electronic rights, which had caused Max, in particular, some agony, for he was the one with living clients who desperately needed the money they'd receive on signing the contract. But my boss, who set the Agency's standards, wouldn't allow any contract to be finalized unless that vague, pernicious clause had been struck. In some contracts, reference was made to something called an "electronic book." When my boss first encountered this term, she'd shouted, "I don't know what an *electronic book* is, but I'm *not* giving away the rights to it."

Hoping to iron this out without bothering my boss, I drafted another letter—"CLAUSE 83.1.a: STRIKE"—and clipped it to the contracts. As I typed up an address label, Hugh came by, picked up the contracts, and glanced over my note. "This might take a while?" he said, half a statement, half a question. I shrugged. "I think he really needs the money."

"Really?" This was somehow disheartening to learn. The Other Client was so established. Not famous, but respected. Established. When Don was sixty, would he still be impoverished? "But he teaches, right? At ——." I named the prestigious MFA program.

Hugh shook his head tersely. "You didn't hear about this? Last spring? It was in all the papers."

"I was in London."

"Right." Hugh breathed in deeply and sighed, one action canceling out the other. "He was embroiled in a sort of"—he waved his hands around as if to conjure the appropriate word—"scandal. It's not clear what happened." I looked at him expectantly. "A student accused him of sexual harassment."

"*What?*" I thought back on my phone conversations with him: terse, polite, sometimes impatient. But not suggestive of sexual harassment. Though what sort of phone behavior exactly *would* indicate a predilection for sexual harassment? Heavy breathing?

"He was put on probation for two years," said Hugh tightly. "Without pay."

That afternoon, I seated myself at the computer and checked the Agency's sole e-mail account, which it was my job to monitor, printing out and delivering to the appropriate agents any notes that arrived. My boss, for her part, dictated responses, which I typed up, presented to her for approval, then retyped into the computer. Sometimes, after I was done, I furtively checked my own e-mail, but today I went directly to the *New York Times*'s Web site, which had launched just a few months before. It was slow and confusing, clunky, and I found it hard to stare at the screen long enough to read an entire article. But now I saw its full value: I typed in the name of the Other Client and immediately his story unfurled. The details weren't as bad as I'd expected. He had, it seemed, grabbed a student's breasts at a departmental party, though some witnesses suggested he had simply looked at her breasts, and others insisted his transgression consisted of making a lewd comment about said breasts. Regardless, this was the age of political correctness, and the Other Client had been thoroughly castigated in a campus tribunal, at which scads of students testified against him. He was sexist, misogynistic, they said. He made crude comments in class and was generally unsupportive of their writing, his criticism so harsh and unconstructive that they were left with no idea how to proceed with their work and despairing of whether they even should.

The strange elation I'd felt about the sale of his novel was fully gone, replaced by an uneasiness. This was, as Don would say, schoolgirl stuff: judging an artist by his actions rather than his work. How many great writers had not been the greatest of humans? Would I dismiss Philip Roth for ripping through wives? Or Hemingway? Or Mailer? And yet why was it the male writers whose behavior we were always having to excuse, or risk seeming prudish and judgmental? Don would say it was their—*his*—prerogative, their biological prerogative.

The Other Client's novel, I realized, takes place in a small town not so different from the town in which he'd lived for years, the town that housed the prestigious MFA program, in which a serial killer gruesomely murders and eviscerates young girls. Was it a coincidence that a man who had been brought down by a woman—in an isolated close-knit town— would immediately begin work on a novel in which the girls of an isolated close-knit town are being picked off before they can reach womanhood?

Suddenly I felt physically ill: parched, nauseated, hot and cold all over. The air-conditioning was running at full blast and I shivered a little in its chill. I looked around to see if anyone had noticed how long I'd been sitting at the computer, but the office was empty. August. Still, I got up and stretched, then made my way to the kitchen for a glass of water, contemplating an Advil.

In doing so, I passed the slim bookcase that held the Other Client's books. They were all, as my boss had remarked back in May, "smaller" than this one. The sorts of novels sometimes described as "quiet." Meaning they were about ordinary people living their lives. Meaning they earned good reviews but didn't sell in vast quantities, as did books about serial killers. Had the Other Client, stripped of his regular paycheck, made a conscious choice—a calculated choice—to write a book that would sell?

And was this worse or better than writing a book as revenge?

Or were the two not, perhaps, mutually exclusive?

That night, as I walked to the subway, I realized that Don, too, had murdered off a girl who had hurt him.

Three Days of Rain

On a stormy Thursday night, Don left for the wedding, duffel slung over his shoulder. "Bye," he said, kissing me roughly, his arms wrapped in my blue waterproof shell. Often, he took my clothing—Levi's, T-shirts, fisherman's sweater, Frye boots—without asking, but I'd offered him the shell to prove that I wasn't upset. He seemed nervous, tense, oddly exhausted by the effort of packing—worried that he had no suit to wear—and I wondered if, for the moment, he regretted disinviting me. Or, well, he'd never actually invited me. I'd just assumed that I was meant to go along. Regardless, I'd refused to help him pack. "Do you think I can wear this to the ceremony?" he'd called, holding up some wrinkled garment.

"I don't know," I murmured, not looking up from my manuscript, the first I'd pulled out of the slush pile. Rumors abounded of great writers pulled from the slush, but the queries my boss received suggested there was no veracity to them. Each week I sifted through letters printed on cloud stationery and cat stationery, letters in novelty fonts like Zapf Dingbats or Lucida Calligraphy, letters that recounted dreams or spoke of astrological charts, letters proposing books on Ayurveda for gerbils or the Tao of parasailing, letters from budding crime novelists and mystery writers, with self-created logos at the top, featuring guns or daggers or blood dripping from the letters of their names, letters from eroticists involving the word "moist," letters from memoirists recounting atrocities. The letter from the writer whose novella I was now reading had stood out in its simplicity. Times New Roman on plain white paper. Stories in small, respected magazines; no MFA but a BA from Barnard. I was halfway through the novella, about a little girl whose alcoholic father drags her to bars with him—rather than sending her to school—and was pleased to find that it was good. Really good. Small in scope, elegiac in tone, precise in language. Good.

"Well, can you take a look?" he asked, irritated.

I looked up and shrugged.

"Come on, Buba, you're good at this kind of thing," he pleaded. "Tell me what to wear. I don't have a suit, so some sort of shirt and pants. With a tie?"

I succumbed. "You can't wear a tie if you're not wearing a jacket. You'll look like a Bible salesman." This was my mother's line. I had never actually seen a Bible salesman.

"Fuck it," said Don, throwing what looked like a guayabera into the duffel.

In the courtyard, he paused for a moment and looked back at me, pursing his lips in a kiss. I raised my hand to wave, but it was too late. He'd already turned away.

It was spooky in the apartment alone, at night. The shadows from the trees in the courtyard moved darkly across our red floors, and the noises from the apartments above and below only reinforced my solitude. I was alone in a big city, in an apartment with a door so flimsy I myself could force it open.

In the morning, though, I felt a strange lightness. Don

was gone. I had no obligation to call him, to check in with him, to align my plans with his. I lingered at home longer than usual, drinking strong coffee made in my little espresso pot—I always felt selfish using it when Don was home, as it only brewed enough for one—and put on a plaid dress I knew he hated, long and loose and comfortable.

In Williamsburg, everything was the same—young people heading for their offices clad in vintage dresses and chunky glasses fogged over from the rain—but in midtown it became clear, suddenly, that it was August. The streets were empty. As a treat, I bought my coffee at the elegant food shop from which I'd heretofore purchased only that single, transformative sandwich and where I was the sole customer, the servers standing with their arms crossed across their crisp white shirts, tapping their feet in boredom. My office, too, was empty. The agents were all at their country houses in Rhinebeck or the North Fork or simply in their air-conditioned apartments, taking reading days. The accountant was on vacation, as was one of the two bookkeepers. Olivia was gone, of course, and Max and Lucy still without an assistant. Even Hugh wasn't in. The office felt off-kilter, spectral, without him. Pam and I and the second bookkeeper were, it seemed, the only people in the office, the world.

Alone, I couldn't sit still. While my coffee grew cold on my desk, I gathered the week's filing and walked through the office, placing contracts and cards and correspondence in their appropriate folders and filing cabinets, which took all of twenty minutes. I had some contracts to go over, some permissions forms to fill out, and, of course, the never-ending piles of slush and Salinger letters. It was ten thirty. I had three hours until the office closed at one thirty. Taking a sip of chilled, murky coffee, I opened the drawer of letters and pulled a handful out at random. A man in the Netherlands—Salinger had a large following among the Dutch, based on his fan mail—who loved *The Catcher in the Rye* and had, on a trip to New York earlier this year, traced Holden's steps around the city. Though it was winter, he had in fact seen ducks in Central Park. Was Salinger aware that the ducks now stayed in Central Park through the winter? A girl at a boarding school who had just read *Franny and Zooey* and was arguing with her friends about whether Franny was pregnant or not. The girl said yes, but some of her friends said no. Could Salinger settle the debate?

Pulling out my letterhead, I typed a form letter to the Dutchman. So many fans referred to those ducks in Central Park. As a kid, I'd fed these ducks with my dad, sometimes well into the cold weather. I distinctly remembered standing at a pond somewhere on the East Side, near the Met, in the Tyrolean-style coat I'd worn around age six, my hands freezing as I tore bread into bits. Could this man be right? *Did* the ducks stay in Central Park through the winter?

Writing to the prep school girl, I couldn't resist adding a line explaining that Mr. Salinger prefers his stories to stand on their own, without explanation or commentary from the author. "Even if I were able to pass on your letter—which, as stated above, I cannot—it's unlikely he would indulge your question with an answer. If there is ambiguity in Mr. Salinger's stories, it is purposeful. As I'm sure you know, he has often been asked whether or not Franny is pregnant"—I knew this to be true, from the letters that came in and from Hugh, though I had no idea what it meant—"but, again, he leaves it to the reader to decide whether or not this is so. In literature, as in life, sometimes there are no right answers." Part of me wanted to keep going, to tell this girl that she needed to be firm in her convictions, to resolve debates herself, without seeking outside authority, that the fact that she'd written to Salinger—who she surely knew would not be likely to write back—showed pluck and gumption, and she should run with those qualities; that the world outside Choate or Exeter or Deerfield Academy was even more complicated, and she would need to know her own mind to get by. And part of me thought that if Salinger were writing this letter himself, he might actually say those things. Or tell her to read poetry instead of *Franny and Zooey*. But I said none of that. I had said enough. "Best," I typed. "Joanna Rakoff."

It was funny, I thought, that I typed my name over and over again at the bottom of these letters. For there was a way in which the me who wrote the letters was not me at all. In the same way that the me who answered the phones, who soothed Roger's anxieties and told producers, in plummy tones, that she was "terribly sorry but Mr. Salinger simply doesn't allow stage or screen adaptations of his work," was not me at all, or was a version of me. Me as an Agency Type of Person.

And then a strange realization arrived: the me who talked to Salinger—nervously, about poetry—was the actual me. Though he still didn't know my real name.

At twelve thirty, the bookkeeper shut off his desk lamp and headed out. A few minutes later, I walked through the reception area en route to the bathroom and saw that Pam had left.

New York in August.

As I walked back to my desk, the phones suddenly began to ring. This was what happened when Pam went home. The phones rang throughout the office. I raced back to my desk and breathlessly picked up the phone. A gravelly voice shouted my boss's name, followed by a "please." It was as if I'd conjured him.

"Jerry," I shouted. "This is Joanne."

"Joanne," he said, in a slightly softer voice. Though I had acclimated to the shouting. It no longer sounded all that loud to me. "They have you answering phones?"

"Pam had to leave early," I explained.

"All right," he said. "Don't get stuck answering phones. You'll never get out. You're a poet."

"My boss actually isn't in today," I said quickly, to stave off any nervous chatter on my part.

"She's been out a lot lately," he said. "Is everything all right?"

He was the first person to notice that she'd been out most of the summer.

"Yes, fine," I said. "She's had a lot of reading."

"Good, good." There was a staticky sound, as if he were rubbing his cheek on the receiver.

"Can I help you with anything?" I knew—I knew—I wasn't supposed to help Salinger with anything.

"No, no," he said. "Just some questions about 'Hapworth.' But it can wait."

"Okay," I said. "I'll be here until 1:30 today if you need anything."

"Okay, then. You take care."

When I hung up the phone, my eyes hit the wall of his books, their titles printed so that I didn't have to twist my head. It was almost 1:30. There was no one in the office. My phone had rung exactly once today. I got up from my desk and pulled down a paperback version of each volume. *The Catcher in the Rye, Nine Stories, Franny and Zooey, Raise High the Roof Beam, Carpenters and Seymour—an Introduction*. For eight months I'd stared at these titles, so much so that they were imprinted on my brain. Sometimes, when I walked along Bedford or Madison, they floated into my head unbidden, like a mantra. "*Seymour*," I'd think, "*an Introduction*." And sometimes as I fell asleep they appeared before me, floating on the insides of my eyelids in their trademark font and colors: maroon, mustard, black on turquoise or creamy white.

I grabbed my bag and slid them in, then slung it over my shoulder and walked out the door.

. . .

I thought about going to the MoMA, or the movies, or up to the Met—all things I loved to do alone and now felt obligated to do with Don—but the lines at the museums were sure to be long and the theaters were filled with summer blockbusters. I thought about calling or dropping in on a friend, but who *were* my friends? *Where* were my friends?

So instead I did what I really wanted to do, what I knew all along I'd do: I went home and read. First *Franny and Zooey*, because I wanted to see if I agreed with the prep school girl or not, or because I knew my father loved it, that he identified with Zooey, who was an actor, as my father had once been. Then *Raise High the Roof Beam, Carpenters and Seymour—an Introduction*, then *Nine Stories,* and then, finally, on Sunday morning, as the rain slicked down, as I drank another cup of coffee from my espresso pot, *The Catcher in the Rye*. I read and read and read. I did not stop for the ringing phone—Allison, who had ducked away from the wedding weekend to check on me—and only occasionally stopped to grab a peach or a piece of cheese or a glass of water. I carried the books into the bath with me—as Zooey carries his script into the bath with him—and on Monday, Labor Day, when I had eaten all the food in the apartment, I brought *Catcher* with me to the Mediterranean place on the corner and read it over eggs with harissa, then went straight home and finished it, with tears rolling down my face.

Salinger was not cutesy. His work was not nostalgic. These were not fairy tales about child geniuses traipsing the streets of Old New York.

Salinger was nothing like I'd thought. Nothing.

Salinger was brutal. Brutal and funny and precise. I loved him. I loved it all.

Fall

Have you read Salinger? Very likely you have. Can you recall that moment you encountered Holden Caulfield for the first time? The sharp intake of breath as you realized that this was a novel, a voice, a character, a way of telling a story, a view of the world unlike any you'd previously encountered. Maybe you were a teenager, brimming with frustration and rage, certain that no one understood the complexities of your soul, and then there was Holden, a conduit for all of that misplaced emotion. Maybe, like the boy from Winston-Salem, you thought about Holden whenever things became too much and he calmed you down, made you grin. Or maybe you, like the doomed young girl—cancerous cells multiplying in her blood as she lay on the couch and read—loved the precision, the million tiny strokes, the sparseness of Salinger's early stories, of "A Perfect Day for Bananafish," or "Uncle Wiggily in Connecticut," or "Just Before the War with the Eskimos," all of them hilarious and heartbreaking, rife with glowing, pulsing symbolism.

Or maybe you, like me, loved it all. I loved Holden, in his

grief-fueled rage. I loved poor Seymour, whispering Taoist tales to his infant sister. I loved Bessie Glass, fretting about the apartment in a housecoat, her pockets laden down with tools. I loved Esmé, of course. Who doesn't? And I especially loved—or was a little in love with—Buddy Glass, second son, who narrates a few of the Glass family stories and whose life is increasingly consumed by grief.

But I suppose I loved Franny—and "Franny"—best of all. Do you recall this story? Do you remember its perfection? Its compression? Let me remind you: In Princeton, a handsome fellow named Lane Coutell stands on a train platform, waiting for his girl—Franny, of course—to arrive for a game weekend. In his pocket, he holds a letter she sent earlier in the week, which he's read so often he's practically memorized it, and as she steps off the train, he's overwhelmed by a wave of emotion that can't quite exactly be described as love—he's too limited a person to truly feel love, at least at twenty-one—but is perhaps a mixture of affection and ownership, with some pride mixed in; pride, of course, at having landed a girl as beautiful and brilliant and *original* as Franny. And yet when she asks, "Did you get my letter?" he pretends at nonchalance. "Which letter?" He is very, very young.

That letter, written in dithering girlspeak, espouses nothing but love for Lane, so much so that any reader—except Lane—would suspect the lady doth protest too much. And indeed once Franny and Lane are seated at lunch, Franny cannot—absolutely cannot—stick with Lane's program. She can't pretend she cares about Lane's paper on Flaubert. Though she doesn't express it this way, the world strikes her as filled with phonies—with egos, to use her term—and she can no longer go along with the enterprise of pretending this isn't so, of pretending that her professors are geniuses, that anyone who publishes in a small magazine is a poet, that bad actors are good. She can, in short, no longer participate in the world, with its web of socially constructed lies. She's dropped out of the play in which she's been cast as the lead. She's stopped doing her reading for class. She's *done*. Done with everything except the little book she's been obsessively reading, *The Way of a Pilgrim*, in which a humble Russian peasant wanders the land trying to figure out how to pray. His answer—which Franny has adopted for herself—is the Jesus Prayer, a simple mantra, which she repeats over and over, trying to synchronize it with her heartbeat, as per the pilgrim's instructions. If you have read the story, then you know: This is not a story about Christianity. Franny's adoption of the Jesus Prayer has less to do with Jesus than with her desire to transcend her own troublesome ego, to stop the superficial thoughts and desires that plague her. To somehow find a way to live in a world that sickens her. To be her authentic self. To not be the person the world is telling her to be, the girl who must bury her intelligence in her letters to Lane, who must compromise herself in order to live.

Maybe you, like me, identified so strongly with Franny Glass, upon first reading, that you wondered if Salinger had somehow—through some sort of bizarre, science-fiction-style maneuver—tunneled into your brain. Or maybe you, like me, found yourself sobbing with recognition, with relief, that there was someone else who had felt such exhaustion, such despair, such frustration with everything, everyone, including yourself, your inability to be properly nice to your well-intentioned father, or your inexplicable ability to shred the heart of the man who loves you most. Someone else who was trying to figure out how to live in this world.

I understood now the various characters and places and questions the Salinger fans mentioned in their letters. The ducks in Central Park. Seymour Glass kissing Sybil's foot. Phoebe. The red hunting cap. I understood now all the "goddam" and "helluva" and "bastard" and "crumb-bum." And the effect was rather like finding the missing pieces of the jigsaw puzzle that has been sitting, half-finished, on your coffee table for months. Suddenly the full picture was clear.

It goes without saying, I suppose, that I now understood why the fans wrote to him, not just wrote to him but confided in him, confided in him with such urgency, with such empathy and compassion, with such *confession*. Because the experience of reading a Salinger story is less like reading a short story and more like having Salinger himself whisper his accounts into your ear. The world he creates is at once palpably real and terrifically heightened, as if he walked the earth with his nerve endings exposed. To read Salinger is to engage in an act of such intimacy that it, at times, makes you uncomfortable. In Salinger, characters don't sit around contemplating suicide. They pick up guns and shoot themselves in the head. All through that weekend, even as I ripped through his entire oeuvre, I kept having to put the books down and breathe. He shows us his characters at their most bald, bares their most private thoughts, most telling actions. It's almost too much. Almost.

And so, of course, his readers felt an urge to write back. To say *this is where it hurts* or *here's how you made it better*.

But I also understood—I did, I did—why he didn't want to receive those letters anymore. I thought, for the millionth time, of the boy from Winston-Salem. *You can't go around revealing your goddam emotions to the world.* No, but you could reveal them to J. D. Salinger. You would presume he'd understand. And perhaps he would; perhaps he did. For years, Hugh told me, he'd tried to respond to his fans. But the emotional toll grew too great. It was, in a way, already too great for me.

Don came home on Monday, buoyant with energy, happy and rested, glad to see me. "How are you?" he said, sitting down

beside me on the bed. I'd just finished *Catcher* and my head
was spinning. "Tell me everything my Buba did."

When I spoke, my voice was hoarse, as if I'd just woken
up. I'd barely uttered a word all weekend, except to order my
eggs and coffee. Outside, the sky was gray, utterly devoid of
color. "Nothing," I said.

"You didn't go to the movies? I know how you love that."
He smiled, trying to cajole me into loquaciousness. *I know
you.* A curious blankness, an apathy, had settled over me. I
watched the sky darken, preparing for rain. I had, in Don's
absence, rather forgotten about him. I had not wondered what
he was doing at the wedding, at the beach, if he was thrilled
to be able to stare at the various young women in attendance
without fear of my censure, if he had woken this morning
with some blonde by his side. I had not really thought about
him at all.

On Tuesday, my boss returned in full force, or with aspira-
tions toward it. She had sold her apartment and was in the
process of selecting another one. The front-runner had a
sunken living room and beautiful views of the East River.
She brought in plans and walked around the office unfurling
them on our desks so that we might weigh in. We all agreed:
the sunken living room looked lovely, elegant, like something
out of a Carole Lombard movie.

She had also been to a spa in the days prior to her return,
and she asked us, all of us, to feel her elbows, which had been
thoroughly exfoliated for, she said, the first time in her life.
"Feel my elbows!" she cried, when anyone asked about her
trip. "Feel!" I felt, and as I felt, I thought of Seymour Glass,
who writes in his journal about the imprints other people
make on his hands, their humanity searing his flesh. "I have
scars on my hands from touching certain people." Seymour
Glass, who is somehow too sensitive, too emotional—"quiet

emotional"—for this world. Seymour Glass, who shoots himself in the head with a revolver, while his wife lies on the bed next to him.

One morning in September, James came over to my desk with his usual mug of coffee in hand. "So, I read Don's novel again," he said, looking at me intently. He was trying not to smile. "And I'd like to take it on. To take him on."

"Really?" I said, rising so I was closer to his height. I had, I realized, been holding my breath while he spoke. "That's amazing."

"I'll call him today and let him know. And we'll send it out." Raising his eyebrows, he allowed himself to smile.

"You won't need him to do edits?" I asked, carefully modulating my voice so as to quell a rising panic. How could the novel go out as is? It wouldn't sell. I knew it wouldn't sell.

"Yeah, I've been thinking about it," said James, taking a small sip of coffee. "And I think this is the kind of novel where an editor is either going to love his style or"—he grimaced—"not love it. There are changes he could make, but I think I may as well just get it out there, find an editor who loves it, and let him direct Don in a rewrite. There are a lot of directions you could go with an edit. I don't want to send him in the wrong direction. I want someone to fall in love with his writing."

I nodded.

"Why?" said James, his grin turning mischievous. "Do you think the novel needs a rewrite?"

"No!" I cried.

"Come on," James said, laughing.

From my boss's office came the squeak of her chair. "What's going on out there?" she called.

"I'm taking on Joanna's boyfriend," James called back. Since the installation of the computer, he had developed an admirable ability to banter with my boss. Or perhaps she had developed the ability to banter with him, for he was no longer merely the junior-most agent—still tied to his Dictaphone and his filing—he was now the Computer Expert, the Agency's conduit to the digital era.

"Really?" asked my boss. I heard the unmistakable flick of her lighter.

"Really. He's written an interesting novel." James rolled his eyes at me, anticipating my boss's tart response, but none came. "Joanna thinks it needs work before I send it out."

"She's probably right," said my boss with a laugh. A moment later, a stream of smoke came swirling out her door, like the trail from a genie's lamp.

The drama over "Hapworth" moved from the inside of the book—the leading, the margins, the running heads—to the outside. Roger had encountered a glitch: despite the ample space he'd given the lines, despite the wide margins, the book was still not thick enough for the title—or Salinger's name, for that matter—to be stamped horizontally across its spine. "The letters run together," he told me, worriedly. "It becomes a blur. It just looks *terrible*."

Salinger was displeased by this, of course, but he understood that Roger could do nothing about it. He decided to take matters into his own hands: he came up with a design for the spine himself. One entire day in October was lost to a flurry of faxing: Jerry faxing my boss designs. My boss looking them over, then faxing them to Roger, who made changes and faxed them back to us. And on and on. My boss did the faxing herself, running back and forth to the machine, which was just beyond the finance wing, catty-corner from the computer, adjacent to the coffeemaker and the photocopier and the microwave, the various reminders that this was 1996 rather than 1956.

By the end of the day, the involved parties had reached a détente, of sorts: Roger agreed to use Salinger's latest design, which was somewhat unusual, involving his name slanting down the spine on a diagonal. This agreement had not come easily. "Bite it, Roger," my boss finally said, or so she reported to Hugh and me.

"You didn't really say that?" asked Hugh, laughing.

"I most certainly did," confirmed my boss. "This would have gone on forever. It's just ridiculous. If he's going to get this book in stores by the New Year"—the pub date was still January 1, though this seemed highly improbable to me and, I knew, to Hugh; we hadn't even finished working out the contracts—"no one cares what the spine looks like. They'll buy the book because it's Salinger."

"True," said Hugh. "But it's Roger's press. I can see why he wants it to look decent."

"It *will* look decent," said my boss, holding out Salinger's rendering to him.

Hugh squinted at it. "Wow," he said. "Can they even do that? Stamp it on the diagonal?"

"Roger's ordered a sample case, so we'll see soon enough," said my boss with a smile that I recognized, belatedly, as utterly wicked.

Sometimes, at lunch, I walked through Rockefeller Center and glimpsed Jenny's old building, a wash of sadness spreading through me. She was no longer inside, e-mailing her colleagues about lunch; she was in Cleveland. Though I rarely saw her when she worked just across town—her life, her world, had been so separate from mine—it comforted me to know she was there, a few blocks west. There was the hope, I supposed, that things would change, go back to the way they were.

She and Brett had rented not a house but an apartment

near the university—real estate in Cleveland was not, it turned out, as cheap as they'd thought—and she had found a job, a part-time job, at the science museum, as an educator, which meant she was one of the cheerful, sweet-natured docent-like people who brought kids to the discovery center—or whatever it was called in Cleveland—to observe ant farms and run their fingers along dinosaur bones and who knows what else, all the things we had done as kids at the Museum of Natural History. It was, I told her over the phone, the perfect job for her, relieved to be able to tell her the simple truth.

After I hung up, though, I thought about Holden, of course. Like the boy from Winston-Salem, I was starting to think about Holden a lot. Holden loved the Museum of Natural History, too, the Indians and the deer drinking from the artificial pond and the birds migrating south in a V. "The best thing, though," he says, " . . . was that everything always stayed right where it was. Nobody'd move." Those Indians, that deer, the birds in flight, they remain utterly the same. "The only thing that would be different would be *you*."

One day my boss handed me a story by a client of hers of whom I'd heard nothing. He was elderly, I gathered, and had published a few acclaimed novels in the distant past, but these novels were long out of print and his name was all but lost to the channels of history. Certainly, it rang no bells with me. Later, I would look for his novels on the Agency's shelves but find none. "Why don't you send this out?" she said.

"Under my own name?" I asked tentatively, certain she would say no. Uncertain as to whether I even wanted her to say yes.

"Yes," she said. "Of course."

The story was good. Good, but quiet, in the parlance of the Agency—which also favored the term "edgy" to describe anything, it seemed, with graphic sex, like the work of some of Max's clients—in that it wasn't particularly plot-driven. But neither were many stories, including Salinger's. It read more like a visitation with a character.

In this day and age, I knew, this story was not, most likely, for the big magazines. But sometimes the unlikely occurred. Sometimes *The New Yorker* ran stories translated from Urdu or written entirely without the letter *e*. Sometimes it, too, ran stories that were merely quiet. The magazine had a new fiction editor, I knew, and he would surely be looking for new writers. I typed up a cover letter, clipped it to the story, and sent it off, into the world.

That afternoon, James sent Don's novel out. He was, of course, an Agency Type of Person, so he would not be holding an auction for the book, but would instead send it to one editor at a time. "If it were a *big* book," he told me, "I'd do an auction." Maybe James was right. We just needed one person to see the strange grandeur in Don's writing, to see, too, how it might be unpacked, loosened, lightened, his story ordered and trimmed. Just one person.

I wondered, though, if holding an auction might signal to editors that this was an important novel. If an auction might *make* it a big book.

No, I thought, as I watched Izzy, the messenger, depart with the manuscript, his slicker ballooning over his gaunt form, no, that had been up to Don.

I'd grown used to the quiet of our wing without my boss, grown used to mapping out my own time, and for those first few days following her return I had to force myself not to regard her as an interloper, an intrusion on my calm, peaceful workday. All the more so when the shouting began. We had all been treading delicately around her—with good reason—so I was shocked when, one afternoon, I heard Max raise his voice in her office. The door was closed, so I had no idea what he was yelling about—something he regarded as "bullshit" and "not acceptable"—and I froze in my chair, unable even to type.

I was saved by the phone, out of which emanated a pleasant English accent. "Is this Joanne?" it asked.

"It is," I confirmed.

The caller explained that she was the assistant to *The New Yorker*'s new fiction editor and she was calling about the story I'd sent. My heart began to beat faster. I'd been expecting a note. This was how rejections usually came. Perhaps they were going to take it? Could this be possible?

"We're going to have to pass on it, I'm afraid," she said with a huge yawn. "Sorry, I have terrible jet lag. I can't get used to the time change. I've been here for ages, but I still wake up ridiculously early and fall asleep at six o'clock."

From my boss's office, the shouting had subsided. Max burst out the door. "All right," he said, shaking his head in exasperation, as he walked away, studiedly not glancing in my direction. My boss sighed and slowly followed him, surely going off to talk to Carolyn.

"Listen, the reason I'm calling is because we really liked this story. If the author has any others, please send them. And please do stay in touch. Send us more." She yawned again, less dramatically. "It was close."

This pleased me more than it should have. I was close. I had aimed high and almost made it.

Don was close, too. Sort of. A few days later, James strolled over to my desk and held a letter up to me. "First rejection," he explained with a huge grin. "And it's a really great one." I had worked at the Agency long enough to understand that there were rejections and there were rejections. There was *not for me* and *I just didn't find these characters sympathetic* and *the story struck me as improbable at best,* and also simply *I'm afraid this is too similar to a novel we're publishing next fall* or *too similar to a writer already on our list.* And then there was *I truly loved the writing but I just didn't feel the story hung together* and *I'm so torn about this novel* and *I'd love to see this writer's next novel,* which was essentially the gist of the note James held in his hand.

I was wrong, I thought, as he walked off to make a Xerox of it for Don.

Walking home through the chilly wind, I remembered that the editor had actually said no. A good rejection letter was still a rejection letter. Perhaps I had been right.

I would've preferred, I supposed, to be wrong. Though I wasn't at all sure.

I thought and thought about the fiction editor's assistant. She had said to send more, and I felt, somehow, that we must send something immediately. I thought about the writer I'd pulled from the slush, the lovely novella about the girl and her alcoholic father. I'd been waiting for the right moment to present this potential client to my boss.

At the end of the day, I rapped softly at my boss's door.

"So, I normally just send form letters back to the slush," I said awkwardly. "But there was one query this summer that seemed interesting. So, I, um, asked for her novel. It's actually a novella." Suddenly I realized that I had potentially broken various rules. I should have brought the query letter to my boss first and asked permission to contact the writer. Seemingly all the blood in my body rushed to my face. "I don't know if it's to your taste. It's quiet. And small in scale. But I think it's good. I think it could sell."

My boss smiled. "You know," she said, "you should have talked to me before you asked to see her work. When you contact an author, you're representing the Agency." *I understand,* I started to say, but before I could make a sound, she'd held out her hand. "Let me see it," she said.

That Friday, the mail contained a bundle of Salinger letters sent over from Little, Brown and several letters for me: the Salinger fans, writing back. I opened one, neatly typed on an ancient typewriter, smiling with delight, for reasons I couldn't quite pinpoint. "Dear Miss Rakoff," the note began, "if that's who you really are." My smile quickly disappeared. "Your name is so ridiculous that I am pretty certain it's fake. I don't know who you really are, but I'm assuming you're using a pseudonym to protect yourself." I laughed so loudly that Hugh shuffled in his chair, disrupted from whatever minutiae occupied him at that moment. "Well, whoever you are, I'm writing to tell you that you have no right to keep my letter, or anyone's letter, from J. D. Salinger. I didn't write to you. I wrote to him. If you think you can keep my letter, you're wrong. Please send it to J. D. Salinger immediately." I had no recollection of this person's name, which probably meant I'd sent him a standard form letter, but I wasn't sure. By this point I'd answered, God, hundreds of—a thousand?— fan letters.

I opened the next, which was addressed in bubbly, girl- ish script: the girl seeking an A via a response from Salin- ger. What was I expecting? An expression of gratitude for my harsh but helpful words? What I found instead were two pages filled with expletives, fired off in a bout of rage. "Who are you to judge me?" she asked. "You don't know anything about me. I bet you're some dried-up bitch who doesn't even remember what it's like to be young, just like all my teachers. I didn't ask you for advice. I didn't write to YOU. I wrote to J. D. Salinger. Probably you're just jealous that you're not young anymore, so you feel like you have to punish kids like me. Or you're jealous of Salinger because he's famous and you're just some person." There was a sort of beautiful truth to her note. I was, indeed, just some person.

Some person who was now beginning to understand why Hugh had handed me that form letter. To save me from myself.

"I'm talking to bigger printers," Roger told me one day in October. There was a slight swagger in his voice that I'd not detected before. The enormity of this project was, it seemed, affecting him. Until now, he had been a publisher of small books, below-the-radar books, books that sold in hundreds rather than thousands. Now—it had hit him—he was publishing Salinger. *Salinger*. Whose books sold in the *millions*. Back in June, Roger had planned an initial print run of ten thousand: larger than any book in his catalog, but still quite modest. My boss had gone a ways toward convincing him that, as Hugh said, collectors could buy up ten thousand books before they even arrived in stores.

"If we go with a bigger print run, I run into another problem as well," he said. "Where to store the books. Now, normally, I stash them in my father-in-law's basement—"

"Wait, what?" I asked, laughing. The situation had now officially crossed the line into the absurd. J. D. Salinger was publishing with a press *that stored books in someone's basement*.

"Yes, well, I store them in *my* basement, too, but it fills up pretty quickly . . ." his voice trailed off. "So if we're talking a print run of thirty, forty, fifty thousand, I'd need to rent a storage facility, so that's next on my list." He sounded troubled, exhausted, as if these calculations were keeping him awake at night. Surely a larger print run meant a larger outlay of cash for Roger, who taught at a state university. Could he even afford any of this?

But there was another problem with the bigger printers, the printers who could handle Salinger-appropriate print runs. "Their bindings look *cheap*," he explained, disgustedly. "Perfect binding, rather than a true sewn binding. They're essentially gluing the book instead of sewing it. I know Jerry won't like it. I remember the contretemps over *For Esmé* years back." Apparently, Jerry had been horrified by the quality of the British paperback of *Nine Stories*—called *For Esmé—with Love and Squalor, and Other Stories* in the U.K.—so horrified that he'd raised a huge fuss and broken with his longtime publisher, a close friend. Roger could endlessly spout this sort of Salingeriana. With each phone call he inched a little closer—in my mind—to the territory occupied by the fans. "I don't want anything like that to happen. It's too dangerous," he said. "I just have to make a decision."

"Why," I asked Roger suddenly, "why do you think Jerry responded to your note?"

"Well, I used a typewriter—" he began.

"I remember," I interrupted, as gently as I could.

"And I know he liked that. But—" He paused for a moment, and I could hear him breathing. He had a slight cold. "I suppose"—he paused again—"well, I didn't tell him how much I loved his stories. I didn't say, 'Oh, *The Catcher in the Rye* is my favorite novel,' or anything like that. Some instinct, something, told me not to fawn over him, not to tell him he was a genius or"—he adopted a stentorian, professorial tone here—"*an important American writer,* or that kind of thing. I mean, I suppose that's why he lives in Cornish, isn't it?" I nodded, forgetting for a moment that I was on the phone, that Roger couldn't see this gesture. "So that he doesn't have people constantly telling him that he's a genius. So that he can just be himself."

"Yes," I agreed. *How lucky,* I thought, *that he knew exactly who that self was.*

Harper's turned down the story, too, as I knew it would, for their editor favored the ironic, the young, the "edgy." *The Atlantic* declined, too. And so I began thinking about small magazines, small *prestigious* magazines, the magazines that would pay less—or little, or nothing—but would draw attention to my boss's client. There was *The Paris Review* and *Story,* where Salinger had gotten his start, and a host of others. But there was one, in particular, that I thought might like this writer's elegant precision. Before I could change my mind, I typed up a cover letter, clipped it to the story, and slipped the sheaf into a mailer. *Done,* I thought, smiling to myself. As I closed the thick *Literary Market Place,* my eye fell on the name of another magazine, a magazine that ran poetry with both rigor and heart, and fiction that was unlike anything one could read elsewhere. There on the page in front of me was the name of the poetry editor. Before I could think better of it, I plopped down in my seat again, pulled a sheet of plain bond out of my drawer, and pounded out a brief letter to him. Then I pulled from my drawer three of my own poems, poems I'd typed in the early hours before my boss arrived, the rest of the office consolingly dark. I clipped the letter to them and slipped them in a manila envelope, just as I did for Agency clients.

The first freeze came quickly, more quickly than I remembered from my youth, when summer seemed to stretch through October. It was now November, but it felt like February: icy winds, icy rain. "We need to ask Kristina to fix the heat," I said one night, huddled in a blanket on the couch, still in the wool skirt and sweater I'd worn to work, contemplating putting my coat back on.

"We can ask," said Don, "but I don't think she's going to do it. I mean"—he laughed and gestured to the little strip that constituted our kitchen—"if she won't install a sink, is she really going to give us a heater?"

"Isn't heat required? Isn't it our legal right, as tenants?" I had no idea where this information was coming from, but I was pretty sure it was correct. "I can't stay here another winter without heat. It's ridiculous." My heart was pounding, strangely, erratically, at the thought of another winter in this apartment, with or without heat. Another winter with Don.

How many times had I been told that I would not meet Salinger? That he would not come in, that he had given up New York. The city—the site of his childhood, the setting for most of his stories—exhausted him. The city had prevented him from working after *Catcher*'s release, when he'd lived in an apartment on Sutton Place, its walls painted black, like that of the filthy communist couple in Mary McCarthy's *The Group*. The city had allowed his second wife, Claire, to abandon him, their baby in tow, on a three-day visit from Cornish, where she spent twelve, fourteen hours alone with that baby, in a snow-blocked house, while Salinger sat in a shed out back and wrote. Salinger still sat in that office—or, well, a different office, across the road from the original one—all day, and I wondered if he still wrote about New York, if his imagination still dwelled in the Glass family's enormous East Side apartment, crammed with end tables and books and relics of Bessie and Les's vaudeville years. Or did his mind now concern itself with the stories of the families that surrounded him in New Hampshire? One small, sad voice inside me wondered if his removal from New York hadn't ultimately silenced him, left him without a subject. "I have a question for you," he often said when he called. But I had questions for him, questions that had accumulated slowly over this year in which I'd tried to console, assuage, and calm his readers, in which I'd earnestly tried to stay true to his intentions, his ideas, his desires.

On a blustery November afternoon, a tall, slender man strode slowly through the finance department, glancing to his left and right with confusion. He wore a pressed flannel shirt tucked into jeans that, too, appeared to have been pressed and his silver hair parted deeply on one side, combed and Brylcreemed in the style of the 1950s and 1960s. *No,* I thought, though even from afar I could see that this man had large, dark eyes and truly enormous ears, the sort of ears I now knew he'd also bequeathed to poor, doomed Seymour Glass. He was making slow, steady progress toward me, a look of mild panic on his face. I stood up with the intention of running over to Salinger—for that had to be who this was, though his visit had not been mentioned to me—and guiding him to my boss's office, then froze, hovering over my typewriter. If I ran over to help him, would I seem like one of those assistants I'd been warned about? The ones who tried to slip Salinger their stories and gleefully leaked his phone number? Before I could resolve this question, my boss came running out of her office. "Jerry," she cried, her voice oddly choked with emotion. He'd not been into the office in years, I knew, and I wondered if he looked visibly older, aged, more frail, than the last time she'd seen him. She took his long arm in one of hers, as if to steady him, and embraced him with the other. "Jerry, there you are! It's so good to see you."

"Good to see you, good to see you," he said, smiling down at her. Arm in arm, they made their way to my desk, behind which I still stood, frozen. I had thought that in such a situation my boss would be tense, nervous, but instead she appeared radiant, relaxed, excited. The obvious occurred to me: She truly liked Salinger. Adored Salinger. Her job—I already knew—was far more than a job to her. But so much of her work involved tending to the interests of the dead I hadn't thought at all about what such devotion meant in terms of her relationship with the living. She was Salinger's conduit to the world, his protector, his explainer, his mouthpiece. She was a part of his life, and he hers. She was his friend.

"Joanna, come out here and meet Jerry," she said, smiling. For the first time since early June, her cheeks had color in them. With a nod, I obeyed, extricating myself from my bulky desk with more care than usual, for I was certain I was going to trip on a wire or bang my shin on a drawer or in some way embarrass all of us with my starstruck clumsiness. My legs seemed to be made of some pliable but heavy substance, like liquid lead. Somehow, though, I found myself standing in front of my boss and Salinger—*Jerry*—resisting the urge to smooth my skirt.

"Jerry," said my boss, gesturing to me. "This is Joanna, my assistant."

"Hello, hello," he said, taking my hand in one of his own and holding it as much as shaking it. His hands were extraordinarily large and warm and dry. "We don't really need an introduction. We've spoken on the phone many times." In person, his speech was less garbled, his voice less loud. He looked at me, dark eyes shining, as if for confirmation.

"We have," I agreed.

"Well, it's wonderful to finally meet you." He still had my hand in his.

"It's wonderful to meet you, too," I parroted back at him, idiotically, resisting a strong and bizarre—and inexplicable— urge to hug him. It was easy to imagine my boss, briefing her next assistant: "No matter how close to his work you feel, you are not to *embrace* him."

I was also thinking about those letters in my desk. There were, at that exact moment, three half-drafted responses sitting in the drawer with the fan letters. Irrationally, I feared that Salinger might somehow open the drawer and discover them, this breach of policy, of his instruction.

"*Well*," my boss said, clapping her hands together as if to startle me out of my misplaced anxiety. "We have a lot to discuss. Let's get to it. Jerry. Why don't you come sit down for a bit, and then we'll go to lunch?"

"That sounds perfect," said Salinger, and he followed my boss into her office, towering over her small form. The contracts for the "Hapworth" book were drawn up. I myself had typed and retyped multiple drafts of the contract until we found a format that was amenable to Salinger. This, of course, also fell under the category of highly irregular: publishers drew up contracts, not agents. But in this case, the publisher was so small it wasn't even clear if he had a standard contract and if he did it certainly wouldn't have applied to a book by J. D. Salinger. My boss had written the contracts herself, and perhaps Jerry was here to sign them, in the dark confines of my boss's office, the door to which, as I watched, closed with a resolute click.

In my desk lay the letter from Winston-Salem, two neatly typed pages, unfurled from a laser printer, and ending:

> *I'll write you again soon. I can hardly wait. Anyway, my line of thought is this: if I was the guy who put myself onto paper and I came out in the form of "The Catcher in the Rye," I'd get a bang out of the bastard who had the nerve to write me a letter pretending (and wanting) to be able to do the same thing.*

As the door clicked, I slid open the cold metal drawer and fingered the ragged white sheets. I'd read this letter a dozen times now, unsure of how to respond. I still wasn't sure what to say. Wouldn't it be better to simply pass the note on to Salinger and let him decide?

My boss's door remained closed for a long time, long enough that I eventually slipped out to buy my sad little salad. When I returned, the door was open and they were gone. An hour later, she returned alone. The letter would remain in my desk.

Two days later, on Saturday, a large, red-faced man with a flat-top arrived at our apartment with a box. "Hello," he said, then gestured inexplicably toward the interior of the apartment. Some hours later, an odd, archaic-looking metal contraption was installed on our front wall. "How do you turn it on?" I asked.

"No!" he said vehemently, with another inexplicable gesture. I held up my hands in surrender.

A moment later, Kristina arrived, as always clad in her red nylon track jacket. "Hello, wife!" she cried, taking my hand. Immediately, she and the man—her husband, presumably—began arguing loudly in Polish. I retreated to the couch. "Wife," she cried, after a good ten minutes. I stood up. "This is the heater. It needs to be hooked up to gas. But my husband forgot pipe. He will come back tomorrow with pipe and hook it up. Okay?"

"Great," I said, trying to muster some enthusiasm. How could this little box heat an entire apartment? I had never seen a heater that looked anything like this.

"But it's warm in here," she cried, smiling. "Whew! So warm! You'll be fine until then, yes?"

Don and I—in shifts—waited home all Sunday, but Kristina's husband never arrived. On Monday, I called Kristina and asked what was going on. "He had trouble finding right pipe, but he has it now," she assured me. "He'll be there tomorrow."

"I'll be at work tomorrow, though," I said. "I won't be able to let him in."

"We have key. He'll let himself in."

"Okay," I said nervously. My parents had a strict policy against unsupervised strangers in the house.

"Oh my God, Buba," Don cried, when I expressed concern. "What? Do you think he's going to steal something?"

All day Tuesday I tried not to worry. The minute the clock hit five thirty, I raced out the door. Half an hour later, I was on our block, where the air had a strange, unprecedented scent, one I couldn't place. I unlocked the door to the front house, grabbed our mail, then walked through the door to the courtyard, where it hit me full on: gas. The courtyard was full of gas. Gas so thick my eyes immediately began to water. Gas so thick I could actually *see* it, swirling through the air. It had happened, I thought, my worst fear. Don had come home and turned on the stove. The wind had knocked the pilot out and gas was pouring out of the stove. Don was possibly dead. Or near dead. Except that Don wasn't supposed to be home until much later. He was working, then going to the gym. But he could have changed plans. Been fired. Anything.

For a moment, I stood in the courtyard—staring dazedly at its cracked concrete center—unsure of what to do. Then I ran up the steps, trying not to breathe, and unlocked the outer door, then the door to our apartment, where the gas was so thick my head immediately began to fog over. The stove was closed. Closed and off. As in a horror movie, I slowly turned around. There was the new heater, a fierce flame burning in the little window on its lower left corner. From its bottom, a thick pale-blue pipe now extruded before jogging and running parallel to the floor. Beneath this pipe lay a puddle, a puddle steadily growing as the pipe above dripped and spurted something that looked like water but thicker. A puddle just perhaps eight inches from that flame.

Brooklyn Union Gas came quickly. "If you had stayed at work an hour later," the serviceman told me, "the building would have blown."

"Was it just installed wrong?" I asked, rubbing my hands together. I'd been sitting on the stoop of the front building waiting for their blue truck to pull up.

"They used water pipe instead of gas pipe," he said. "Kind of unbelievable. The gas ate right through the pipe. And with that open flame—" He shook his head. "I've never seen a heater like that before. I can't imagine where they bought it. Definitely not the local hardware store." With a thumb, he gestured to the corner, where there was, in fact, a hardware store. "Looks like it was manufactured forty, fifty years ago. Or in another country." *Poland,* I thought.

"Is it safe?" I asked.

"Safe?" He looked at me as if I'd just asked whether the sky was blue, squinting one eye and smiling a little. He had a broad jaw and blue eyes set amid a spray of creases. "No, I wouldn't say that heater is safe. I mean, it has an open flame. You walk by it, poof, your coat's on fire. And that's just the most basic problem. Even if they set it up properly, what if there's a leak somewhere else? You're better off with a space heater. Or just being cold." He looked at me, standing up a bit straighter and cocking his head to the side. "You live there alone? In that"—sucking in a bit of gas-tinged air, he cocked his head toward the house—"*place?*" I sensed that he had been restraining himself from saying "dump."

"No, no," I told him quickly. "I live with my boyfriend."

His head was still cocked slightly toward the house as he continued to look at me, nodding. Then, in one sudden, elegant gesture, he stood up straight again and placed his hands in his pockets, so his arms curved out like wings. "Your boy-friend should take better care of you," he said, pulling his keys out of his pocket. "All right. Let the place air out for at least two hours. We opened all the windows for you. You have somewhere to go?" I nodded. I could go to the L, I supposed, or around the corner, where my friend Cate had just taken a huge railroad flat. "Good night," he said. "Keep the windows open all night. Let the place air out. You need fresh air, even if it's cold."

"Fresh air," I called as he got in the truck and started it. "Got it. Fresh air."

At the end of the month, Max again took me along to a read-ing at KGB, where we sat with a convivial group of young editors and writers who lingered—as was not often the case—long after the reading ended, drinking whiskey with soda backs. "What the hell do you do all day for your boss?" he asked. "I mean, what does *she* do all day back there? Other than smoke and talk on the phone." I stared at him, blinking, a smile frozen on my face, unsure of what to say. My silence must have cowed him, for he took a bracing sip of whiskey and waved his hands in a gesture of apology. "Forget I said that. Things have been a little tense lately." He'd been in and out of my boss's office more often recently, often shouting. Max was up for partner, and it seemed that there were issues with the negotiations. I wasn't sure, but I suspected this had something to do with the Agency's old-fashioned coopera-tive system, in which agents' salaries were based on seniority rather than sales. At any other agency, Max—with his vast, fantastic client list and his million-dollar deals—would be among the highest-paid agents, but not so at the Agency, where the pot was divided equally. To become a partner, too, he would have to pay into the Agency, though I didn't know how much. Surely more than my entire salary. I wasn't entirely sure why he stayed. "I *do* wonder," he said, looking not at me but at the wall, where a Soviet-era poster—a woodblock print of a worker holding some sort of hammer-like implement—hung just above our heads. "I do wonder what she does. 'Cause she's certainly not selling books." A muscle tensed in his jaw. Suddenly he turned to me, a terse smile creating creases at the sides of his mouth. He looked tired. "What? Is she just, you know, sending threatening letters to everyone who mentions Salinger's name on his Web page?"

I laughed. She sort of was. "There's the 'Hapworth' deal."

"Right," he said, swishing the dregs of his drink. "The 'Hapworth' deal. That's a doozy." Max, I now knew, had been an actor in his youth—like my father—and he retained the precise articulation of the trade. "Wait!" he cried. "You were here for the—" He wrinkled his lips in thought. "Were you here for the letter thing? Or did that happen right before you started?" I shrugged. I wasn't sure. There were a lot of letter things. He banged his hands down on the table. "Listen to this." His dark eyes now glistened with pleasure. "Sometime, I guess right before you started, I'm leafing through your boss's circulating folder and it's all, you know, 'Please delete the following clauses from this contract' and whatever." I laughed. I knew this language all too well. "And then there's this letter that's addressed to a Ms. Ryder." He paused to let it sink in. "So I started reading, and the letter basically said, 'Dear Ms. Ryder, Many thanks for your recent letter to J. D. Salinger. As you may know, Mr. Salinger does not wish to receive mail from his readers'"—this was, of course, the language of the form letter I had been given; I nodded—"'thus, we cannot pass your kind note on to him. Thank you, also, for returning Mr. Salinger's letter from'"—he waved his hand around—"'1958 or whatever. But, again, Mr. Salinger has specifically asked us not to forward any mail to him, so I am returning it to you.'"

"So, someone had sent Salinger one of his own letters?" I asked, confused.

Max held up a hand. Wait. "So, I looked at the address at the top of your boss's letter and it's Beverly Hills or Laurel Canyon or somewhere like that. Los Angeles. Hollywood." He gave me a significant look, his eyelids lowered. "Then I look back at the letter your boss was responding to and it says, 'Dear Mr. Salinger, I'm a huge fan of your work. *Franny and Zooey,* in particular, has long been a favorite of mine, and I've reread it many times over the years.'" Max shrugged. "Something like that. And then: 'I know how highly you value your privacy and I know, too, that you don't want your personal letters out in the world. Last month, I was at an auction and a letter of yours came up for sale. I bid on it—and won—with the intention of returning the letter to you. The letter is attached.'"

"That's lovely!" I interjected, if not drunkenly, then a bit tipsily. Salinger's letters, I knew, were enormously valuable. Former friends and acquaintances had sold their caches for huge sums, incurring Salinger's wrath. At one point, he'd asked Dorothy Olding to burn their correspondence. She'd complied, which amazed me, in part because of the Agency's obsessive record keeping and in part because, well, did she not feel some sort of obligation to scholars, to literary history? No, I supposed, she felt an obligation to her client. "What a nice thing to do."

Max put up his hand again. "So the letter ends: 'I hope this gives you even a small amount of peace of mind. Sincerely'"—he paused, widening his eyes—"'*Winona Ryder.*'"

"You're kidding!" I cried.

"I am not kidding." Max crossed his arms and smiled. "Winona Ryder."

"I don't understand, though." I sipped at my drink, which now consisted purely of ice. "My boss knows, of course, that

Salinger would want that letter returned to him. I mean, he would, right? Didn't he sue people for selling his letters?"

"Of course he would want the letter," said Max, shaking his head and looking at me as if I were slightly dim. "Of course."

"But why didn't my boss just send it on to him?" I knew the answer to this question, but I wanted to hear Max say it.

"Because that's the Agency way." He sighed and slumped a little. He had just closed a frantic auction that had resulted in a two-million-dollar, two-book deal. He had two little babies at home now, twins. His life, actually, no longer consisted of book parties. This was a rare night for him. But something else, I knew, was troubling him. "We follow the letter of the law without any thought given to its subtleties. Salinger doesn't want any mail? We're not going to send him any mail, even if it's mail he would probably want. It's like"—he sighed again and ran his hands through his fluffy hair—"your boss doesn't get it."

"Get Salinger?" I asked.

"Salinger," agreed Max. He looked away again, at the woodblock print of the man holding the hammer or anvil or whatever it was. Then he smiled sadly. "Publishing. Books. Life."

Publishing, books, life, I thought as I walked, through the cool air, up to the L at Third Avenue. It seemed possible to get *one* right. But not all three.

The next day, while I was sleepily filing some cards, I found myself in *S* and—as Hugh had suggested I do so long ago—thumbed through the long drawer until I found the submission record for *The Catcher in the Rye*. There it was. A pink card just like the pink cards I typed up for my boss every day, preprinted with the names of all the publishers. I knew, of course, that publishing was a different, more ferocious beast than it had been in 1950, but I still expected—what?—evidence of the type of fierce bidding war Max conducted, the sort I read about in *Publishers Weekly*, editors fighting over nonfiction accounts of Ivy League murders or first novels from Iowa grads? A card marked all over with submission dates and editors' initials? But the *Catcher* card was almost pristine. The novel, it seemed, had gone to one other editor before Little, Brown—*months* before going to Little, Brown—who had eventually turned it down. Someone had rejected *The Catcher in the Rye.*

Neither had the advance for the novel been extravagant or even particularly large. Salinger, I knew now, had not been unknown when Dorothy Olding sold *Catcher*. His *New Yorker* stories had already won him a following, though nothing like the popularity that would come, with readers lining up at newsstands the morning a new Salinger story was to appear in the magazine. But this was an era—forty-five years prior, not so long ago, really—when novelists didn't receive lavish advances. Regardless, there was something about that modest advance, that initial rejection, that soothed me. Salinger had not always been Salinger. Salinger had once sat at his desk, trying to figure out what made a story, how to structure a novel, how to be a writer, how to be.

The next morning, my boss summoned me to her office. "That novella you passed on to me," she said, her voice so low I could barely hear her. "It's very good."

If I spoke, I knew I'd break into a smile, so I merely nodded.

"It's small, though. Quiet. As you said." She pulled a cigarette out of her pack and tapped it thoughtfully on the desk. "I don't know if I can sell it alone, as is. Give her a call and ask her if she has anything else? A full novel, ideally. Stories. Another novella, even."

My boss would have flinched, I thought, at the little gasp of joy the writer gave when I explained that I was from the Agency and my boss would like to see more. "I have a novel," she said. "A short novel."

"Send it on," I told her. "Send it on."

One cold, cold night I met Allison for a drink at a dark, elegant lounge by her apartment. "Why are you doing this?" she asked me suddenly, halfway through a martini. "I've wanted to ask you that pretty much since we met. Why are you with Don? Seriously."

"Oh," I said, my voice sounding strange and hollow and far away, as if someone other than myself were speaking. Reflexively, my mind turned to Franny and Lane. Why *was* I doing this? And why had I never asked myself the same question?

The next night, still feeling the effects of that martini—and the one that had come after—I forced myself to stay home. From the gray couch, piled under blankets, I called Jenny, who was bogged down in wedding preparations. The boathouse: nixed once and for all. A former dance hall in midtown, with its red candy-box interior: booked for a date two Julys hence, the first available opening, a full three and a half years after Brett's storybook proposal. "Maybe you should just elope," I told her, the phone growing warmer from proximity to my ear. The wind blew fiercely, stray leaves flying in gusts against the window like moths. I wore a woolen bathrobe over which I'd fashioned a shawl out of an old afghan. Tonight, Don was out running—running in the cold, the dark, which sounded utterly unpleasant to me—in another effort to get his weight down for a fight. He had to fight as a flyweight, otherwise, he'd be pummeled. His novel had now amassed half a dozen rejections, which he had pinned to the fridge with magnets; they winked at me from the corner of my eye, the familiar logos of various publishers, the blocks of black text.

"I think Brett's parents would die if we did that," she said.

"Hmm," I said, annoyance welling up. I tried to tamp it down, unsuccessfully. "But *you* want a big wedding," I blurted. "Right?" Why did I need to call her out on this? Why couldn't I just pretend that the Big Event was for Brett's conservative parents?

"I do," she admitted warily. "I think there's value in taking vows in front of all your family and friends. And celebrating with them, too." She took a sip of something. Very likely something sweet. She and Brett drank like middle schoolers: Malibu and Coke. Fuzzy navels. As if they were purposefully trying to appear unsophisticated, to mock the pretensions of the creative class, our craft beers and local wines. In Staten Island, they'd kept the bottle of Malibu right on their kitchen counter. "A wedding is kind of an excuse to have a big party."

"And to buy an amazing dress?" I suggested, willing cheer into my voice. I wanted—I did—to get in the spirit of things. But I still didn't understand why all this was so important to her. Why did she need to bankrupt her parents? Why was she devoting so much time and energy to what, as she herself said, amounted to a big party? And then, all of a sudden—like a curtain drawing away—it all became clear to me. I heard her words as something more than platitudes: *to take your vows in front of friends and family.* And my heart melted. She needed this wedding—this perfect, minutely orchestrated wedding—to shout, *This is who I am.* To tell us all that she was not that girl who'd tried to kill herself freshman year, the girl who developed an unhealthy obsession with her poetry professor junior year, the girl who had baffled psychiatrists and mystified her parents, for she had once been so perfect, so good, so obedient.

Just as Franny Glass had once been, before she collapsed in a Princeton restaurant and installed herself on her parents' couch.

Just as I had once been.

It had taken a few more years for my house of cards to collapse. Or, well, for me to knock it down. With Don. Don: my implement of destruction. Jenny had dated her share of Don-like guys. In fact, she'd been involved with one—obsessively, all consumingly so—when she met Brett. In fact, Brett was the guy's roommate. The wedding would whitewash *that* mess, too, I supposed. But: No wonder Jenny hated Don. No wonder my life frightened and disturbed and repelled her.

In a few years, would I be marrying a law student who exclusively read histories of the Great War? I tried to imagine devoting the time and energy that Jenny had put into her wedding. Or, more important, choosing a partner, for *life*, who didn't share my interests, my own particular view of the world. I could picture none of it. For a moment, I allowed my mind to turn to my college boyfriend, whom I had not been brave enough to call, who was surely in his Berkeley apartment, jotting notes on manuscript paper or reading Lermontov, and my breath caught with longing. In a year, would I be there with him, walking along Telegraph with his arms wrapped around me? If not there, then where? And then, suddenly, I knew. Not here. I would not be in this apartment, with its missing sink. I would not be typing letters for my boss. And I would not, most definitely would not, be waiting for Don to return from a run.

"It's going to be great," I told Jenny. "It's going to be perfect." And again, I wasn't lying.

·   ·   ·

One morning, as I pored over yet another contract, I heard my boss cry, "Darn it!" A moment later, she came sauntering over to my desk. "What are your plans for lunch?" she asked.

"I'm not sure," I said nervously. Was she going to ask me to have lunch with her? This seemed highly improbable.

"Do you think you could drop something off at *The New Yorker* for me?" I sat up a little straighter at the mention of *The New Yorker*. "Izzy is out again." Izzy was the Agency's wizened, cheroot-smoking messenger, who communicated purely through grunt and hand gesture and whose deep, chesty cough kept him home three days out of five. "I tried the messenger service, but they won't have anyone until the end of the day, and then I realized, well, the Condé Nast building is just across the street really. Why not just walk it over?"

"Of course," I said, my heart now thunking crazily in my chest. *The New Yorker*. I was going to the offices of *The New Yorker*. Should I call the auburn-haired editor and let him know I was stopping by? Or the fiction editor's assistant? No, I thought, I wouldn't be giving them enough notice. I would be putting them in an awkward position, having to tell me, "Sorry, I'm swamped today." But a Brown Derby sort of scenario occurred to me: I would drop off the package with a kind, interested editor who would engage me in conversation about the author or the Agency—surely he would know the Agency—or Salinger. Or, I'd run into the auburn-haired editor and he'd say, "Hey, let me introduce you to my boss!" And maybe one of them would say, "Well, if you ever want to leave the Agency, just give me a call."

An hour later, I dashed out—without even putting on my coat—a brown paper package under my arm. On Madison, the sun shone in jagged beams and the air held the promise, the hint, of warmth, but it was still cold, icy gusts blowing up my sleeves, and I quickened my pace as I crossed the avenue to the gray building, which housed all the magazines owned by Condé Nast. I'd imagined *The New Yorker* operating out of a brownstone on some genteel, tree-lined block, the editors gathering at four for tea in the parlor. I had imagined it, I supposed, as an operation akin to the Agency.

But the Condé Nast building was just a dully anonymous office tower, like all the buildings on Madison and Park and Lex. I walked quickly through the sleek gray lobby and boarded the appropriate elevator, trying not to smile to myself—*The New Yorker!*—when the doors closed with a thunderous ding. On my designated floor, I found a reception desk with *The New Yorker*'s distinctive logo discreetly hung above it and handed over my package to the older lady—her face sweetly powdered—at its helm. I glanced around, thinking perhaps I'd see one of the editors from the party, passing through on his way to lunch. But the area was empty. "This is from my boss," I told her. "At the Agency."

"Of course," said the receptionist, smiling kindly. She had the rheumy voice of a longtime smoker and wore her hair pulled back in a bun. "I'll have it delivered right away."

And then I got back in the elevator without so much as a word, a glance, exchanged with another soul. In the lobby, I fought a crushing disappointment. *That was it? Really?* I thought as I walked up Madison, the wind sneaking through the weave of my sweater. The feverish anticipation of the morning dissolved in a haze of anguish and regret.

Across the avenue stood the entrance to the Agency's building, but I couldn't bear the thought of returning to my desk just yet. I had imagined—what?—spending an hour chatting with witty editors? Oh God, how *stupid*. With a shiver, I turned west on Forty-Ninth, where the wind hit me full in the face. It was just noon, still early for lunch, and the streets were eerily empty, the workers of midtown safely ensconced in their overheated offices, endlessly picking up the ringing phone, sending out missives via optic cable, closing deals and crunching numbers and cutting film, their minds on where they would pick up their sandwiches or sushi half an hour hence.

At the corner of Fifth, I paused by the windows of Saks, already dressed for the holidays, with mannequins in beautifully draped crepe dresses, the deeply saturated colors of the season: red, maroon, pine green. Tourists flowed past me in clusters of four and five and six, en route to more elaborate window displays—Tiffany's, Bergdorf's, Bendel's—or Central Park, so close and yet I'd never ventured up there on my lunch break. I'd eaten lunch at my desk pretty much every day during my year at the Agency. Why had I never thought of taking my salads to a bench, sitting in the sun, or walking around the pond, or up to the zoo?

In five minutes I was at the southeast entrance—past the Paris Theatre and the Plaza, and the rows of horse-drawn carriages, sidestepping piles of manure. There it was: the park. The acres of fields, the winding, intersecting paths, unfolding before me. I had played here as a kid, too, climbing the Alice in Wonderland statue, clambering through various playgrounds, feeding the ducks. Holden's ducks. The huge, beautiful willows that dipped low over the pond were bare of leaves, their frilly branches spinning in the wind. I was freezing by now, my hands red and raw, my fingers numb. Tucking them under my arms, I walked down the sloping path to the pond. Holden calls it the lagoon—a word that for me connoted magic, the mermaids of *Peter Pan*—but in my family we'd just called it the pond. And there it was, the water black and sluggish, foreboding, a few rays of sun slicing across its center. Brown sparrows hopped around the path in front of me, and a pigeon or two fluttered down from the back of a bench at the prospect of food. But there were, indeed, no ducks. It was colder here, in the pond's little vale, the wind whipping down from the top of the park. *The wind clicks around to the north*, I thought. Merwin's most beautiful, most compressed, most perfect poem, written for his second wife, Dido. I walked into it, my eyes watering, to the little curved bridge that crosses the pond, and looked up, toward the grand buildings on Fifth, the trees that stretched beyond, the path that led to the zoo—where Holden takes Phoebe, and where I, too, had watched the seals bark for fish, water sloshing over the edge of their tank. And then, suddenly, from the north—yes—came the unmistakable sound of moving water. Ducks. A fleet of them coming toward me with calm fortitude, brown mallard females of varying sizes. Fifteen, twenty of them, their feathers lush and fluffed. They swam under the bridge and I turned to watch them enter the pond proper, circling its perimeter in search of insects or tiny fish or scraps of sandwiches left by hearty cold-weather picnickers. They were so beautiful, the ducks, so beautiful and sweet, gliding with regal grandeur across the black depths of the pond, their million tiny feathers protecting them from the cold.

That afternoon, when the mail came in, there was a letter for me, with a Nebraska return address. Inside, I unfolded two sheets of small white paper covered over in large, shaky letters. The veteran. "Dear Miss Rakoff," he wrote.

I was very pleased to receive your letter last week. Of course, I'm sorry that Mr. Salinger isn't interested in seeing his mail, but I'm not surprised either. I didn't really expect or even want a response. I just wanted him to know how much his work meant to me. I very much appreciate the time you took to write back and I enjoyed reading your thoughts on Mr. Salinger's work. I'm sure you're too young to have lived through World War II, but it was a terrible time for those of us who served. Maybe your father served? Or your grandfather? In fact,

> *I knew a man named Rakoff during my time in the air*
> *force. We were stationed together in Germany just after*
> *the war. Was this perhaps your father or grandfather*
> *or uncle? It's an unusual name. I'd never met another*
> *person named Rakoff until your letter came.*

My heart began to speed up a little. My father had, in fact, been in the air force and had, in fact, *been stationed in Germany*. In Stuttgart. But years later, during the Korean War. He'd enlisted, I believed, in 1952, a year after *Catcher* came out and a year after he and my mother married. Could the veteran have done another tour, during the Korean War, and met my father? Now, in his dotage, was he conflating the two?

I set the letter aside, heart still beating. Could my father have met this man? How I wanted this to be so. Quietly, I picked up the phone's heavy receiver and began to punch in the numbers of my father's office. From her sanctum, my boss coughed heavily and shuffled some papers. I put the phone down. Before I could take my hand away, it rang, and I jumped a little in my seat. "I'm calling for Joanna Rakoff," announced an unfamiliar voice.

"This is she," I said.

"Yes, this is ——." The caller uttered a name that meant nothing to me, but in such a tone that I understood he thought us acquainted. I racked my brain trying to think who this might be. "You sent us a story a few weeks ago. I'm sorry it's taken me so long to get back to you." The editor of the small magazine. I'd expected a letter from him, or his assistant, not a call. "Well, I finally read it last night and I can't get it out of my head. We'd be very pleased to accept it for the magazine."

"Wonderful." I wasn't sure what else to say. "Thank you so much for taking a look at it."

"Thank you for thinking of us." He had the sort of gruff

voice I associated with the Far West. "We'd love to see more from your writers." *My writers,* I thought, smiling. *My writers.*

"Oh my goodness," my boss cried, when I told her. "I knew you could do it." She beamed at me. "You're on your way." Then she stood—with a heaviness that had not been evident when I'd started—and motioned for me to walk out into my antechamber with her. Her gait reminded me of Leigh, those long draggy walks through the apartment. "Hugh," she called, smiling. "Joanna sold a story."

"That's great," said Hugh, with an avuncular smile.

"Yep, a hard sell. Very quiet story." She nodded for emphasis. "She found me a new client, too." My eyes widened at this. "I'm taking on that girl you pulled from the slush. The second novella is very good. I'm not sure how I'm going to sell it. I have to think. Apparently, she has a novel." She turned to Hugh. "These are very spare, eerie tales. Very good. Very elegant." They both turned and smiled at me, as if they were my parents. "I knew from the moment you walked in the door," said my boss, lighting a cigarette, "that you were an Agency Type of Person."

That night, I raced to meet Don at the L, only to find the small, makeshift room filled to capacity, with people standing by the door, waiting for tables to open up. Our neighborhood, all of a sudden, was teeming with the young and underemployed, scads of twenty-two-year-olds, fresh out of Brown and Wesleyan and Bard, having arrived after summers backpacking through France or surfing in Mexico. Increasingly, people we knew were moving north, to Greenpoint—the little neighborhood just above Williamsburg, still predominantly Polish, where good deals could still be had on linoleum-floored railroad apartments—or east, to the Italian neighborhood one stop farther in on the train, the Lorimer Street stop, by Leigh and Don's old apartment. Just a year earlier, when I'd camped out there, the latter had been considered a murky, marginal neighborhood.

Don waved to me from a table at the front window, usually our favorite, a rarely won prize. But tonight the waiting throng kept jostling him and knocking his bag down. Every few minutes someone opened the door, letting in a gust of freezing air. I ordered coffee, though what I really wanted was food, food and wine. Not a bagel. Real food. Dinner. Don jostled his leg up and down, gnawed on a hangnail; his fingers were bitten to bloody stubs. He had his journal out, open in front of him, the pages moist from the tips of his fingers.

"So, I have news," I told him as the waitress set my coffee down. The coffee at the L was terrible, actually, though this apparently didn't dissuade people from lining up for it. But the coffee at the L was beside the point, I supposed, glancing around me. Everyone was so attractive. Had they been this attractive a year ago? Don, I realized, was older than most everyone in the room. No, the point of the L was not the coffee. The point of the L was to be at the L. "I have news," I said again, though this was not a phrase I habitually used. I just wanted his attention. "So, I sold a story."

Don glanced—unhappily, irritably—toward the counter, where a troupe of young girls—or, well, girls my age—congregated, ordering coffees in anticipation of a table, but he seemed to be staring past them. "This is bullshit," he said. "Let's get out of here. I can't think straight."

Out on Bedford, in the frigid air, he smiled. "Much better," he said. "What was going on in there?"

Across the street, at Planet Thailand, it was also crowded, but we found a tiny table across from the stove. A few feet away, the chef shook a wide silver wok, enormous flames shooting up its sides. "I sold a story," I told Don, again, after we'd ordered papaya salad and rice noodles.

"What?" he said, looking at me with unvarnished hostility. "One of *your* stories? I didn't even know you'd ever actually finished a story. Not since college."

"A *client's* story," I said. "One of my boss's clients."

"Oh," said Don, letting out an enormous breath. His face broke into a smile. "That's completely different. As long as you're not a threat to me. We can't have that." He let out one of his cackles.

"Of course not," I said, prying apart my chopsticks with a snap.

"I thought all your boss's clients were dead," he said, wiping his glasses with the edge of his T-shirt.

"This one is almost dead, I think," I said, with a pang of disloyalty to my boss, to her client.

"Like the Agency." Something in Don's voice had changed. At the L, I was invisible to him. This happened all too frequently. But he could see me now. I had reappeared for him. It scared me—and it bothered me—the way I could disappear right in front of his eyes. "That's really great, Buba. Maybe you're going to be a big agent. Like Max." He took a long swallow of ice water. "Maybe you can represent me. Since James doesn't seem to be doing a very good job."

I lifted my water glass and took a sip. There was no way I could speak. The thoughts coursing through my brain were too horrible, too disloyal to acknowledge: that I wouldn't represent him, for I knew—I *knew*—that his book wouldn't sell. This was why I'd approached James rather than Max about Don's novel. I knew Max wouldn't take it on. I was Max's reader. If the manuscript had come to me cold—if it hadn't been my *boyfriend's* novel—I would have recommended a form rejection.

I didn't say this, though. Of course not. I smiled and lifted a few strands of papaya into my mouth. Just then something strange happened, something that seemed, in a way, to have been lifted out of a Salinger story: The chef spilled a spray of chili powder into the flame at his waist, sending a thick fug of smoke directly to our table. Our eyes watered and turned red, and my throat constricted—a terrible, helpless feeling—and, most remarkably, I saw Don for a moment as if from across an abyss, his face distorted by the reddish smoke. How far away he was. How far.

When we got home, there was a small envelope waiting for me, hand addressed. I turned it over: the logo of the small magazine to which I'd sent my poems. "What's that?" asked Don.

"Nothing," I said, and slipped it in my bag.

When he seated himself at his desk—the more rejections came in, the more he stared at the screen of his computer—I got into bed and opened it up. The note was from the poetry editor, accepting one of my poems.

That night, I couldn't sleep. Don, as always, fell like a stone, on his side, earplugs in, mask pulled over his eyes. But my mind wouldn't stop churning. Maybe I *would* be an agent, a big agent. Maybe I would seek out new clients for my boss, and eventually she'd let me take one on myself. Maybe. I thought back to that night, just a month or so before, when I'd talked to Jenny—we'd not spoken since—and the thought of being at the Agency in a year had struck me as incomprehensible, nonsensical. And yet—and *yet*—how could I leave now? I was, as my boss said, on my way.

Quietly, so as not to wake Don, I heated some milk on the stove, then sat down at my desk—a few feet from the bed—turned on my computer and, with some confusion, our little modem, and—with a chorus of blips and bleeps and staticky feedback—went online. In my in-box, I found a note from my college boyfriend. My heart thrummed merely at the sight of his name. "I've not heard from you in a while," he wrote. "I just wanted to check and see if you're okay. I'm worried that you're afraid to be in touch with me. Jo, I'm really not mad. I just miss you." He was mad. I knew he was mad. He deserved to be mad. *It's okay,* I wanted to write to him. *Be angry at me. Yell and scream. This would all be so much easier if you would just be angry. I don't deserve your forgiveness.* But I couldn't; I didn't. Instead, I told him that I'd sold a story. *It's the most thrilling feeling. I can't quite explain it. I don't understand it. Rationally, I know that it's just a business transaction. But I can't help feeling that there's more to it: that I brought this story into the world. People will read it because I placed it. Until I placed it, the story belonged only to the writer. Now it will belong to the world. (Also, a magazine just accepted one of my poems. I'm almost afraid to mention it, afraid that if I tell anyone, I'll jinx everything.)*

In the morning, I woke to find I'd left the modem on. Our phone had been busy all night. I began to shut it off, to close my various windows, then noticed there was a new message. "You're participating in the production of art," my college boyfriend told me. "Whether you're making it yourself or shepherding it into the world. You're doing the right thing. Just stay in the world. If I could come to New York, I would."

Come, I thought, as I brushed my teeth, *please come.* I thought of how he had saved me in London, from a crumbling student house off Cartwright Gardens and a terrible, aching loneliness, a loneliness that it seemed only he had the power to cure. He had found for us a beautiful flat in Belsize Park, with wedding-cake moldings and double-height ceilings, a world away from the sink-less, freezing apartment I shared with Don. After he left—to visit his parents before moving to Berkeley for school—I'd cried and cried, but it was only in those months, alone, that I'd truly been able to write. The poems had come, one after another, as I jogged through Hampstead Heath, the stories, too. Why, why? I had missed him so terribly, sobbing on the phone, counting the days until I came back to the States; I had opted not to go on to doctoral work, in part, because I missed him, because London without him seemed like a movie set, the beautiful row houses and gardens, mere props for a life that didn't exist. Because I loved him, truly loved him, had loved him from the moment I met him, at eighteen.

And then, unbidden, I thought of Salinger. My whole life seemed to have narrowed down to Salinger, Salinger, Salinger, in this case a line from "De Daumier-Smith's Blue Period." The narrator of the story, a teacher at a correspondence-based art school, writes a letter to his one talented pupil, urging her to invest in good oils and brushes, to commit to the life of the artist. "The worst that being an artist could do to you would be that it would make you slightly unhappy constantly."

Could I allow myself to be slightly unhappy constantly? I thought about the way my college boyfriend looked at me—I had never, not ever, disappeared before his eyes—and the way his skin felt in the morning, warm and loamy, and the long nights we'd spent talking, ever since we'd met, the vibration of his low voice in my ear. For a moment, I allowed myself to miss him—to truly miss him—and the pain that shot through me was almost physical. I ached for him. I loved him. I wanted him. But right now I needed to be slightly unhappy constantly.

Slightly unhappy constantly alone.

One afternoon in November, my boss came running out of her office, cigarette in hand, calling for Hugh. *What happened?* I wondered. It had been ages since the last yelling-for-Hugh incident. She'd been subdued since the summer, understandably. This time, she seemed less panicked, more shocked. Before Hugh could emerge from his office, she turned to me, tapping her slender foot. "Do you know who that was on the phone?" I shook my head as Hugh—with a great rustling of paper—hustled out of his office, smoothing his hair.

"What happened?" asked Hugh.

"A reporter just called for me," said my boss. "From some paper in D.C."

"The *Post*?" asked Hugh. I could see him trying to make sense of the situation without having to be told. The mark of a genius assistant.

A stream of smoke swirled into my boss's face and she stepped back, waving it away, flecks of ash dropping onto the carpet. "Not the *Post*. The *Journal*? Some paper I've never heard of." She looked at us. "It seems Roger Lathbury talked to them. About 'Hapworth.'"

"You're kidding." Hugh had that look on his face, as if he had bitten into something spoiled and wasn't sure if he should spit it out or swallow.

"Nope." My boss smiled grimly, her mouth closed.

"Did you talk to them?" asked Hugh.

"Of course I didn't talk to them," she cried. With a laugh, she shook her head. "I can't believe Pam even tried to put that *person* through."

"Are you sure Roger talked to them?" Hugh scratched his chin.

"How else would they know about the book?" With one swift gesture, my boss stubbed her cigarette out in the ashtray that sat on the credenza by Hugh's office. "Jerry certainly didn't tell them about it!"

Hugh said nothing, his mouth sealed into a tight line. He had known this would happen. He had not trusted Roger from the start.

I had, though. I had trusted Roger. I'd not thought he'd do something like this. I *had*, it was true, feared that he'd mess the deal up through some sort of weird nervous behavior. I'd not thought, though, that he'd do the thing Salinger most abhorred: talk to the press.

"Do I tell Jerry about this?" my boss mused, tapping a long finger on the credenza.

Hugh raised his eyebrows in a gesture of befuddlement. "I guess you have to," he said. "He's not going to be happy."

No, I supposed he wouldn't. Part of me wondered why exactly we had to tell Jerry. He would never see the story, would he? In some obscure paper? No. But I supposed this had more to do with Roger: If he was talking to this little paper, then he would certainly talk to bigger ones. And then there was the larger issue—what was really at stake—that Roger simply couldn't be trusted. He wasn't the kindred spirit Jerry had thought him. He was a phony, just like everyone else.

My boss retreated to her office without ceremony and closed the door. It was a long time before she emerged again. "What did he say?" Hugh called.

"Nothing," said my boss. "He thanked me for telling him. He sounded a little sad." She herself sounded a little sad.

"Well, he thought this guy was a friend," said Hugh, appearing in his doorway. Hugh, I knew, had not believed in any of this from the start. He thought it all ridiculous. He didn't, however, seem pleased to have been proven correct. He, too, seemed simply sad.

A few days later, as dark closed in around me, my boss already gone—her smoke still lingering viscously in the air—Salinger called. "I'm so sorry, Jerry," I said. I had only recently been able to actually call him "Jerry" and it still felt strange. "My boss has left for the day."

"That's okay," he said in his pleasant way. "I can talk to her tomorrow. Could she call me in the morning?"

"I'll have her call you first thing," I said.

"Hey, Joanne, let me ask you a question." For the first time, this sentence did not fill me with anxiety. "What do you think of this Roger Lathbury fellow?"

I didn't question why he was asking me again. "I like him," I said. "I think he's a good guy."

"I do, too," he said, his voice a bit more hoarse than usual. A bit sad, I supposed. "I do, too." It was over. I knew. The deal was off. The contracts were signed, but they gave Jerry full power, full control. Jerry could call off the deal at any time.

"Take care, Joanne," he said.

"Jerry," I said. For the first time, his name felt comfortable coming out of my mouth. There was so much more I wanted to say. "Jerry, good-bye."

Winter, Again

I never wrote back to the boy from Winston-Salem.

I never wrote back to the veteran in Nebraska, for I could not bear to tell him that his friend was no relation to me. My father had confirmed this, with some disappointment—no one in his small family had served in Germany during World War II. Perhaps this was where I got it from—my belief in fate, in magic, in felicity, the mermaid lagoon. From my father.

Nor did I write again to the high school girl. Her rage was too enormous for me to bear. And what could I say to her but *Wait, wait, and you'll see. It gets easier once you're no longer graded, once you have to assess your actions for yourself.*

I should have, I suppose. I should have written and told her exactly that, though surely I would have only fanned her flames. But she's haunted me all these years, as has the veteran, and the boy from Winston-Salem, whose letter I still have, its creases soft from wear. I keep it pinned to the corkboard above my desk, a talisman, a reminder. In some ways, I wish I'd taken them all. The thought of them, those letters, those documents of so many people's lives, just tossed away, grows more and more unbearable as the years pass. I could have saved them and I didn't.

When I gave notice, my boss stared at me in disbelief. "But you were doing so well," she said. "You sold that story and—" She didn't finish. "I was so sure you were an Agency Type of Person." The sadness in her pale eyes was too much for me, though I knew this sadness was not really to do with me. She had lost so much, so many, in the last year. Max had just left, too, in a storm of rancor, his office abandoned nearly overnight. Losing her assistant was nothing in comparison. I was eminently replaceable. The city was full of boys and girls like me, clamoring at the gates of literature. And yet— and yet—I wavered, as she tried to dissuade me. "Why?" she asked me.

"I just—" Could I tell her I wanted to be a writer? I wasn't sure that I could. "There are things I want to do. I love this"—I held my hands up, gesturing to the books, the very walls around me—"I love it here. But there are things that if I don't do now, I'll never do."

"I understand," she said, and I truly believed she did.

With Don, I wavered, too. Of course I did. James had not found that editor who would fall in love with his novel. I went home with him for Christmas, as planned. We returned to Brooklyn in time for New Year's Eve. Another party at which I had nothing to say. The next morning I woke up and the first thing I thought was *Jerry's birthday*. He would be turning seventy-eight. It was also the original publication date for the "Hapworth" book, the book that would never happen, the book that would always consist of one single case of sample covers, stored, I presumed, in Roger's basement. He didn't seem the type to throw such relics away. Around the time I left, a story about the book appeared in a paper we'd heard of: the *Post*. Salinger never officially told my boss that the deal was off. His silence told us all we needed to know. I had used the same trick with my college boyfriend, I supposed. He had recovered from it, or so he said, but I wasn't sure I had. Would the same, I wondered, be true of Jerry and Roger?

Regardless, with Don, I told the truth. "I feel like a different person from that girl you met," I said.

"It's not you, it's me," said Don with a laugh. Not a cackle. Just a laugh.

"Sort of," I told him. This was true and not true. Maybe he was right. There *was* no one truth. Truth: a schoolgirl thing.

When I left, I packed up a bag of clothing to drop off at Goodwill: my plaid skirts, my loafers. I was not a schoolgirl anymore.

Thirteen years later, I tiptoed out of my children's room and collapsed into my own bed, with a book. Through the bedroom window came the dull rush of traffic on the Williamsburg Bridge, the cars bound for Brooklyn, for my old neighborhood. Less than a year after I left the Agency, my grandmother died, leaving me her apartment on the Lower East Side. Like her, I was raising two children there, children who played in the same parks my father and his brother played in, and my grandmother and her sisters before him. Like my father, they walked across the Williamsburg Bridge to visit their friends, who were the children of my friends. And like Holden—and like me—their childhood played out against, was defined by, the city's grand institutions. They, too, spent Saturdays passing under the great whale at the Museum of Natural History and inspecting the armor at the Met. They, too, rode the carousel in Central Park. They tossed crumbs to the ducks in the pond.

From the hallway, I heard the pad of my husband's feet. "You're awake!" he said. All too often, I fell asleep with the children. Though I also rose hours before they woke to write in my closet-sized office, a lesson I'd learned all those years before, during my year at the Agency, from Salinger.

"I know," I said, with a yawn. "I don't know how it happened."

Leaving his post by the doorjamb, he came over and sat down next to me. "I'm afraid I have some bad news."

I sat up, suddenly fully awake. Three thousand miles away, in the foothills of San Jose, my father lay dying. Within a few months of my parents' retiring to California—also not long after I left the Agency—his doctors diagnosed a syndrome similar to Parkinson's. A syndrome whose effects he'd, apparently, felt for years. "Some patients are experts at masking the symptoms," one of his doctors told us. "Your father was an actor, wasn't he?"

"Is it my father?" I asked. I hadn't heard the phone ring, but that didn't mean anything.

"No, no," said my husband. "J. D. Salinger. Died."

"Oh." I let out a long breath. "Oh."

"I know he was—" His hazel eyes blinked behind his glasses as he tried to formulate this thought. What *was* Salinger in the tableau of my life? In the twelve years he'd known me, I'd reread *Franny and Zooey* and *Raise High the Roof Beam, Carpenters* annually, *Catcher* every two or three years. My Salinger paperbacks were falling apart, their pages yellow and crumbling, their covers taped together. I could buy new copies, but I didn't. "I know he was important to you."

"He was," I said, allowing myself to be embraced. "He was."

"You should go to sleep," he said, finally. "It's late." Our two-year-old had taken forever to get to bed, a not-uncommon occurrence.

"Yes," I agreed. But a few minutes later I found myself in the living room, pulling *Franny and Zooey* off the shelf. Our edition was a hardback, actually, bequeathed to me—along with paperbacks of *Catcher* and *Seymour*—when my parents moved to California, the same edition I'd stared at, day in and day out, during my year at the Agency.

Here's the thing: People say you outgrow Salinger. That he's a writer whose work speaks to the particular themes and frustrations of adolescence. The latter might be true. Certainly, I can attest to the fact that many of the people who wrote letters to him ranged in age from approximately twelve to twenty-two. I don't know how I would have regarded Salinger had I read him in middle school. But I encountered Salinger as a grown-up or rather, someone who, like Franny, was just sloughing off my childhood, my received ideas about how to live in the world. And, thus, with each passing year—each rereading—his stories, his characters, have changed and deepened.

At twenty-four, I identified so strongly with Franny—her exasperation with the world, with the men like Lane who dominated it—that the story's structural perfection, its gorgeous precision and symbolism, its balance of social satire and psychological realism, its dead-on dialogue, eluded me. At twenty-four, I'd thought, *I want to write like that*. At thirty-seven, I still wanted to write like that, but I had a better understanding of *why*, a hope that someday that "why" would become a "how."

All these years later, I still—*still*—felt like Franny, overwhelmed by the suffering around me, by all those egos. Perhaps, like Holden Caulfield, "I act quite young for my age." Perhaps I'll always be a person who gets "quiet emotional," like the boy from Winston-Salem, who knows you can't go around bleeding all over the world, but can't manage to stanch myself. Perhaps I had married someone rather too much like Lane Coutell. Three years later, I would pack up my children and leave him for my college boyfriend.

But now I equally love—my heart truly breaks for—

Bessie Glass, who's lost two of her seven children, one to his own hand. Bessie, who wanders through her apartment like a ghost, who fears—so much that she can't think straight—that whatever demons plagued Seymour might plague Franny, too. There is a point in "Zooey" that is almost unbearable, a point at which I always have to put the book down and take a breath: Zooey is haranguing Bessie for not recognizing *The Way of a Pilgrim* as belonging to Seymour. Franny, you see, had told her mother that she happened upon the book at her college library. "You're so stupid, Bessie," Zooey says furiously. "She got [it] out of Seymour and Buddy's old room, where [it's] been sitting on Seymour's desk for as long as I can remember." And then Bessie says, "I don't go in that room if I can help it, and you know it . . . I don't look at Seymour's old—at his things."

That was the point at which the tears arrived. A few pages later, Zooey asks Franny if she wants to talk to Buddy. "I want," Franny says, "to talk to Seymour."

That was the point at which my husband found me sobbing, loudly, phlegmily, haplessly trying not to wet the pages of this book that had passed from my father's hand to my mother's and now to mine.

Salinger's stories, to a one, are anatomies of loss, every inch of them, from the start to the finish. Even *Raise High the Roof Beam, Carpenters*—one of the funniest stories in the English language—is soaked with the fact of Seymour's death, Seymour's suicide. Seven years later, Buddy is still mourning. Even *Catcher* is ultimately a portrait in grief: Holden's madness has all to do with his brother Allie's death. And Franny is not pregnant. She's in mourning. As is the entire Glass family. A family in mourning, never to recover. A world in mourning, never to recover.

My husband stared at me, shocked, from the doorjamb. "This is about your dad, isn't it?" he said. "It's making you think about your dad. About what's going to happen." My father, we knew, was not going to recover. He would grow worse and worse, until he couldn't move and couldn't talk, and then: the end. "It's reminding you of your dad."

With the back of my hand, I wiped the tears from my face and swiped my nose. "No," I said. "It's just about Salinger."

Acknowledgments

My most profound thanks to: Jordan Pavlin, Tina Bennett, Stephanie Koven, Alexandra Pringle, Anne Michel. Kathy Zuckerman, Laura Brooke, Brendan Fredericks, Diya Kar Hazra, Caroline Bleeke, Svetlana Katz, Nicholas Latimer, Brittany Morrongiello, Katie Burns, Sally Willcox. Thank you to everyone at Knopf, Bloomsbury, WME, and Janklow & Nesbit.

Thank you to Allison Powell and Carolyn Murnick, to Joanna Hershon, Stacey Gottlieb, and Abby Rasminsky for such insightful early reads. To Lauren Sandler, for everything. To Kate Bolick, Evan Hughes, Adelle Waldman, Matthew Thomas, Dylan Landis, and, most of all, Charles Bock.

Thank you, also, to the wonderful editors and producers with whom I worked on the pieces that evolved into this book: Jeffrey Frank, John Swansberg, James Crawford, David Krasnow. And thank you to Slate, BBC Radio 4, and Studio 360.

Thank you, thank you to PEN for providing the funding that allowed me to finish this book. To Ledig House for a place to work, and to Ofri Cnaani and Claire Hughes for the same. To Paragraph, where most of this book was written, and to Joy, Lila, Sara, and Amy.

Thank you to Kenneth Slawenski and Ian Hamilton, whose impeccable research filled holes in my knowledge of Salinger's life.

Thank you to Claire Dederer, Cheryl Strayed, and Carlene Bauer for examples of what a memoir can be, and straightforward guidance about writing one.

I am enormously grateful, of course, to the Agency for giving me the best first job a girl could have, and to my boss and the person known in these pages as Hugh for teaching me more than I ever could have hoped to learn about books, business, literature, and, yes, life. Also thank you to the person known in these pages as Lucy.

Thank you to Henry Dunow, Anne Edelstein, Jen Carlson, Corinna Snyder, and Chris Byrne. Thank you to Roger Lathbury, Robert Anasi, and Billy Bano.

Thank you to Coleman and Pearl.

This book would not exist were it not for the generosity, support, and editorial acumen of Amy Rosenberg. Thank you.

Keeril: There are no words.

A NOTE ON THE TYPE

This book was set in Scala, a typeface designed by the Dutch designer
Martin Majoor (b. 1960) in 1988 and released by the FontFont foundry in
1990. While designed as a fully modern family of fonts containing both a
serif and a sans serif alphabet, Scala retains many refinements normally
associated with traditional fonts.

Composed by North Market Street Graphics,
Lancaster, Pennsylvania

Designed by Soonyoung Kwon